Journal of
Philosophy and the Visual Arts

ACADEMY EDITIONS · LONDON/ST MARTIN'S PRESS · NEW YORK

Acknowledgements

Front Cover: Thérèse Oulton, *Song of Deceit*, 1988, oil, courtesy the artist. *Frontispiece:* Kazimir Malevich, *An Englishman in Moscow*, 1914, oil, Stedelijk Museum Amsterdam.

Andrew Benjamin
pp 6-7: Illustration by Adami courtesy the artist, engraving by P Magne from B Faujas de Saint Fonds, *Essai de Geologie.*

Jean-François Lyotard
pp 8-18: Translation from the French by David Macey, illustration courtesy Karel Appel.

Joseph Margolis
pp 19-27: Pont des Arts project by Peter Wilson reproduced courtesy the architect.

Wendy Steiner
pp 28-33: Illustrations by Varo supplied by the author.

Julia Kristeva
pp 34-9: Translation from the French by David Macey. Paintings by Jackson Pollock:

The Blue Unconscious, private collection; *Night Mist,* courtesy Norton Gallery and School of Art Florida; *Alchemy,* Peggy Guggenheim Collection Venice/Solomon Guggenheim Museum New York; *Sea Change,* Seattle Art Museum.

Clive Dilnot and Maruja Garcia-Padilla
pp 40-55: Vermeer's *Woman in Blue*, the Rijksmuseum Amsterdam, and *Allegory of Faith*, Metropolitan Museum New York.

Paul Crowther
pp 54-9: David's *The Death of Marat*, the Musées Royaux des Beaux-Arts, Brussels.

Chlöe Chard
pp 60-69: Illustrations supplied by the author. Illustration on page 60, the British Library; illustrations on page 69, the Trustees of the Sir John Soane Museum.

Irit Rogoff
pp 70-75: Illustrations by Mandieta and Neustein supplied by the author.

David Wood
pp 76-80: Escher's *Ascending and Descending*. Escher Foundation.

First published in Great Britain in 1989 by *Journal of Philosophy & the Visual Arts*
an imprint of the
ACADEMY GROUP LTD, 7 HOLLAND STREET, LONDON W8 4NA
ISBN: 0-85670-966-2 (UK)

The Publishers and Editor do not hold themselves
responsible for the options expressed by the writers
of articles or letters in this magazine
Copyright of articles and illustrations
may belong to individual writers or artists
Published in the United States of America by
ST MARTIN'S PRESS, 175 FIFTH AVENUE, NEW YORK 10010
ISBN: 0-312-03066-5 (USA)

Printed and bound in Singapore

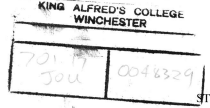

Journal of
Philosophy and the Visual Arts

Co-ordinating Editor: Andrew Benjamin

VALERIO ADAMI, *BACK TO BOMBAY*, 1977, ACRYLIC

ANDREW BENJAMIN
INTRODUCTION

B FAUJAS DE SAINT-FOND, *SPHERICAL LAVA AMID IRREGULAR PRISMS*, FROM *ESSAI DE GEOLOGIE*, 1803-1809, ENGRAVING BY P MAGNE AFTER A E G DAGOTY

Within philosophy and within those fields or areas of study stimulated by or responding to its recent developments, the visual arts are coming to play an increasingly significant role. The aim of the first issue of the *Journal of Philosophy and the Visual Arts* is to present examples of the different ways in which this is taking place. It is clear that the continual confrontation between philosophy and the visual arts is going to lead to a re-examination of the self-conceptions of both. This will take place despite their inherent plurality. The importance of this relationship is therefore twofold. On the one hand it does not concern the simple development of the arts themselves but rather the way in which the visual arts are understood and hence the way development within them is conceived and formulated. The greater the philosophical and intellectual sophistication of writings on the visual arts becomes, the more it is likely that the radical force of the visual arts – its capacity in its effectuation to question the premises and presupposition of art itself – will have found a language within which that force can be expressed. This in itself would already be an important development since what is usually the case is that criticism stills that force by refusing to allow it to impinge on the nature and practice of criticism and aesthetics.

It is precisely this formulation that brings to the fore the other important aspect stemming from thinking anew the relationship between philosophy and visual arts. Here what will be at stake is allowing the force of art to bear on the writing about art. This will occasion the need for a constant reassessment both of the style and practice of that writing as well as the philosophical premises or foundations on which it is based. The necessity to move away from a simple historical art criticism as well as the aesthetics sanctioned by analytic philosophy is demanded not only by the impasse within which both these approaches find themselves but also by the developments within contemporary art.

These developments give rise to two different avenues of approach, although there are, of course, important points of contact. The first concerns that which stems from an interpretative confrontation where the object of interpretation resists – if not forbids – an understanding that would take place within the terms handed down by tradition and thereby within which understanding is envisaged as being constrained to take place. The challenge, here, is extremely complex. It involves, amongst other things, rethinking the relationship between art and its history; the place of philosophy being here the means whereby that relationship is rethought. In addition it demands a further rethinking,

this time concerning the relationship between mode of interpretation and object of interpretation. It goes without saying that 'rethinking' is once again, and of necessity, of a philosophical nature.

The other effect that can be noted concerns the history of art; the writing of art history. The developments within art and the developments within philosophy have allowed for a reconsideration of the practice of art history. It is a practice which exemplifies the scholarship that has always been associated with art history but incorporates within it a recognition of contemporary philosophical debates and thus of the impossibility of maintaining, via repetition, the very complacency that abounds within the unexamined retention of traditional concepts and categories. The tradition need not be written about within its own terms.

All of the papers within this volume can be situated to a greater or lesser degree within the terms sketched above. Style, history, gender, psychoanalysis, pragmatism, literature, deconstruction, etc, all figure within and as attempts to *think* the visual arts. They provide therefore the first in a number of moves to be made in this domain. The next two issues of the *Journal* will concern the 'topics' of architecture, and the avant-garde. Within the issue on architecture what will emerge as central is space; but emerging in terms of the demand located as much in recent architecture as in philosophy for a philosophical reconsideration of space. It is only by operating outside any clear and unproblematic distinction between theory and practice that it will be possible to bring philosophy and architecture into a creative confrontation.

The problems posed by the avant-garde are of major importance. What needs to be investigated is both the historicity as well as the actuality of this term. If, for example, it can be argued that the avant-garde or rather the term 'avant-garde' marks a unique historical moment that has passed, then a new vocabulary – one having both philosophical and political force – must be developed in order to chart, discuss, analyse, judge, etc, experimentations within the arts. It may be, of course, that history need not limit the term and it can come to be redeployed, redefined and hence redeemed. There are no obvious answers to these questions. That, however, does not diminish their urgency.

While it is always difficult to define a project in advance, the orientation of the *Journal of Philosophy and the Visual Arts* will be always towards developing, tracing and enacting the consequences, for both philosophy and the visual arts, of the attempt within them to rethink and reformulate their specific projects.

JEAN-FRANÇOIS LYOTARD
Sans Appel

He writes.

Theories
Are things, and neither idealism,
religions, nor stories
nor slogans.
The complexity of things themselves: that's what
theories are

The thing exists, without ever letting itself
be seen in its entirety; it does not
appear. Theory is the thing

Would like to be a thing, the Thing
What about me, me, says thought

    says thought to itself as it tries to think Appel
    I want to be the Appel thing
    to respond to Appel's appeal.

The problem is that in painting, in matter,
the Thing is called colour. What about me,
says thought, how can I be matter?
How can I be colour?
Not: thinking colour. Nor the colour of thought.
Thought as matter itself. It too must be colour
because

    there is therefore no opposition
    between spirit and matter.

Does colour say: what about me,
me? What's to become of me? What
am I destined for? Who will call me?
mustn't form call me and come to tame me?
(at least that's what thought thinks about me, and
had done for a very long time in the Northern and
Western parts of the globe)
Or, to put it in more flattering terms, am I not
destined to generate forms? Would I be anything at all
if I wasn't informed about myself by the mirror of forms?
Would I even know that I am colour, matter
without the generation of a form? Where
would I be reflected? or rather, where would be
the flection of the matter I had yet to become, which
had yet to be I, that makes me me, me,
the red, the Prussian blue,
which makes me visible, sayable? A form which generates me?
Would I – colour – be colour if there were no eye
to reflect me? No object in which I could be laid down? Does
the amorphous *exist* in itself?
Says thought to itself, reassuring itself, asking questions in matter's
place,

answering on its behalf.
Colour? Just like that, no frame, no surround,
just colour laid down on nothing? Colour as the tone in which
all objects, faces, and landscapes are bathed, from which they take on
their individual colours? To such an extent that
the judgement could never know their colour in itself,
could never know what colour they would be if they did not
merge into the bath of colour.
according to this view, colour 'turns' so as to appear to be, in our eyes,
what it appears to be
in its 'real' visual appearance, an appearance which is false, falsified
by its very origins. Whereas the eye does not even see
the general tone, the tonality which is, however, the key (a musical
key)
to all local chromatic timbres, simply because it can only
sense them if they are all that is 'laid down',
all that occupies determinable, visible surfaces.

But even so, says thought to itself, I could rediscover
the tone of this impalpable Great Colour
by looking at coloured objects. I can easily work out the key from
the notes of a melody. So I could easily rediscover the key to timbre
by trying out local colours and seeing which ones clash
with the dominant tone that provides the range of all visible tones.

So I could even succeed in deducing this immaterial general chromatic
matter
from visible colours, even if I did have to do so indirectly, absurdly,
by
introducing variations. All I have to do is find tones that cannot be
obtained by working with it.
Jam the lock in order to find the key.

But there again, that would mean reflection,
a mental experiment using the little mirrors known
as coloured objects.
Yes, yes, says thought to itself, I have only
limited means at my disposal.
I have my limitations. But overcoming them is part of
the job-description.

It's like 'light' in baroque, classical or romantic
painting.
The thinking eye deduces it
from the tone taken on by the coloured object. The tone
of that facade changes, depending on whether it is bathed
in the water of the rising sun, in the blazing midday sun, or in
the vapours of the dying evening. In the course of a single
summer's day. Monet's Cathedrals. Appel mentions them. But I can
still
differentiate between two or three shades within that general tone
at any given moment of the day, even though the eye never sees it
in itself. In painting and the visual arts, that tone

is known as light.
It lets you see without being seen.
But it can be imagined, named.

I know perfectly well, says the thought of colours to itself,
that it is only because the tone is never the same that I can
succeed in imagining it, naming it. I have to assume the existence of
objects with constant local colours. And I also know that
it is the difference between the changing time of day (and the
changing seasons), together with the assumption that every object 'is'
always the same colour, which inspires the idea that a dominant
optical colour suddenly affects every individual tone at any given
time of day (or season of the year)

But what would happen, asks Appel, following the example set by
Rembrandt, Vermeer and Cézanne
What would happen, asks matter,
if thought could not use variation in light
to help the eye construct the hypothesis of an immaterial
colour which is in itself invisible.
After all, the question applies to any local colour:
the yellow of a metro ticket,
the red of a London bus
the green of Californian eucalyptus.
They are not definite at all.
It is the mind which forgets to forget
their chromatic inconsistency because it is
content to identify the objects they colour,
the objects they dress
and which it claims to be able to grasp.
It grasps a coloured garment as though it were an identity card.

We say yellow in the same way that we say rectangular,
green in the same way that we say leaf.
It's part of the definition.
It allows us to recognise things. That is not seeing; that
is the thought of seeing, and it can only recognise.

The eye of the painter has always tried
to form an alliance with the Thing
in order to combat this abstraction

    in that unique instant
    which transcends time and place (. . .)
    an art of
    'what is not there' (p 98)

he says. The object is
there, but the Thing is not there.
Colour, the raw material of painting, raw material
for vision, is not a given, like a nice little object,
or like one of its properties. And nor can it be
deduced from the good old colours laid down on objects,
the colours which indicate them by dissimulating them
(colour, *celare, cacher*) because those tonalities themselves
are only signals
insofar as the eye escapes their control
and allows the purely vital bustle of the mind to use them as markers
in action which have to be performed properly. With ends in view.
Adaptation. Or, which amounts to much the same thing,
to allow spirituality
to tame their materiality
in a symbolic semantics,
as Kandinsky tried to do. With a view to an end. Elation.

And considered in that light, he says, accommodated in that way,

colours have to be removed, stripped off like masks
by the hand of the painter
if he is to go beyond appearances
beyond the norms of the good life or edifying thoughts.
Here, on the threshold of
appearance; on the point of touching 'what is not there'
the art of painting is subject to serious threats.

    Basically, it is a matter of expressing
    the essence of the tree . . . In a word, what does not
    appear in what does appear, what remains hidden, concealed
    retreats into what does appear.

Theories are a threat. The spirit whispers
to him that, by going beneath appearance, visual art
can only encounter pure Form, absolute Grey or White, or
the Concept, and Grey, Form and White are no more
than visual transcriptions of the Concept – that theory is
Platonism – or, on the other hand, the multi-hued singular Unconscious,
Expression, Will, the theory of Dionysianism.

All those capital letters. Thought
uses them to try to intimidate colour
and to tame it.
Tries to strengthen the grip of the
colouring hand in its fumbling attempts to go beyond
the accommodating eye. It whispers
to the hand, telling it how and what to paint,
how to lay things out, and it whispers to the eye,
telling it what rules it should prescribe for
gestures, once it has got past the descriptive stage.
No, no,

    the eye has to keep listening,
    like a radar . . . (p 63)

listening to the nothingness which,
from the other side of the threshold, calls
upon the hand to honour
matter.

    basically, the brush starts
    with nothing and ends on a nothing (p 142)

What? says thought. Nothing
is unthinkable. Well,
that is what has to be thought,
points out matter-colour.
The threshold of appearances cannot be crossed.
There is no other side. If you paint
the other side, you just form more appearances, remain
in the realm of appearance.
And that is the humility of painting.

The object of my appeal is certainly not to make you
break through the wall of appearances, to vent your surplus anger
on the conventional and the accommodating,
colour tells thought.
I am appealing for nothing, for a light, untouchable commutation
in the nothingness of appearances. The brush
which carries me, transports me and
sets me down in the movement known as
'the gesture of painting'.
It owes me protection and homage.
By taking me away from here,

it reveals the non-existence of here when
I leave it, and by applying me there,
it shows that there was not there,
that it is only there thanks to my appearance-there.
In itself, the gesture metabolises
my being-as-colour, my function.
I no longer hide the object
as I make it visible,
and I begin to make myself visible,
to give myself away, like anything else
that can only give itself away by being
given (a place, an object). Neither on
this side of objects, beyond them nor on them, but in them.
And so I am made matter
rather than substance,

first substance, then
matter

I quite understand, says colour laughingly,
that before I could be transported,
before I could be metabolised into a sign,
the mind, Appel's mind, had to be tempted
to break through. To be tempted by violent tactics.
It's true that thought finds me irritating.
That, at first, he needed a knife and a spatula
to puncture the coloured appearance of objects,

 fighting in front of my paintings with great knives,
 and then I said:
 I am working like a barbarian in a barbarian age.
 In about 1957-58, it seemed to me that I was still
 slashing at pictorial matter with great knives (pp 14, 134).

Needed to disembowel the visible
so as to make the chromatic matter
inside it flow. Needed
to make it bleed.

 The red itself changed. At first, my
 red was blood. Then it became freedom,
 space, light (. . .) the period of the tragic, lost
 Nudes . . . At that time the blood really did flow!
 All that come about because the artist is struck by life.
 In every sense of the word. (. . .) When I was young, I would slit open
 whole tubes of red with a razor blade just to watch the dazzling paint
 flow. (p 92)

But the gesture I need, the gesture that
I don't even demand, has nothing to do with exploits,
says the Thing. I don't give myself to heroes.
I am still the Res, nothing [*rien*]. Endlessly.

 The difficult question of the end,
 of how to complete the work.
 I never really finish a painting (pp 24, 26)

I do not call upon thought to want me.
To want to have me, to want to show me. I call
upon it to know that it is matter.
But do I even call upon it?
Why should I address myself to thought?
As though I expected it to grant me a remission, to make reparation.
It's not my fault if the one thing about me that appeals to thought
is the fact that I have no call for thought. My blues and pinks
are indifferent to all the plots thought can dream up about them.

And thought knows that knowing it is matter is the lesser of two evils.
It must confess to paying tribute to the massive indifference
of being-there for nothing (why yellow, why greyish-brown?)
Confess that even within it, something fails to answer the call because
it
is too old, or too young. That it too is of the Thing. Has no appeal.
Gives rise to things.

And words are this for-nothing-in-itself, this inanity,
words are colour-matter. Always in the way, just like colours.
Saying something other than what thought means to say.
They are its non-will, its mass. As innumerable as
colours. They come to us from the depths of time; they do not come;
they are there.
You can philologise them, just as you can chromatologise colours.
But, like colours, they are always in the process of being born.
Thought means arranging them, coming to an arrangement with them.
Not very
disciplined, these elderly children. Writing respects their candour.
Painting has the same difficulties with colour, provided that it reveres
it.

Because thought habitually objectivises. It's a habit of ours.
It sets its sights on something far away, then sets up objects,
Vis à vis itself. Sets its sights and visualises.
And when it thinks of itself, and thinks itself,
Sets its sights on itself, sets up internal objects.
Concepts, schemata, operators, regulators
and rules. It regroups what it receives – matter – by regrouping
its forces so as to take it all in as an object
that stands before it. A visile constitution of the object.
And, consciously or otherwise, it defines the object it has constituted
in exactly the same way that it defines a sonic or chromatic timbre
it analyses it and reduces it to its distinctive components,
both qualitative and quantitative.
Intensity, duration, frequency.
When it conceives of matter,
thought is, so to speak, forced to exhaust
its properties. But the result of this endurance test,
this time-trial that pits it against the Thing
is never anything more than an approximation.

Theorising simply means seeing properly.
Having a true, complete vision.
Having appropriated the improper.

Now movement,

 'the kinetic moment'
 the very rhythm of the mind as it comes to grips
 with the fluctuating world of matter, starting with
 pictorial matter (p 63)

the movement that is matter,
and that thought thinks is matter
expects of it,

 Painting itself responds
 to a sort of appeal, even a
 sort of interrogation (p 63)

the repercussions of matter on thought
challenge propriety. They destroy the properties. And therefore
deobjectivise.
Discourages thought from looking to closely. What is the point
of violently breaking in if the object is no longer there,

not yet there, already not there, already somewhere else, still
other? If it is no more than an arbitrarily-interrupted dancestep?
A wave or a vibration (matter) that appears
to have stopped. The movement that Appel is trying to launch,
his gesture, should not be seen as an attempt on the part of thought
to grasp chromatic properties, to handle them or embrace them,
Nor as the 'response' the power of mind
makes to matter's implied 'Will you every know me?'
But this gesture is an attempted entry. Thought enters the material
dance. This is a spontaneous response. Sponta sponsa.
It promises itself to matter of its own accord. The matter that is
thought, the undulation of thought,
allows itself to be shaken, to be made to vibrate by the matter
that is colour, by its waves. And it has no
intention of going back over them
to make them objects of knowledge, of vision. No going back, no
looking back.
No reply, no replay, no folding back

> In my paintings form
> becomes vibratino,
> a form without form wells up,
> the formless existence that I paint –
> the vibrations of colours (p 107)

The Great Colour that thought was just thinking about
is not the colour of the light which floods all that is visible.
Not the colour that tints objects and allows them to be seen, and
whose properties – invisible properties, even – thought might
be able to reconstitute by comparing, reflecting and calculating. Appel
calls it matter, not light.
The Great Colour is not optical.
The Thing is not a trick of the light.
Of course the light sheds no light on itself. Even so,
visible or not, it is conjoined with sight, with the eyes, *vis à vis* them.

> I am not trying to understand the force that powers
> my own hand . . . Perhaps it is the 'ecstatic eye'?
> This is the moment of the third eye! . . . Ecstasy has its
> role to play in all this. The ecstasy of the third eye!
> It's not always easy to adopt an other gaze.
> You have to be firm with yourself (pp 96, 104, 111, 97)

You might find that there is an atmospheric tone in a thought,
or perhaps in thought. It may or may not be unique, and, by acting
incognito, it might shed light on its cognitive process, on the objects
it
knows. It might. By analogy. But it is not in that sense
that thought is colour.
It is colour in the way that it is matter,
in the sense that it has no destiny.
An undulation without a destiny.
A dance in itself, before space-time.
And it is on the basis of this dance, the dance of the photons,
that space-time is reckoned. The unity of movement wherein
places and moments are generated.

Colour-matter does not say: what about me,
what I am destined for? Thought makes it say that
and says it on its behalf. And the fact that it has no destiny
that makes matter alien to all thought. The fact that it does not
expect to have any destiny. It asks questions, but not because it is short
of answers, conceptions, forms or measurements. It questions thought
to the
precise extent that it expects nothing from it and asks it no questions.
The absence and non-existence of theories;

that's what things are.

The big question for thought, or the question full stop, is
the absence of questions: matter
It is in that way that the thing is present for thought.
As a non-question. It is not a question asked by matter or by the Thing,
a question arising out of matter, or one referred to a matter,
as one might speak of the Middle East question
Matter is a question for thought
because it poses thought no questions.
Thought progresses by asking questions, because thought simply
means
examining the case, studying the file,
judging. It always inevitably presupposes that a complaint has
been referred to it. A complaint, a request for an
opinion, from the other side.
It presumes that it has to decide the question of the true, the beautiful,
the just. Colour has to lay a complaint and plead.
It is assumed that the court is in session, that colour has filed a
complaint.
But colour has never laid a single complaint.
Matter wants to have nothing to do with thought and wants nothing
form it.
Colour is. Fine. But what can thought do about that?
Can explain what it is. But not the fact of its being.
That has nothing to do with existence, whatever Appel may write
about it

> *The thing is existential*
> *the thing exists without letting itself*
> *be seen in its entirety*

it's more a matter of
the colour-Thing insisting, or perhaps simply
sisting.
If it existed, it would already be appealing to its other,
to thought, and expecting an answer,
expecting its fate to settled. Its whole destiny hangs on
that *ek-*, that *ex-*
It is neither a small other
nor a great Other. I mean that it is neither the lure
that demand procures itself, nor the unknown law
that governs desire. I say that for the benefit of my friends of the couch.
That topography belongs to thought, to the thought of a knowing,
willing,
intriguing mind, and it knows nothing of matter
If thought should perchance place matter in that topography,
if it should ordain an end for it, even an indeterminate end,
and if it uses matter as a pretext for smuggling that end into
'objects', thought is thinking matter in such a way
as to deflate its self-importance

Matter is the in-itself. That says it all.
That is unthinkable, we only think the accessible,
that which relates to, relates for

You know, as though you loved someone for the colours
of their eyes, the skin on their wrist. As though that
master-colour had been the pretext for that iris, the skin of that joint to
precipitate the great desire (the Other) that haunts you into
   a small object capable of capturing your demand.

I am not saying that solely for the benefit of the couch, I am also saying
it
for the benefit
of the picture. The thought of painting was, and is, in the habit of

taking colour as its material and using it to dress up
its silence, its being out of the question. Is there any
techne, any art that does not require that division of labour?
The West has almost always conceived and practised its art
by reshaping materials. So called because, like the matter of the ancient
philosophers, it is initially no more than an indeterminate potentiality
which awaits the formal and final act which will really bring it into
being. If it does have a form before that technical act is performed, its
form is not appropriate and the act elevates the material, produces a
closer affinity. Remakes it, promotes it.

Affinity with what? There's not a lot of choice.
With the use men will make of it, or think they will make of it.
With the pleasure that the work will give the soul. With the end, known or
unknown – and in art it is by definition unknown – which inspires men to
reshape ('create') in general, or in other words with the techne or art. The
impulse, the *physis* of nature, is believed to work towards that end.
Physein: to grow. One can argue about the various affinities and
articulations that exist between at and impulse.
If we think of matter in terms of materials, we inevitably evoke an
impulse. What I mean is this: just as the final form of a tree appeals to
vegetable matter to
direct its impulses towards it, so the final form of a painting calls upon
chromatic matter to achieve perfection.

(It cannot be any other way; if it were, there would not be that immediate,
spontaneous affinity between appeal and impulse, no nature,
and no work of art, but only what me might call
the work of technique. Conception, conceiver and concept mediate
between the act and the potentiality. But that's another story).

The word material implies both an appeal and a potentiality.
That is the other source of its potential power.
Its power to push on to the end which appeals for it.
An impulse may be always-already
determined by it 'natural' end, but it is still capable
of responding to the appeal of art,
provided that its appeal is not essentially different
to the appeal of nature.
Has the same spontaneity.
Appeals to the material in the same way
as its 'natural end'.

The model which governs the thought
of shaping its educational, pedagogic,
cultural. Children grow up naturally,
like wild flowers. But it is only in the eyes
of what is known as reasonable culture that
flowers are wild. But cultural reason
is also part of nature. Human nature.
And it appeals to children because they are growing things.

> Once more, my painting
> says: we are nature . . .
> Nature forced itself upon them
> with such intensity that they had
> no option but to paint as they did. They
> responded to a sort of appeal (pp 186, 145)

that is why 'they' – Rembrandt,
Goya, Van Gogh, Cézanne, Picasso,

Pollock, 'for example' – had
no need of style. They had
no style at all.

Oh come on . . . the differences . . . Surely
they all have their own manner. We may as well say
that a weeping willow's manner of being
a tree is its style.
Nature appeals in many different manners.
There again, there are many manners of telling it:
Here. To tell the truth, it's a very general appeal. Aristotle
called it the Prime Mover and, as its name indicates,
its power (matter-materials) is capable of responding
in many different ways. It's the same with the arts:
a lot of genres and families, and a lot of individuality,
even singularity, within a collection.

But there is still the immediate affinity.
It takes dialogue as its model – and dialogue
is not and never can be an exchange between equals:
it means that one partner educates the other –,
and demands that one must conduct (*du-cere*) the other out (*e-*)
of his present state. As he awakens, the other will awaken and begin to ask
questions. Isn't that how it works?
This means that the material must have at least a potential destination,
if only in that it now lacks a form and an end,
a real form or end, and that the fact of its being addressed *to*
endows it with that destination.

Appel's gesture, the transporting of colours, singular as it may be,
could be classified within this economy, metaphysic or mythology,
and it can be related to a family of painters – and Appel himself
mentions the most important names. His gesture might in fact be nothing
less than the coming together of an impulse and an appeal, a dialectic
between the power and expectations of a form (that of the colour-material)
and the appeal that the end (the final work in its completion)
addresses to the material.
Impel, impulse, propellere.
Appel, ad-pellere. The mechanics of
affinity, of abduction and of
adduction. Distrated into the
material, attracted by form.
And the position of the painter: fitting his gesture
in a universal interaction.
A Socratic gesture. You are on my side, decides
thought, confronted with the restive in-itself.

Painting is an intermediary situation

Thought's great effort to think
what happens to it because there is colour in
the art of painting. Is there anything
that cannot be caught in the snares of its intrigues?
Nature: what an intrigue!
The whole relationship between address and
destination cast like a fishing net
over the infinite variety, the wild innocence of colours
and the way they are captured or transported
by the gesture of painting. Of course

> I said to myself: 'Van Gogh painted more
> with his brush than nature could paint. He literally
> plunged into the secrets of nature.' (p 139)

12

he 'adds' to nature,
but only because
he hears the call more clearly
because he

    frees matter (p 187)

he frees, that is, the powerful impulses
that lie within the material and
destins them to his work.
His work is nature because it is
truer than nature.
The power of colours
unleashed. The chaos that creates
is

    a positive chaos (p 14)

chaos to the accommodating eye,
but for the third eye, it is a secret explosion
of colour in all its truth.
Like Socrates, the painter begins by
destroying. He seems to begin by
seeming to destroy. But that
is the work of nature.
She too constructs by destroying.
Or does she deconstruct?

In loving Appel's works, our eyes
cause nature to increase. Cause growth to grow.
Reveal that there will always be conjunctions
between the chromatic matter we abandon
– and it has to be abandoned because it is
made up of countless shades, and because it is impossible
for all colour tones to be realised, to have been realised –
between matter, which will always be a potentiality, and
its destination in a final form,
conjunctions and a dialogue to be begun anew,
both the destruction of the given to release potential chromatic
material, and the positivisation of chaos in the shape of a painting.
There will always be art to be made.

But why painting? Because
nature is constantly being made complete by
colours.

    The point of poetic creation if not
    to overcome matter, as the empty aesthetic preached
    by so many people would have it, but to free matter (p 187).

Thought thinks of all that, and it thinks as it pleases,
in accordance with its own definition of wisdom.
When Appel is not painting, when he thinks about colour,
he thinks about it and thinks it in accordance with the great old schema
of appeal and impulse, of to and for.

Indeed, it is that same schema that motivates him to resist
contemporary 'barbarism'

    I am afraid of the new barbarism which is killing
    man's freedom (p 179)

Appel is (a) *résistant*. It might be thought
that he resists in the name of chromatic 'sistance'.
That is not always the case. He also resists
in the name of a 'reparation'.

by a sort of symbolic life-saving
operation . . . truly hope that we
will avoid disaster (p 166)

the reparation owed to a nature,
devastated by modern civilisation

    In my paintings, I tried to show, above all,
    that we ourselves are part of nature, and that we must never
    forget that because – make no mistake about it – nature, inevitably,
    is always stronger than us, and always will be.
    Beware her wrath!
    In the towns, nature's colours are disappearing.
    The sea is turning yellow. The coloured canvasses of the world
    are being displayed differently.
    the work of colour allows
    a painter to gain a rapid insight
    what is happening to a planet of
    robot-technicians, a planet
    worn out by pollution and scorn for nature.
    I can see the colours of pollution very clearly (pp 186, 94, 94)

But do you know how he 'makes reparation?', colour asks thought,
he makes reparation by 'destroying', by 'holing' the canvas.
It seemed to be complete, to be properly finished,
to have found its end-user, it end-user certificate, as
the arms-dealers say
Appel prevents pictures from coming to a happy end by splashing them
with drops of colour, by dirtying them. His brush spits on them

    I scatter spots of colour over my pictures.
    They often have nothing at all to do
    with the painting itself in terms of
    colour, form or any kind of necessity (p 50)

without any kind of finality, uncalled for.

    In a sense, they (the spots) are only there to destroy
    the picture, but once they have been put there, they
    belong to it (p 50)

But don't they acquire a new destiny once
they are inscribed in the picture?
Yes, says thought to colour, they re-address it or
redress it, they stop it from looking beautiful, from creating beauty,
and they make a hole in it, but an appeal makes itself heard through the
hole,
It is eccentric to the work, and puts it out of work so as to give it a
better destiny.
For the work itself is sus-pect, suspected of taking its place
in the supermarket where colours are polluted and where matter is
degraded
by being turned into materials

    Its as though it were an act of reparation
    for our age.
    It creates a breach, lets the air in
    so that our civilisation can go on (p 50)

Allowing nature to go on in our civilisation, which mortifies
it so dangerously. The disorder of the spots, the sacrifice of the painting
are dedicated to the nature that lives in man, so that he may be
forgiven for having made such poor use of it. He uses nature
like a dustbin

    an exploded planet, or a polluted planet,

the huge dustbin of the cosmos! (p 166)

Precisely, thought goes on, and if the picture isn't to go
in the dustbin, isn't to contribute to bureaucratic pollution,
to disenchantment with the world of techno-science and insurance
companies,
precisely because it is so conventionally, so primly beautiful
. . . you have to make the painting a dirty object, a besplattered object.
Thrown away. Into the dustbin of the world with it! Let it show signs
of
cultural wear and tear,
of being carelessly used, and let it come to a bad end.
And what about you, a colour thrown on to the canvas? There is
nothing
'necessary' about you either, but you do have a finality. Your dejection
makes reparation, pays homage to the life of the chromatic matter
known as
nature.
And chance, which is given the task of projecting you on to a
canvas that had, you thought, come to a good end, the chance element
in the
gesture is still governed by faith in the life of nature. Hope governs this
gesture, with all its desperate poverty. A dialectic of sacrifice, that's
all, concludes thought, with amusement.
Appel has always resisted, that's true. But he has always needed that
faith
in order to be able to resist.

Colour objects to the idea that Appel is resisting.
He knew what poverty meant, and he still knows. A poverty bordering
on madness. Amsterdam, a totally Jewish town, cosmopolitan, as he
describes
it, fond of a laugh, fond of a good time, bustling, meditative – wiped
out
by Nazism. He left
his family just before the occupation
(his father told him, either you become a barber like me, or you make
your
own way in life).
The language of his childhood, a mixture of Yiddish and Amsterdam
slang,
hunted down. Not a penny, and famine raging. On top of all that

there was not a lot of love

Just a 'little blonde', at the end of the occupation,
and she died of galloping consumption. It took her only a week to die.

Everything is mad
mad everything
Because everything is mad
Mad everything, even.
Even not being mad is mad
Nothing is mad (after all)
Non-madmen are mad
Madmen are not mad
Madness is mad

Written in '47. No difference between
yes and no. Madness is degree zero, thought
at its most wretched. What thought is left
when there is no more yes and no.
Thought-matter, says colour, and then
she is my sister. Appel didn't turn to colour
to save the world. Colour was given to him
because he was refused everything. Not like a

scrap that no power could refuse him. Poverty
can blind you. It can close you in on yourself,
and shut you up. In hatred. Victimise.
Make you proud. Strengthen the ego. But colour
enters into matter like something that
vibrates before there is any yes and no,
like something that is there before there is any form, any concept,
and destination. In the depths of the holes, of the spots:
the animal, the child, the madman,
the clown, and their gaze.

If I had not become a painter,
I would definitely have become a clown.
All my life, I've wanted to be a clown,
because I make people laugh wherever
I go . . . Faces distorted by suffering, laughter
or work. Many of them crazy. Then they become imaginary
when I decorate them with movements, and free colours,
depending on how they look. The colours become clownlike.
A human being drawn by the huge foot of some great
prehistoric animal, like a dinosaur. The child is the
strongest element within man. He looks at everything as though
he were seeing it for the very first time (p 90-92, 23)

What did Goya, Rembrandt and Van Gogh
paint in their late periods?

The gaze of a human animal (p 22)

A wretched animal. Perhaps even a vegetable. A tree, a flower
face-scapes. Mad because they have no destination, because
they are no more than a vibrating movement addressed to nothing.
This is no animal drawn instinctively to its ends, no a
plant fulfilling its destiny as a complete form.
A cat, a horse, a tree, a flower totally transformed
into vibrating matter, pure movement on the spot, timbre.
Their gaze is not in their eyes; it *is* their eyes,
their fur, their veins, their fronds, the dustbin of the sense,
material splendour.
And that means that you – thought – can come near enough
to take them, to understand them, to apprehend them, you will
abandon them, throw them on the tip.
They are too stupid.

He goes through dustbins. When he was
very young, in Amsterdam, he began to collect
found objects, to stick them together, to assemble them.
Objects lost and found. All that Dada, surrealist, Negro art,
And now, especially when he is in New York, he wanders
around like a tramp, picking things up. Anything that usual thought
casts aside, has no further use for. Anything
that the modern ego, in its enjoyment of the world, casts out
when it is done with it.
And doesn't recycle. Not because it does not know how to,
but because recycling costs too much. It only recycles
dangerous rubbish. The old themes of will, calculation and safety.
A sad ecology for an oikos, for a home run on
rational lines. Rational and rationed. Like those grand old
paleolithic sites that are surrounded by a belt of bones that
were thrown away after meals. At least the leftovers were
biodegradable. They went back into nature's machinery.
Being industrious, nature recycled them herself.
Now we throw away everything that we cannot assimilate. Anything
without a destiny.

The things that Appel picks up

14

are documents about
ontological desolation. About a flaw
in the project of will, safety and skill.
And they are not just objects, like
broken TVs, ruined automatic coffee makers,
worn tires, mattresses whose springs have gone . .
He also picks up the unemployed, the
unnatural offspring of so-called human nature,
those who are too old, too young,
the unqualified, those who can't speak properly,
those who arrived only recently, those
who are hurt in body and soul.

What has that to do with colour?
They have no destination. Not that
the poor are nomadic by vocation. They
have no vocation. And colour-matter has
no vocation either.
That is what the painter sees in them.
And when he throws spots of colour on to
his pictures and repeats the gesture
of revocation and imperfection
when he ruins the entire finished
picture with a final brush stroke,
he is telling thought: there, that's the matter
that you can never call your own,
there, that's your disgust, that's what's
left of colour after the meal of colour
that you call painting.

If there is an element of sacrifice involved,
it is none of Appel's doing.
Thought, or a certain thought,
sacrifices nature (human nature included)
to itself. And he resists, but not by
sublimating something that has not
received the call,
and which remains without any destiny
in the rubbish dumps and the shanty towns,
or returning it to the movement
of nature, of the affinity
between appeal and impulse. That is something
very different: populism, pauperism,
tachisme, perhaps a form of minimalism.
No, he wants only the non-will
of colour-matter. He wants non-destiny
to manifest itself.

That's all very well, says thought-nature
to colour-matter. A very good apologia
for your cause.
But let me make one point.
In digging through dustbins, your
defender admits that you, yes you colour,
can be grasped only to the extent to which you are, a supplement,
a cast-off, a dead letter in my life,
in the life of thought. The loss of energy caused by friction,
and the heat involved in all movement. Nothing primal
about that. The splendour, the radiance
and the eruption

    Pollock . . . I too feel like
    an erupting volcano (p 26)
come after the event. Nature and affinity
are the rule, non-affinity can only
exist if it 'sists', only if it is put

in the margin. We begin by thinking,
arranging objects in response to the impulse
and the appeal; we need nature first.
We have no direct purchase on matter.
According to your notion of the non-destined,
it is in itself no more than an idea that I produce,
and I produce it because I am thought. And it is my duty
to think, to go beyond. Your animals,
trees and landscapes do not know
that they are pleading a cause, the cause
of those who have no appeal, issue no call.
The cats, the face-scapes,
the 'big animals', the bouquets
that Appel paints are his thoughts
about the Thing, his thought about
what cannot be thought, about you,
colour, in your being-there. It is by
dint of thinking about them that he calls
upon them to bear witness. Being a cat and
being a picture of a cat are two different things.
It takes the whole of culture
to destroy culture.
Let me go on. It is all too easy to say
that the painter resists our bad culture
and perversion, that this gesture rubs the
techno-scientific world of business up the wrong way.
And that he is therefore struggling against
thought in general. I am thought, and I am
not merely a matter of calculating probable effects,
programming, safety and initiative.
I can do all that, but I can do the opposite
too. Work is within my capabilities, but so is non-work.
Taste and distaste, Human and inhuman. Calculation
and feeling.

    There are always two 'sides' to painting.
    Van Gogh and Cézanne.
    Rembrandt and Vermeer.
    Picasso and Mondrian.

There is matter and light
in both thought and painting.
Writing and style, if you like.

    Van Gogh, Goya
    That is my side in painting, if I can put it that way.
    The expressionist side (p 18)

Rimbaud and Madame de la Fayette, Hartmann
and Goethe. It's the same in the sciences,
contingency and necessity. Intuitionism and
axiomatics. And in philosophy,
perhaps. And ultimately these oppositions are stupid.
Always the same name traversed by the thought
of the appeal, and of the uncalled-for
the same thought invoked and revoked.
coming to terms with its own differences of opinion.
Appel calls himself an expressionist, but

    I recently realised the extent to
    which I have become a baroque painter,
    especially in my paintings of face-landscapes,
    the use of colour and form is almost too rich . . . Must
    make more effort to be disciplined
    Van Gogh could teach us a lesson in will-power
    and asceticism It is possible to find your balance

in a contradiction (pp 138-142)

A well-tempered expressionist, then?

    far removed from German expressionism,
    which is usually devoid of any contemplative
    vision, sometimes vulgar,
    a bit heavy, too realistic (p 103)

No, not well-tempered, an expression
of matter traversed by meditation.

    a typically European inner struggle
    the struggle between will and meditation (p 102)

a materialism in which, as in Monet,
who is on the other 'side', there is

    no constraining materialism: if
    he paints a street, a church, a boat or
    a landscape, everything is dematerialised (p 103)

A dinosaur walking with the delicacy of
a dove. That's Appel when he
says that he paints 'what isn't there' and
when he says that

    the essential operation starts with
    pictorial matter itself (. . .) I
    look for the 'idea' in the mass of plasticity
    itself (pp 145, 89)

you mean that the great animal paw
dripping with red that has just made
its mark on the canvas and which is daubing it
is motivated by the infinite delicacy
of a spiritual dance. And I do mean
spiritual: thought
struggling towards non-thought

    and what has not yet been lived

Matter, your defender is
more ambiguous that you think.
He may well say that

    in painting a brushstroke is purely and simply
    what it is – rhythm, colour, matter (p 187)

but he immediately contradicts
that pure simplicity by adding

    and at the same time, it is something else
    . . . a transparent matter, and therefore a negation
    of the utilitarian world
    and a work that communicates
    without ever ceasing to be paint,
    a painting which goes beyond paint (p 187)

Why 'a work that communicates?'
wonders matter-colour. Can you communicate
ecstasy, the other gaze? Perhaps he simply means
that it transmit vibrations to thought. The silent
communication of my vibration to you, with you,
thought as vibration.
Ultimately, there is only

dance. As in Action Painting,
in Pollock. Resenberg said of them
that they had broken the old link
between painting and literature, and
associated painting with dance. De Kooning's dance
Pollock's dance, Matisse's dance, and Karel Appel's dance.

    I am trying to show the movement
    that swirls through
    things and the mind
    the movement itself (p 68)

If thought can know itself
as colour-matter thought itself
must be able to dance. It is because it is an undulation
that thought is material. And thought is an undulation
if it is material. A free undulation which is
determined only in certain cosmic zones where it 'sets'
and stabilises into effects, into objects.
Perhaps the Thing he talks about and tries to paint
is simply vibration.
Of course one can use colour like an object,
think of it as an object:
stable, extended in our terrestial space,
something permanent in our terrestial time. But the
colour with which his gestures gambles is merely one kind of vibration.
And thought is another. Between the two, there lies
a field of light where particles are distributed
A network of receptors and nerves, where the rhythm
of photons is transcribed into the rhythm of
electrons. Then there are the waves which sweep across
this other universe, the microcosm of the cortex, the beaches
of the great neurones.

If it is merely called upon to recognise, the cortex
identifies the waves and records their arrival in its memory bank
by giving them a name. But it may also take an interest in
waves and wave patterns for their own sake. It might be distracted
from its task of identifying and recognising them.
Of wondering what possible use might be made of them.
It might try to actualise in the immediate
the rhythm in which it is caught up. Acting rather than thinking,
if you like. Inscribe the rhythm on a support,
on canvas, or on paper. It has to hurry. It has to
outwit its own power to hold back, to inhibit
to recognise and store for future use.
Make its nerve energy beat faster against the eyes,
the arms, the fingers, the whole body.
Appel standing.
The Pollock film shows that very well
the whole body dancing, inscribing itself
on a support which lies flat,
by means of dripping paint. Dance is not
depicted as it is in Degas or even in
Matisse; it is not mediated by a concept,
by images, schemata or memories.
Colour itself, both liquid and solidified,
dances on the support and leaves its trace
behind. The brain gripped by the dance of colour,
half seen, imagined.
    It is difficult to know where
    a painting comes from. Chance has a
    role in it of course, the most important thing is the 'third' eye,
    if people are on the alert (p 64)
rapidly transmitted to the shoulders, the

knees, the wrists which inscribe
Pollock on the canvas with splashes and streaks. And Appel with
broad strokes of the brush.

    the brush – I use a brush when I paint
    in oils – allows a sort of . . . a more direct manual
    contact with the painting. It is as though I could
    feel the painting through the brush (p 142)

He has to work fast

    Van Gogh worked with terrible power, at
    extraordinary speed. By working quickly, I gamble
    with chance, and suddenly, without being surprised, I find
    another unexpected answer
    in the way the spots arrange themselves, in the expressive
    force of the colours (pp 16, 89)

Haste frees the
central nervous rhythm
from recognition and control. A meditative asceticism,
the opening of the third eye,
the lesson taught by animals and children.
That's it: let the rhythm of the undulations
flow without filtering them through
the sieve of the known, the knowable,
the permitted and the forbidden.

That is not sufficient, but it is necessary
if we are to cross the threshold of appearances
and venture towards matter in its dancing immateriality.

    At moments like that, I no longer 'filter' anything

The brush makes colour cast off its moorings, leave
the calm polluted water of the port, and set sail for
where the great waves roll in one after the other,
with nothing to hold them back.

Escape

    A mill is a tool for the wind . . .
    A mill is like human being
    who has escaped (p 47)

The face can escape. The important thing
about a face is that is an open vista. That is scapes the
the limits of the known, the familiar. That the potential matter within
it
punctures its form, springs forth, spills out
over it, dislocates it,
That the face becomes dilated into
a landscape, one of the countless landscapes
concealed in its good, recognisable form, a form with a definite
destiny. Let it loses its destiny. Let it elude
the addressee of faces, the socius,
the right-thinking, homologised community.
The roar of faces emerges
from a ouquet of countenances.

    It was dark. I was walking down
    Broadway, towards Time Square.
    The pimps, the sixteen-year old whores,
    the foxy ladies, the screeching taxis,
    and the neon signs were being tossed around,
    as though by a centrifuge. Suddenly a

    a blood-curdling roar was heard from the virgin forest,
    drowning out the traffic and the turbulence:
    a black had recognised another
    black on the opposite side of the street!
    Like a volcano erupting. Friend answered friend from
    one side of the great avenue to the other, with the
    same jungle cry. They went their parallel ways,
    still screaming about their lives in slang (. . .)
    What a clamour on the scale of New York!
    How do you paint that? (p 116)

Place your trust in the howls you hear by chance.
in the first touch of colour
on the canvas, the first stroke of the brush.
The rest comes later, as a perk,
like the racket set up by the two blacks
on opposite sides of Broadway.
Colours scream out their lives.
They use slang. They understand
each other. They create a landscape
a vista, an eruption
Countenances talk proper,
and use the polite language of town centres and
residential areas. Colours pour out of it,
like invisible faces
Any landscape is an escape, any landscape
is a scapeland.
A landscape can erupt anywhere,
in any object, and make it pulsate
radiantly.

    Can you hold water in your hand,
    catch it in your fingers? What fascinated
    me about what the tree told me is that, even though
    is 'was' all those possible metamorphoses, it was
    in reality situated nowhere (. . .) What I mean is
    that the tree is not there. But it is definitely present.
    If someone in the middle of the sea (. . .) plunges his hand
    into the water, what is he left with? (. . .)
    You cannot catch water, and nor will the
    tree allow itself to be caught (pp 137-138)

They escape, but they do so by going forwards.
They offend. They offend against all controls,
against the thought that masters.
A cat might have fifty different faces.
A animal is closer to its faces than a
human being. And the God of the Bible
is mad up of nothing but faces, and that is why He is
invisible. He screams out his colours,
a pillar of fire by night, a column of smoke by day,
in the desert of Broadway, on the highway of
the exodus. He is water, timbre, and nothing
can hold Him. Present and not there.

On a different scale, on the scale of our poor bodies,
dance breaks down silhouettes and propriety. It allows
vibratory powers to break loose from their roots.
It is a 'tool for the wind'.
Gestural matter spills out of a sturdy body.
It must cease to be there, must no longer be anywhere.
Dance does not increase the body's power
over space, or over itself.
But it does shatter subtleties.
And in doing so it opens up space.
The body is not more than a support for the

inscription of rhythms, just as a canvas is a support
for liberated colours.
The canvas is ruled by the dance
of the paint that drips from the paw of the painter.
The body is ruled by the dance of sonorities
that are in excess of it.

The presence which haunts Appel
is thought acceding to something which is not
destined for it, and never will be.

Impression of being on a tightrope, of being
a high wire artiste, a wire dance (. . .)
A game played out in the very bosom of matter, in
the world and in front of the canvas, between life
and death (p 150)

He demands poetry, in the world,
on paper, and in words.

March 1987

Notes

Page references given in the text to page numbers are to Karel Appel, *Propos en liberté. Entretiens avec Frédéric de Towarnicki et André Vernet*, Edition Galilée, Paris, 1985.

It should be noted that in French the name Appel is indistinguishable form the noun *appel*, meaning 'appeal', 'call'.

KAREL APPEL, *BOAT WITH CLOUDS*, 1984

JOSEPH MARGOLIS
The Interconnection Of Art and History

It is a fact worth pondering that, in his wide-ranging Mellon Lectures in the Fine Arts for 1984, Richard Wollheim has nothing to say about the nature of history or art history. What he does say in the published version of the Lectures is confined to two pages of the Preface of a volume of nearly 400 pages. There he makes it clear that, for him, 'the objective study of an art [is not] the history of that art [but what] we call . . . criticism': 'given the small progress that art-history has made in explaining the visual arts, I am inclined [he says] to think that the belief that there is such a feature is itself something that needs historical explanation: it is an historical accident.'[1] This has all the earmarks of what, in the developing jargon of our age, may be called the 'premodernist' conception of art and history: in effect, the reduction of the history of art to mere transience or temporal persistence or chronic contingency.

The now-familiar array of notions – premodernism, modernism, postmodernism – do not figure at all in Wollheim's account, a fact that is actually more symptomatic than surprising for a commentator who gladly shares with Ernst Gombrich the truth that 'there is no such thing as "the innocent eye".'[2] *That* admission, in the hands of theorists impressed with the profoundly historicised nature of human culture and human existence, would have irresistibly ushered in the kind of distinction the modernism/postmodernism controversy has recently made so engaging. But in Wollheim's hands, as in Gombrich's and (even more significantly) in Freud's – the genius Wollheim most admires – the rejection of the 'innocent eye' merely introduces an appropriate caution for a complex discipline (art criticism or psychoanalysis) that rightly supposes its field of inquiry to be stable, to be composed of determinate objects the properties of which may be discerned with a certain necessary skill, and to be relatively unchanging (though surely enlarged) by the processes of history. Gombrich and Freud, of course, are exemplars of the so-called premodernist mentality.

It may also help to say that Jürgen Habermas' reading of Freud shows how Freud may be construed in the modernist way, just as Jacques Lacan's reading shows how he may be read in the postmodernist, even post-structuralist, way.[3] In fact, although he does not discuss modernism frontally, Wollheim does chide the so-called 'institutional theory' of art, which, as he says, attributes 'legendary powers' to certain self-appointed 'representatives of the art-world' who can make a work of art merely by thinking that something is art; probably the best-known modernists are historians, and he points expressly to Clement Greenberg, as one who could 'make and unmake the reputations and prices of works of art' but *not* 'that they were works of art.'[4]

In the same spirit but tactfully, Wollheim repudiates 'the tradition of social or sociological explanation of the arts' (exhibited, for instance, in the work of T J Clark and Francis Haskell) as well as the methodological bias of 'the structuralist and post-structuralist tradition': apparently, the first mistakenly encourages the thesis that there is 'a social function that all works of visual art universally and of necessity discharge'; and the second is marred by its 'seeming indifference to the particularity of the works they engage with and the readiness with which they allow their perceptions to be blurred by what is called by their adherents, quite inappropriately, 'theory' –

inappropriately because the term 'theory is in place only when some distinction is respected between description and explanation.'[5] Wollheim is frank to say that 'the art-history [he] most admire[s] is art-history in its most traditional mode. Connoisseurship, or the science of attribution, still seems [he says] the best hope for the objective study of painting.'[6] He means to favour what is perhaps a fair analogue of what Thomas Kuhn has labelled 'internal history', (speaking of the advanced sciences of course), which Kuhn somewhat unsatisfactorily means to reconcile with 'external history' (Marxist or Mertonian history, for instance, or the kind of history that has fairly recently been designated 'the science of science'.)[7] Kuhn speaks as a modernist, of course, with unusually strong (even incoherent) longings in the direction of a premodernist conception of science – in particular, with longings for a science in accord with the spirit of the unity-of-science model, softened considerably, it is true, for the sake of the discontinuities of actual scientific discovery. Kuhn is drawn to a conception of an effective science that does not ideally require the admission of an inherently historicised reading of its valid findings (premodernism); whereas it is true, nevertheless, that the actual local work and serial discovery of nests of scientists forever threaten to be radically historicised (modernism). Kuhn never satisfactorily addressed the question of the conceptual relationship between the two. To some extent, the same uncertainty appears under various guises in the views of Karl Popper and Imre Lakatos: all three obviously thought to resolve the puzzle by embracing one or another version of progressivism (which is simply, of course, one of the master forms of modernism).

Wollheim is more unequivocally premodernist than Kuhn, even though he is explicitly opposed (as is Kuhn in a parallel way) to the intrusion of positivism into art history and art criticism. Positivism, Wollheim says, is 'a pernicious disease', marred and marked by an 'over-estimation of fact, the rejection of cause, and the failure to grasp the centrality of explanation.' For all that, there is more in common between Wollheim and the positivists than Wollheim would care to admit – just as there is a great deal in common between positivism and the views on art of Monroe Beardsley (the philosopher of the American New Critics, a theorist very different from Wollheim, but one who would also not wish to be called a positivist – since thinkers of these sorts (premodernists all, let us say) are inclined to view the field of inquiry they favour as one that is reliably populated by well-defined, well-behaved, stable, boundaried objects the intrinsic properties of which (quite like those of the physical objects of the positivist or unity world) remain fairly unaffected or unaltered by the vagaries of history (even if, because of intentional features, artworks are not reducible to such objects). Beardsley certainly does not speak for Wollheim. But when he utters his two well-known principles of literary interpretation and ontology (generalisable, one supposes, to all the arts as well as to the sciences) he captures a premodernist conviction that Wollheim (and Gombrich and Clark and Freud, and possibly even Kuhn when he is most uneasy) surely share: namely, first, 'that literary works are self-sufficient entities, whose properties are decisive in checking interpretations and judgments' (the Principle of Autonomy); and second, that 'if two [interpretations of literary works] are logically incompatible, they cannot both be true' (the principle of the Intolerability of Incompatibles).[9]

These initial observations on Wollheim must be allowed to percolate as we proceed through our reading of very different views of art and history. We may in fact anticipate that they will guide us in a surprisingly apt way when we finally reach an assessment of Arthur Danto's theory of art. For Danto's account is surely the most advanced version of an analytic philosophy of art attentive to the complexities of cultural history. And yet, for all that, as we may anticipate, it is an account that does not satisfactorily escape from the premodernist and modernist limitations of thinkers like Wollheim and Kuhn. It may, for that reason, serve to facilitate a small prophecy about how we are bound to come to conceive the nature of art and history.

II

Western thought has turned sharply away from premodernist, even modernist, assumptions, or has been willing to worry them unmercifully in terms of an increasing radicalisation of history. It would not be unfair to urge that the general drift of current philosophical reflection of every influential sort (*pace* Wollheim) subscribes to the following general doctrines to one degree or another: (a) that all cognitive transparency and privilege is indefensible and must be rejected; (b) that human persons and the phenomena of their cultural or intelligible world are, as such, socially constituted or constructed in an indissolubly complex way from the materials of physical and biological nature; (c) that the range of human conception and understanding is horizontally and tacitly constrained by the ultimately unfathomable limits of the actual condition of life – preeminently, the praxical conditions – of the society in which given persons are first formed and acquire their cultural aptitudes; and (d) that human agency is capable, nevertheless, by reflection and actual commitment, of altering, even transforming, the conceptual horizon of its own society; of the sedimented, somewhat essentialised, nature its usual membership is said to exhibit; and the further real possibilities of improvisation that society's history may yet manifest as a result of the interventions of its own apt members.[10]

We may say that *modernism* is the result of combining (a)-(d) – roughly, intransparency and historicity – without losing the confidence that truth claims and truth-like claims are objective, open to rational legitimation, ideally collected in the form of a gradually coherent, systematic, and uniquely adequate account of the real world. *Postmodernism* also subscribes to (a)-(d), but it does so with the distinct purpose of disclaiming objectivity or the cognitive accessibility of an independent world, or with the purpose of disclaiming at least legitimating objectivity or progressively approximating an encompassing system of what is timelessly true or right or good. It is reasonably clear that modernism and postmodernism are by no means exhaustive options, though they are exclusive of one another. On the contrary, modernism is incoherent on its own grounds; and postmodernism is either incoherent or utterly arbitrary in disallowing questions of truth. Certainly, the admission of (a)-(d) is incompatible with the denial of some form of relativism at least, must be incompatible with the defensibility of nonconverging, even incompatible, but realist claims; nevertheless, modernism – for example, on the arguments of Habermas and Gadamer and Popper and Charles Taylor and Alasdair MacIntyre and Richard Bernstein and Thomas Kuhn and Hilary Putnam and many others – is incompatible with such a relativism, with strong incommensurabilities, and with the denial of progressivism.[11]

We may, in fact, construct a *passage* of theories regarding the nature and relevance of intentionality and history, drawn from the most extreme premodernism to the most attenuated modernism, bearing largely on conceptions of art that have straddled the last 40 years, that will help us see how the perception of the historicity of art and culture has changed in that interval. In Monroe Beardsley, for example, history and intentionality are all but irrelevant to the cognitive work of the art or literary critic, though they may qualify the content of what the critic discerns.[12] Beardsley's is probably the most extreme version of a premodernist theory of art that our own age has favoured. It is very

much in accord with the well-known account of historical explanation offered by C G Hempel, which is itself critical of narrowly positivist and empiricist conceptions of science but which pretty well disallow any ramified historical or intentional features to colour the methodology (and what we would now call the ontology) of culture.[13] Accordingly, Beardsley construes the objectivity of criticism as leading ideally to a uniquely correct and adequate account of particular artworks. It is the point of his Principle of the Intolerability of Incompatibles. His is a thesis that supposes that, in principle, a correct reading of a poem can be achieved, complated, and uniquely specified for all historical times. Wollheim's view is only marginally softer than Beardsley's, primarily because Wollheim does not share Beardsley's strong empiricism. Addressing expressive properties, for instance, Wollheim accords a more substantive role to intentional considerations, which, matched with his penchant for psychoanalytic explanation, colours his own premodernist picture of the methodology of criticism and the human sciences. In this, as already remarked, Wollheim shares a theoretical orientation with Gombrich and Freud. But he never wavers on the question of objectivity.

Karl Popper holds a view of historical laws that converges decidedly with Hempel's, though he is an even stronger critic of postitivism than Hempel. In effect, Popper captures by his doctrine of verisimilitude – regarding what is unfathomably essential and lawlike in nature (in effect, progressivism) – a modernist analogue of Hempel's premodernist conception of history. It is also true that, in his general opposition to reductive physicalism, in his otherwise inchoate account of so-called World 3 phenomena, Popper is more hospitable to the ontic import of intentionality along lines linked to Wollheim's position despite his own well-known animus against Freud.[14] All of these thinkers are strongly opposed, of course, to relativism and effective conceptual incommensurabilities. The resemblance between thinkers like Beardsley, Wolheim and Hempel, on the one hand, and Popper, Kuhn, Gadamer and Greenberg, on the other, confirms the ulterior convergence between premodernism and modernism: in effect, modernists are concerned to recover within the flux and intransparencies of history what the ahistorical premodernists had thought to fix as the objectivity of factual knowledge. Both tend to think of the world as populated by aggregates of determinate, well-founded, and logically well-behaved objects.

Romantic hermeneutics, progressing from Schleiermacher's instruction and regressing from Heidegger's account of history (opposing Heidegger, in fact, and those Heidegger influenced – Gadamer preeminently), represents, particularly in the work of literary theorist like E D Hirsch, Jr (or, even more extremely, P D Juhl) or, among more general hermeneuts, Emilio Betti, the boldest and most systematic effort to date to bring history and intentionality within the full compass of premodernism.[15] A distant analogue appears in R G Collingwood's rather Cartesian account of history and, somewhat closer in spirit, in Wilhelm Dilthey's account of history – both of which, along different lines, affect their respective authors' accommodation of historical change in the context of theorising about the arts.[16] In both, there is movement in the direction of modernism. But it is really only after Heidegger, though not entirely in accord with Heidegger, that Hans-Georg Gadamer effectively formulated the classic form of modernist historicism. The mark of Gadamer's modernism lies with its emphasis on the strong historicity of human nature, the absence of a *telos* or universal law of history, and (despite that) the full recoverability of 'the' essential human tradition – classical Greek humanism – that, through all historical change and among all peoples, constantly recovers the trans-historical change and norms and values of mankind.[17] The incoherence and arbitrariness of Gadamer's view is patent. It is an essentialism and teleologism *manqué*. But it is also, it must be said, the master influence on such theorists as Charles Taylor (who quite loosely relies on a sense of history to restore us uniquely to a correct grasp of the distributed conceptual puzzles of humanity), Alasdair McIntyre (who finds an unchanging, if de-essentialised, Aristotelian formal structure guiding our normative concerns through all the changes of human history), Richard Bernstein (who yields increasingly along Kuhnian lines to accommodate incommensurabilities in which he happily discovers a liberal convergence among the achievements of science and the normative direction of practical life).[18] Once again, all of these theorists strongly oppose the sort of relativism mentioned earlier; they also believe, with equal conviction, in the uniquely (or at least strongly convergent) truths of science and normative discourse. In this sense, as already suggested, Thomas Kuhn is the somewhat pale analogue of hermeneutic modernism developing out of the tradition of Anglo-American philosophy of science – for Kuhn similarly attempts to recover the assurance of premodernist science from within the threatening historical flux and attendant incommensurabilities modernist theorists cannot altogether ignore.[19]

The most extreme and (therefore) the most doubtful form of modernism appears, without question, in the thesis espoused by Jürgen Habermas. For it is Habermas, precisely, who seeks to recover a universal model of rationality (affecting the prospects of both science and practical life) along the lines of the Enlightenment vision – but only *by way of* a progressivist reading of the dialectics of human communication under all conceivable historical conditions. In effect, Habermas unites universalism and historicism by the ingenious (but entirely obvious and indefensible) strategy of liberating his master notion of 'emancipatory reason' from the fluidities of history itself.[20] Effectively, Habermas cheats on his own modernism. It is for this reason that, in a spirit rather more premodernist than modernist, Karl-Otto Apel shows (again indefensibly) how to reconcile Kantianism and an attenuated historicism that calls to mind the related bridging efforts of Dilthey.[21] Clement Greenberg, the preeminent modernist art historian, is also a genuine exemplar, inasmuch as, through the processes of history, Greenberg claims to recover the inflexible immanent logic of art history (incidentally subverting the kitsch and bad taste of postmodernism) by which successive artists have affirmed, even discontinuously, what is unique and essential (and unchanging through change) in the flatness of the medium of painting. Greenberg's view, therefore, shows clear affinities with the divergent (but still fatal) tendencies of Gadamer and Habermas.[22] And Heinrich Klotz, one of the best-known champions of modernist architecture, has, subscribing in some measure apparently to Habermas' *Discourse of Modernity*, actually now endorsed (as an expression of 'neo-modernism') the reversal of modernist architecture's preference for 'the vocabulary of the present' (as opposed to a sense of continuous history): he now maintains, within the space of a revived Constructivism (largely Russian in inspiration), that 'the history of Modernism leads us back to history in general.'[23] Klotz implies that a pertinent invariance has been recovered.

III

Step back, now, to reconsider matters more analytically. What we mean or could mean or should mean by the history of any of the arts or the history of the history of the arts or the history of the history of the criticism and interpretation of the arts is too difficult a matter for high expectations about the benefits of honest, direct, uncluttered, instant answers. A certain indirection is advisable if, by testing false options however briefly, we manage to delimit the conceptual acreage we need. Nevertheless, the conceit of defending a few theses nailed up very early on the academic door is much too alluring to be altogether resisted. So let us use our nails first and then our devious strategems – although, with that directness, we shall not yet address the nature of artworks or the full connection between art and history.

Here, then are three claims that, construed as intended, may serve to signal a small reformation beyond both modernism and postmodernism:

1 A *history* is a narratised account of whatever may be individuated, regarding changes among, or the persistence of, its intentional prop-

erties; or, it is the actual narratised career of such referents collecting such properties;

2 *Intentional* properties, like all properties, are, or are rightly ascribed as, the properties possessed by a given referent only if those properties and that referrent are, mutually, *ontically adequated*;

3 Natural discourse, is, minimally, *constative*, stable enough in a formal sense to function referentially and predicatively, without prejudice to the nature of whatever the world contains. Silly, of course, our terms of art – 'intentional properties', 'ontic adequation', 'constative', 'narratised' – remain as yet actually undefined. They are, however, the golden keys.

The point of these three theses is to bring together the conserving and liberating possibilities of theorising about the history of the arts and about the history of theorising about the arts: in part, in a global sense, since everything that may be said to have a history should conform with theses 1-3; in part, quite locally, since artworks are uncontroversially thought to be distinctive, rather unlike much else that we find in the world. So we must risk a little more.

By 'intentional,' we shall understand an array of predicables that characteristically cannot be regimented in canonically extensional ways and that still form the actual properties, for instance, ascribed to artworks). By 'narratised,' we shall understand an intentionally significant temporal ordering of the intentional features of some referent or entity, either as an account of its career or as a distinct property of that career itself (the development of Cubism, say). By 'ontic adequation,' we shall understand the conceptual congruity between what we ascribe as the nature of a given referent and what may be truly predicated of it – what it may be said to possess as a property or quality or attribute supportable by or ascribable to something of that nature (the intentional nature of Michelangelo's *Pietà*, say, in virtue of which it may actually possess, not merely have attributed to it, heuristically or rhetorically, the property of representing Christ's *pietà*). And by 'constative,' we shall understand that form of speech act, implicit or explicit, by which we utter what we permit or require to take truth values or truth-like values – as 'true,' 'probably', 'plausible', 'reasonable', 'right', 'valid', and the like – statements, propositions, *énoncés*, on various theories, that identify numerically individuated referents and that ascribe pertinent predicables to them.

The simple governing conception in all of this is that, since natural discourse must, minimally, preserve a constative function, the formal constraints of language yield *some* metaphysical constraints on what we admit to be in the world – quite apart from any cognitive privilege we may think to exercise in describing the things of the world distributively. In short, we must separate a 'metaphysics of constatation' from a 'metaphysics of privilege.' The first is invariant only in the benign sense that the saliencies of human experience do not (or do not yet) appear to yield a way of understanding discourse without implicating constation. The invariances of constatation, like the invariances of theses 1-3 taken together, are, we may say, merely 'indicative' or provisional – that is, *are themselves historicised* – thought they are still noticeably persistent. Thesis 3 prepares the ground for specific metaphysical claims going beyond the formal consequences of viable discourse (constatation). Theses 1 and 2 are just such stronger claims. The first presupposes that there is no known conceptual strategy adequate and convincing for eliminating or neutralising intentional complexities; the second may be construed as a quasi-formal condition of coherent discourse when read in accord with thesis 3. The second is substantive in the additional sense that intentional properties are to be treated as actual properties actually possessed by individuatable entities; hence, the first is substantive as well, particularly when joined to the thesis that historical properties are real properties.

Taken together, these concessions trivially signify that actual entities are not restricted to the possession of extensional properties only. The manoeuvre remains important, because intentional properties are known to exhibit rather peculiar logical features and because they appear to be intrinsic to artworks. They challenge our prejudices about the nature of reality: they are decidedly quarrelsome. For the moment, however, we may take note of the fact that, admitting theses 1 and 2 – now, specifications within the range of 3 – we are resisting all physicalist or physicalist-like accounts (whether reductive or nonreductive) of persons, artworks, words and sentences, human actions, institutions, societies and the like. This affords an enormous economy at one stroke, because it sets out very severe constraints on any wouldbe theories of artworks or of history – particularly, theories of the nature of the history of artworks – that we might be tempted to advance. Effectively, then, we are making out the world of human culture as populated by entities and phenomena that exhibit strongly intentional properties and that include, among those properties, strongly historicised ones.

We must think here of quite ordinary examples. The *Pietà* does represent Christ's *pietà*: the marble sculpture *possesses* that property. The sculpture and its properties are real enough; but what we should mean (both ontologically and interpretatively) by that representational property is open to quarrel and to historicised change without, as such, threatening the reality of the property in question. That's all. The point is that only a certain number of theories can accommodate the facts of this sort. For instance, Beardsley's theory cannot, and Wollheim's probably cannot (though it struggles to do so). If we add other complexities of the sort indicated, affecting both art and history, then it will turn out (as we may anticipate) that nearly all the dominant theories of art and history (and the history of art in the double sense intended) are demonstrably defective – defective in a way that, as it fortunately happens, also indicates an easy escape from the modernism/postmodernism impasse. One hopes the threatening benefit is worth the labour.

IV

These are the nails. Now for the strategems of dispute. It will perhaps not seem obvious, but what we have already laid out leads directly to the defeat of three very powerful models of history (*a fortiori*, of the history of art). Compendiously put: (i) *physicalist* theories of history fail, because they do not accommodate history's intentional complexities; (ii) *world* (unified histories of the entire world) fail, or are fictions or myths of some sort that logically depend on actual prior histories, because they violate the minimal requirements of constatation; and (iii) *relational* histories, that is, theories that treat history as only relationally attributed to actual entities, or as constructed only in virtue of *our* interest in certain actual entities, fail, because they do not account adequationally for our own histories and because they treat history as invariably no more than a form of rhetoric, a mere *façon de parler*.

In a good sense, therefore, the theses nailed on the door have anticipated the failure of the three sorts of history just tallied. By an additional economy, we may say that any physicalist theory of art (Wollheim's, for example, at least with respect to painting and music[24]) must fail, because, where (as with Wollheim) intentional properties (representational and expressive properties) are admitted, the physicalist theory cannot account adequationally for their ascription to given artworks. Whether the same would be true for the rhetorical or relational theory of art (notably, as in Arthur Danto's account[25]) remains to be seen: that is, the theory that intentional properties are only relationally ascribed to physical objects (or workaday artifacts) in virtue of a certain interest we take in them. The theory of art that is the mate of the theory of world history must fail in a trivial sense (if the theory of world history fails) since, as in Hegel's theory of the arts (the supreme exemplar), the very meaning of the intentional properties of particular artworks can only be specified in terms of the unfolding history of the *Weltgeist*.[26]

Characteristically, physicalist histories are premodernist in spirit, as, for instance, are the views of C G Hempel and Adolf Grünbaum; Beardsley's and Wollheim's theories of history, theories *manqués*, are

plainly akin to these, though they are also only partly physicalist in temperament. Hegel's conception of history, the paradigm of world history – our category (ii) – fails because it substitutes *Geist*, a totally encompassing Subject, for distributed, actual historical agents; that is, it substitutes what logically lacks number for what is individuatable: hence, it can only construct, parasitically, a mythic history *on* what may be constatively claimed and confirmed in a world of denumerably many entities. Once that particular failing is grasped, it is but a step to demonstrate that the *telos* of world history is also a fiction *and* that the purposes of individuated human agents cannot themselves ever yield (functioning consciously or unconsciously, in Hegel's or Marx's sense) a unified historical *telos*. Hegel himself is against it, of course.[27] But it requires no very great acumen to appreciate that Hegel, standing at the very dawn of post-Revolutionary modernity, is the very model of a modern major modernist; or to appreciate that Habermas, criticising Hegel's 'wrong turn' – that is, Hegel's preference of the totalised *geistlich* (the 'subjective') rather than the aggregatively social – claims, (as Hegel's and Marx's rightful successor) to have found the correct formula for reconciling modernist and premodernist objectives.[28]

The relational theory is, from our present point of view, the most interesting of the three models, because it happens to have been formulated in our own time in a fully ramified way by one of the most knowledgeable critics any analytic philosophers or art. Arthur Danto's theory, the one we have in mind, is most unusual in being very nearly the only currently developed account to attempt to reconcile elements of all three conceptions of history that promises to escape the limitations of the physicalist and world versions, that is strongly modernist in spirit but tempered by sympathies for both premodernist and postmodernist concerns, and that brings together in one explicit statement the analysis of history and the analysis of artworks. Still, *on the assumption of the theses originally nailed to our door* – arguably unavoidable for anyone who subscribes to the intransparency and historicity of human existence (the dual themes of post-Revolutionary modernity) – Danto's theory must, demonstrably, fail. With *that* failure and the failure of the general strategies of premodernism, modernism, and postmodernism, the attempt to theorise about art and history and the history of art must turn to consider entirely different options made possible by interpreting our three theses in the context of modernity. The marvel and irony remain that such an effort would reveal both the power of postmodernist criticisms of modernism and a way of escaping the self-defeating drive of postmodernism itself.

Turn back for a moment to physicalism and the physicalist theory of history. Consider, by way of a small aside, the possible significance of the difference (on a physicalist reading) between what we could possibly mean in speaking of the history of the events of our universe and the history of the sciences that endeavour to understand and explain them. On the prevailing view, the actual world can be adequately and exhaustively described (as far as objective truth claims are concerned) in purely physicalist terms; or, more strenuously, the actual world is nothing but the physical world (however picturesquely it may otherwise be described). Such theories are said to be *physicalist*: the first mentioned, non-reductive, in the sense that non-physicalist descriptions may be true in their own right but extensionally replaceable everywhere (*not* translated) by physicalist descriptions, *salve veritate*; the second, reductive, in the double sense that scientific truth is rigorously captured only by physicalist descriptions and that nonphysicalist descriptions are meaningless, unconfirmable, heuristic, entirely fictional, or actually translatable in physicalist terms.[29] (Extreme postmodernists, of course, Lyotard preminently, sensing the gathering conceptual trap of admitting the systematic achievement of the sciences and their entitlement to claims of objective truth, repudiate in an utterly irresponsible way the very admission of first-order truth claims [the empirical sciences] and [consequently] the very relevance of second-order legitimative explanations [philosophies] of such first-order marvels. Nevertheless, charming though this *beau guests* surely is, it fails to address or explain [within whatever resources we can command], or it fails to explain why we need not bother to explain, the evident stability and power of the empirical sciences. The sciences cannot be dismissed as a mere ideology or political or religious commitment: we must understand them pertinently if we are to understand the worlds of history and art. At the very least, the postmodernists have lost their philosophical nerve.[30])

On the physicalist view, we may experience difficulty in formulating (whether reductively or non-reductively) a suitable description of our *science*, but (it is claimed) we experience no such difficulty with regard to the actual *domain* of physics. The naivety of this disjunction and the force of questions regarding the scope of would-be physics (ranging over biology and psychology, say) need not detain us here.[31] The relevant point is that the real history of *events* (as opposed to history as the *representation* of those events) could be formulable without recourse to intentional categories of any kind; also, ideally though not yet, the history of our *science* could, where wanted, be (so the physicalist argues) similarly recast (whether reductively or non-reductively). The important consideration is simply that, for the physicalist, physical events *have* actual histories and those histories preclude intentional complexities, regardless of whatever other difficulty we may have with a physicalist rendering of our historical *representations* of scientific findings. Physicalists and non-physicalists (dualists, idealists, neutral monists, possibly other more ingenious theorists, even materialists) cannot share the same conception of history. Even the non-reductive physicalist (the theorist who claims to be able to replace in extensionally equivalent ways every true non-physicalist description without actually translating such descriptions and without insisting on a reductive analysis of the phenomena in question), must admit that there may – possibly even must – be an impoverishment in the resulting conception of history *if* (by our thesis 1) histories *are* narratised orderings, or representations of such orderings, of actual intentional properties.

When, therefore, a theorist like Adolf Grünbaum – however effectively he may attack the views (on science) held by such discussants as Gadamer and Habermas and Paul Ricoeur (who obviously do not subscribe to the physicalist's notion of *history*) – must either be quite mistaken about what a history is or must mean something utterly different (in speaking of the '*history*' of physical events) from whatever his hermeneut targets mean when *they* speak of history. Grünbaum claims that the phenomena of the physical sciences (and the laws governing them) *are* historical and context-bound in precisely (even paradigmatically) the same sense in which the phenomena of human culture are historical.[32]

But this cannot be true unless physicalism – perhaps reductive physicalism – is also true. Grünbaum never directly addresses the conceptual relationship between physical and intentional properties. It is clear, of course, that when he speaks of history and context affecting electrodynamic phenomena (and the formal properties of the laws of such phenomena), *he* favours a position very much like the physicalist's, whether or not he actually subscribes the physicalism; hence, when he treats of the materials of the human sciences (notoriously: when he treats of psychoanalysis as a science), he means to examine those materials methodologically in whatever way the treatment of certain exemplary part of the *physical* sciences (electrodynamics) normatively *dictate*. On Grünbaum's view, the exemplary sciences do yield criteria for the 'proper' discipline of the *human* sciences (including the management of history). It follows at once that, for Grünbaum, histories are not or need not be intentional in structure at all, are actually not intentional among the best paradigms of science. Intentionality itself (we now see) can never affecting principle the logic of history even where (as in psychoanalysis) intentionality stubbornly resists canonical regimentation. Grünbaum, it must be said in all fairness, is committed to a uniform methodological extensionalism among all would-be sciences, not to a reductive physicalism. But the result is the same as far as the analysis of history is concerned, because

the 'histories' of electrodynamic phenomena *are* paradigmatic *and* lack intentional features. The argument in support of Grünbaum's general methodological claim is simply utterly lacking. The same sort of lacuna, we may remark, infects the views of Wollheim and Beardsley.

It needs also to be said that there is no known convincing strategy for eliminating or reducing by translation or extensional equivalence the complex intentional phenomena of the human world – in the arts, in history, in action, in psychology and the social sciences, in interpretation and criticism. There are armies of enthusiasts who dream of the imminences of such an achievement. But for the time being at least we must treat the histories of these domains as profoundly qualified by the intentionality of their phenomena. In fact, on the gathering argument, *historicity* is itself an intrinsic ontological feature *of* cultural entities and phenomena; and, because of that, *histories* (as representations of the careers of cultural phenomena: persons, artworks, actions, institutions, practices, societies) are methodologically affected in a distinctive way. The intriguing thing is that this summary finding is quite indifferent to the fortunes of modernism and postmodernism. It is, of course, still implicitly contested by what we had earlier labelled the relational theory of history and art – Danto's particular theory – which we have not yet examined. So let us make a fresh start to see whether Danto's alternative suffices in its own terms and what, if it does not suffice, may still be recovered for a theory of art and history and a history of art that escapes the indicated weaknesses of modernism and postmodernism.

VI

Danto's theories of art and history are neatly matched and unusually flexible. They centre, as does indeed his further theories of knowledge and action, on the unavoidability of intentional ascriptions in speaking of human life and cultural history. They admit such *ascriptions*; but they raise and resolve the question of *placing* (in a grammatical sense) whatever *properties* they impute, in a way distinctly congruent with physicalism. The result is that the striking flexibility of Danto's schema is bought at the price of an extreme, initially unnoticed slackness. Applied to the arts, it appears initially quite supple in the context of the modernist/postmodernist debate – and it *is* supple. But a theory of art and history adequate at the present time is bound to reconcile what it says about modernism with what it offers respecting the ontic nature of art and history and the cognitive aspects of critical and historical claims. Danto avoids or neglects the connection, or resolves it (implicitly) by an ingenious *relational* use of the physicalist thesis.

Broadly speaking, Danto answers the question by restricting the intentional to what is merely internal to certain acts of ascribing, and then characterises *that* to which *those* ascriptions are made in physicalist or near-physicalist terms – or, at any rate, in terms that preclude the intentional in a strongly realist sense. The exception to this practice may be the human person himself. Danto nowhere provides an explicitly analysis of the nature of human beings in terms of which we may be sure that intentional ascriptions made of humans do or do not designate real intrinsic properties. Since the question is a reflective one and since the entire world of human culture is inseparable from and seemingly as real as man (in fact, it is the very condition on which man achieves his distinctive form of existence), the admission that intentional ascriptions (when applied to humans) affirm something about man's intrinsic properties would seem to subvert any argument opposing a congruent account of actions, artworks, histories and the like; on the other hand, if the intentional is no more than a grammatically or heuristically specified internal *attributum* of a speech act or thought relationally or referentially addressed to something the real nature of which is essentially describable in physicalist terms alone (whether reductively or not), then by the same token it would seem impossible to resist applying that line of analysis to man himself. Danto has certainly never favoured the latter move; nor does he seem inclined to. Nevertheless, in his sustained discussion of actions, artworks, and history, he does favour a physicalist characterisation of what is real, *if* we allow (or can make persuasive) the charge that his *relational* use of intentionality does not disturb a fundamentally physicalist orientation (in fact, confirms it). Reviewing a justly famous array of red canvases which he asks us to imagine, by way of a very agreeable joke, Danto adds warningly:

> Though it is tempting to say, in a Wittgensteinian echo, that nothing is left over [from any red square of canvas that counts as a painting, an artwork], that [the imagined painting] 'Red Square' [for instance] *just is* that red square of canvas, or, more portentiously and more generally, that the artwork just is the material from which it is made, it is difficult to see how this creditable theory can survive an example in which something like a red square of canvas underdetermines the differences between [two further imagined paintings] 'The Israelites Crossing the Red Sea' and 'Kierkegaard's Mood,' as well as the philosophically deeper differences between either of them and that red square [previously introduce] which was not an artwork but a mere thing . . .[34]

Danto is certainly right to press the point. But it remains true nevertheless (so we are claiming) that *his* resolution of the puzzle remains entirely physicalist in spirit or at least fails to show clearly the sense in which it is not. (One may usefully recall, here, Wilfrid Sellars' physicalism, which appears to make similar concessions.[35])

Two preliminary clues may be offered. For one, comparing human actions and physical movements – more particularly, comparing 'basic actions' (that is, actions not mediated by other actions) and 'bodily processes' – Danto holds that the 'the complex event' that is the basic action (characterised intentionally) just '*is identical with*' some 'physiological series' of events: it is numerically 'one and the same event.'[36] The second clue is this. By the term 'historical language', Danto explains that he has 'in mind an open class of sentences which purport when asserted to describe events which have taken place anterior to their utterance or inscription.'[37] He is still concerned with the *relationship* between historical language and historical reality, but that relationship is now essentially coloured by the characterisation just given. The force of the first clue rests with the fact that Danto favours a reductive identity involving action and physical movement: hence, that he *must* treat intentional ascriptions *of actions* as purely heuristic or worse. The implication looms that Danto holds a similar view of artworks and history. The force of the second clue rests with the fact that historical ascriptions, whatever their apparent intentional content, are ultimately and adequately anchored in the contingencies of mere physical time: hence, that they are identified in ways that do not entail intentional factors. The implication spreads that the intentional complexities of history (as of art and action) are restricted *relationally* to whatever may be ascribed *to* physical phenomena *as* a result of our interest in those phenomena, without ever providing a further analysis of our own nature or of the ontic nature of cultural phenomena.

The strange consequence is that, although they seem worlds apart, Danto's treatment of art and history is extraordinarily similar to Grünbaum's treatment of science and history – except that Danto explicitly treats the intentional in a grammatically relational way and Grünbaum ignores the analysis of the issue on what appear to be methodological grounds. Hence, Danto is freed at once to take whatever limber view of the history of art he can and wishes to defend, without the least danger of any serious ontic or methodological constraints. For, he is never committed ontically with respect to art and history – except by default; and he cannot be constrained methodologically – for the intentional discourse of art and history is (now) merely relational or heuristic, entirely dictated by our interest *in* particular entities and phenomena (indifferently identified as artworks or physical objects) that (on the argument) lack real intentional properties. (It is hard to see how the artworld could survive in a robust sense on the vagaries of ascriptions to objects that themselves lack the intrinsic properties answering to what those ascriptions only relationally impute to them.)

Now, the marvel of all this is that Danto employs the device – seemingly physicalist in nature but cleverly outfitted with the additional wild card of a relational idiom (intentionality) that the physicalists would have insisted on explaining reductively or non-reductively – in order to convey what proves to be a distinctly Hegelian reading of the history we are repudiating; and, in doing that, he also manages to address (implicitly at least) what (one supposes) he regards as the modernist/postmodernist dispute – the 'end of art'[38] – in a decidedly teleological and *geistlich* (Hegelian) way.

We need to have the relevant passage before us in order to appreciate its attraction and economy. After introducing Hegel's account of history, Danto says that 'we may speculate historically on the future of art without committing ourselves on what the artworks of the future are to be like . . . it is even possible [he says] to suppose that art itself has no future, though artworks may still be produced post-historically, as it were, in the aftershock of a vanished vitality.' 'I want to take Hegel quite seriously,' he adds, 'and to sketch a model of the history of art in which something like it may be said to make sense' – and even to be true.[39]

The essential point to remember, which the charm of the intended (and delivered) history may deflect us from noticing, is simply this: the Hegelian amplification of history is an amplification made only within the terms *of the relationalised analysis of history and art we are resisting.* The force of the historical thesis could not but be adversely affected if the Hegelianised theory of history Danto constructs, as well as the rhetorically relationalised theory of art we have ascribed to him, were challenged; and the latter theories could not possibly be pertinently strengthened by the independent plausibility of the particular story of art Danto happens to have presented in the complex idiom he favours.

To put the issue in a word: Danto's theory of history – similarly, his theory of art, of action, of knowledge – does not plausibly satisfy the requirements of ontic adequation that we originally introduced. His only possible options are these: (a) on the reductive view (favouring the identity thesis that he explicitly embraces when he speaks of actions), history and art are, *qua* real, mere physical phenomena or physical aspects of physical phenomena – recall the characterisation of 'historical language'; (b) on the non-reductive physicalist view (admitting that Danto does not explicitly embrace reductionism), talk about art and history is, when true, extensionally replaceable by physicalist talk – in which case, it is either heuristic or introduced in an entirely agnostic way regarding its own ontic standing; or (c) on the relational view (Danto's own), talk about art and history is permitted to float free of all ontic constraint; and it is not clear then what may be said to be its particular rigour in cognitive respects (that is, as determinate historical or critical claims), one in which case it threatens to dwindle (in a pejorative sense) to a mere form of rhetoric and (for that reason) it fails to come to grips with the adequation of human agents (interested in art and history) on which the full import of his theory depends. Marx, we may remember, effectively formulated a principled alternative to Hegel's particular histories as well as to Hegel's idealist conception of a totalised *geistlich* history.[40] Danto's account cannot possibly be firmer than Hegel's since it lacks altogether any explicit rationale drawn from the ontology of art or history. Danto acknowledges, furthermore, that his own Hegelian thesis 'can hardly be pondered outside the framework of a philosophy of history it would be difficult to take seriously were the urgency of art's future not somehow raised from within the artworld itself, which can be seen today as having lost any historical direction, and we have to ask whether this is temporary, whether art will regain the path of history – or whether this destructed condition *is* its future: a kind of cultural entropy.[41] But, for one thing, the 'exhaustion' of art may only be an artifact of Danto's Hegelianised vision of history; it is hardly an independent brute fact. For another, it may (such as it is) by due to local

24

eddies of exhaustion and not to the teleology of the history of art: it need not implicate any Hegelian *malaise*. And for a third, the alleged exhaustion may be disputed (as in Heinrich Klotz's attempt to redirect modernism against Charles Jencks' optimism for the postmodern, both of which speculations beckon from 'within the art-world itself.'[42] Also, the mere fact that recent discussions of modernism and postmodernism have not fastened on clear definitions of those terms – either philosophically or in art-historical terms – hardly shows that they have not sensed those sources of social energy that could escape the modernist strictures Danto places on art history.[43] Only a teleologised and totalised conception of history could possibly risk precluding the defeat of prophecy from that quarter.

VII

We must bring this account to a careful close. If we return to the school door's theses, we may say that there are two decisive issues that any responsive theory linking art and history will want to consider. One is the matter of ontic adequation, in particular, of what we may convincingly claim is the most reasonable substantive view of the nature of artworks could be (in virtue of art's possessing intentional properties) while still satisfying the formal constraint of numerical identity. The two conditions interlock, of course: the adequation of designata and their predicables cannot be permitted to violate the requirements of numerical identity. But that itself explains why *descriptions* satisfy two hard masters: for the minima of natural-language discourse – the minima of constatation – include, as already remarked, provision for stable referents as well as for stable arrays of predicables. The mere admission of describability and identifiability, therefore, need not signify any concessions to cognitive privilege: they are, rather, conditions of intelligibility.

Danto's sole response to the question of how to manage the reidentification of numerically individuated artworks rests with his well-known distinction between the 'is' of numerical identity and the 'is' of 'artistic identification'.[44] Here is what he says in what may well be his most sustained recent account of the notion, offered on the occasion of objecting to Susan Sontag's own objection to certain ways of interpreting artworks. It is worth citing at length:

I believe we cannot be deeply wrong if we suppose that the correct interpretation of object-as-artwork is the one which coincides most closely with the artist's own interpretation . . . [Sontag's objection] is against a notion of interpretation which makes the artwork as an expandum – as a symptom. My theory of interpretation is instead constitutive, for an object is an artwork *at all* only in relation to an interpretation. We may bring this out in a somewhat logical way. Interpretation in my sense is transfigurative. It transforms objects into works of art, and depends upon the 'is' of artistic identification. [Sontag's] interpretations, which are explanatory, use instead the 'is' of ordinary identity. Her despised interpreters see works as signs, symptoms, expressions of ulterior or subjacent realities, states of which are what the artwork 'really' refer to . . . Mine is a theory which is not in the spirit of science but of philosophy. If interpretations are what constitute works, there are no works without them and works are misconstituted when interpretation is wrong. And knowing the artist's interpretation is in effect identifying what he or she has made. The interpretation is not something outside the work: work and interpretation arise together in aesthetic consciousness. As interpretation is inseparable from work, it is inseparable from the artist if it is the artist's work . . . The possible interpretations are constrained by the artist's location in the world . . . There is a truth to interpretation and a stability to works of art which are not relative at all.[45]

Now, this *sounds* promising; but of course the constitutive or transfigurative use of 'is' (the 'is' of artistic identification) does not in the least – in fact, cannot, for logical reasons – preclude the use and the need for the use of the 'is' of numerical identity. On the contrary,

'once' constituted (whatever that may mean: it will of course mean different things for modernists and postmodernists), we shall have to fall back to the 'is' of identity *applied* to *what* is constituted in accord with the use of the 'is' of artistic identification. But Danto nowhere explains this connection or even what we should understand *as* thus, and *how* thus, constituted.

It is just here that Danto's own clues regarding art, action, history, artifacts suggest the relational (now, perhaps more pointedly intentional) conception of *taking* a physical object or artifact *to be* an artwork. It is (it seems) in just this sense that Danto mentions 'a work such as Duchamp's *In Advance of the Broken Arm*, which [he says], even when accepted as a work of art, retained its identity as a quite ordinary snow shovel. Comparable examples [he adds] can be drawn from the other arts, especially as we approach our own century, when music and poetry and dance have yielded examplars which could not have been perceived as art had anything like them appeared in earlier times, as sets of words or sounds or movements.'[46] It looks very much as if: (1) either Duchamp's artwork is identical with the artifactual snow shovel (in which case, for the sake of consistency, the intentional *ascriptions* made in the artworld can only be heuristic uses of the would-be artist's intentions *relating to* that artifact or physical object *that is what the ascriptions are about*; or (2) the artwork is *not* identical with the artifact or physical object thus designated, but *is* something altogether different from the *pre*transfigured object: for (for consistency's sake again) the intentional *properties* of the artwork *cannot* be the intrinsic properties of any mere physical object unless the intentional can be reduced to the physical. Solution (1) subverts the reality of the artworld – although it does so without bothering to explain the reality of human thought and existence within the space of which artists' intentions might yet be said to be real; and solution (2) *is* a formal solution that Danto nowhere develops and may even resist. Solution (2) cannot be responsibly acknowledged without going on to address the conditions of individuation and adequation affecting *what* would then be taken to be suitably constituted *by* transfiguration. Solution (2) concedes a substantive transfiguration; and solution (1) introduces no more than a heuristic use of transfigurative discourse relationally projected onto physical objects or quotidian artifacts in accord with the interests humans take in particular physical objects and artifacts.

Once we concede this much, it is very difficult to see how to construe favourably Danto's further 'cunning of reason' would be against it. Secondly, it hovers dangerously close to what we have already termed the premodernism of the romantic hermeneuts. Thirdly, it commits Danto (on the best reading) to a very strong form of modernism that he nowhere defends and that may well be indefensible once a literal reading of the Hegelian model of history is set aside. Fourthly, *if*, as seems reasonable, the artworld or the world of human culture is robustly *real* prior to any particular aritst's or speaker's or agent's intervention, then the plausibility of restricting the very constitution of any given 'object-as-artwork' to 'the artist's own interpretation' (on any theory of interpretation) seems remarkably thin, fraught with well-known difficulties that are nowhere examined, utterly undefended, and hardly responsive to the deeper historicity of the cultural world (the theme of our thesis 1) that a figurative use of Hegel would itself seem to recommend.

Opposing Danto's theory is not a matter for a mere local skirmish. It is the most skilfully attenuated current analytic version of the connection between art and history. But it either denies, implies that it denies, ignores, refuses to admit, or else believes it can proceed without needing to address, *the realist reading of man's cultural world*. It is, if not actually a form of physicalism, at any rate an agnostic thesis designed to be especially hospitable to whatever (it may be supposed) the sciences require in the way of physicalism, while yet permitting the most resilient handling of the language of history, intention, rhetoric, significance, purpose and the like. It succeeds superbly in this, but it succeeds at the price of making a complete mystery of how, with respect to artworks, we should address the question of individuation and adequation. That is much too heavy a price to pay.

The minimal answer required, conceding some form of cultural realism – that is, conceding at least our three original theses – must pursue some version of solution (2): we must concede that artworks *are* individuated as objects of some distinctive kind, *are* constituted by human work or creation or by transfiguring something else, *do* exist emergently as such in a historical and cultural space (just as human persons do), and *do* possess (for that reason) intrinsic intentional properties adequated to the natures we assign them.

Two very brief final clues may suggest the best prospects for this new solution. First of all, fixing the logical stability of reference and reidentification – that is, satisfying part of the formal requirements of constative discourse – sets no limits whatsoever on *what* we should regard as the substantive nature of particular artworks thus identified. We are entirely free, for instance, to resist the analogy (so strenuously favoured by premodernist and modernists) between the closed and bounded objects of the physical worlds and the would-be bounded particulars of the artworld.[47] We may, in short, hold (as we must) to the formal *unicity* of artworks (their individuatability and reidentifiability) and permit their substantive *unity* (their internal or intrinsic nature) to be specified in whatever way we require in order to accommodate their historical existence, their possessing intentional properties, their

being what they are as a result of the iterated and reflexive sequence of interpretation and reinterpretation practised on them. Here, we must move in sympathy with postmodernism's critique of modernism but not at the price of losing the very coherence of discourse. Here, too, we must depart from Danto's modernist loyalty to artists intentions.

Secondly, we are free to explore the nature of the historicised intentional attributes we do ascribe to artworks. The truth is that there is as yet no ramified or developed theory that rejects premodernist and modernist fixities as well as postmodernist anarchies. The answer must lie with the fact that, in understanding a particular artwork, we may validly attribute to it determinate intentional properties, properties manifested in (incarnated in, we may say[48]) the physical properties of those particular works; but that, in attributing such properties, we may consistently admit the further historically open-ended – *not* any uniquely fixed or determinate or bounded – meaning or semiotic significance of those very properties. We may also admit that, as a result of possessing such properties, determinate artworks may, through the social consensus of an evolving practice of interpretation and reinterpretation, *come to possess further such properties* similarly open-ended. There is, on our argument, no other way to accommodate the historicity of the artworld. *There* is the point of pressing Danto's theory in the strenuous way we have. But there, also, is to be found a largely unexplored conceptual continent.

Notes

1   Richard Wollheim, *Painting as an Art,* Princeton University Press, Princeton, 1987, p 9.
2   *ibid,* p 16.
3   See Jürgen Habermas, *Knowledge and Human Interests,* trans Jeremy J Shapiro, Beacon Press, Boston, 1971; and Jacques Lacan, *The Four Fundamental Concepts of Psycho-Analysis,* ed Jacques-Alain Miller, trans Alan Sheridan, W W Norton, New York, 1978.
4   Wollheim, *op cit,* p 14.
5   *ibid,* p 10.
6   *ibid,* p 10.
7   See Thomas S Kuhn 'The History of Science,' *The Essential Tension; Selected Studies in Scientific Tradition and Change,* University of Chicago Press, Chicago, 1977; and Derek J de Solla Price, 'The Science of Scientists,' *Medical Opinion and Review* I 1966, cited by Kuhn.
8   Wollheim, *op cit,* p 9.
9   Monroe C Beardsley, *The Possibility of Criticism ,* Wayne State University Press, Detroit, 1970, pp 16, 44.
10 The principal lines of defence of (a) - (d) are sketched in Joseph Margolis, *Texts Without Referents; Reconciling Science and Narrative,* Basil Blackwell, Oxford, 1988.
11 See Joseph Margolis, *Pragmatism without Foundations; Reconciling Realism and Relativism,* Basil Blackwell, Oxford, 1986.
12 See William K Wimsatt, Jr and Monroe C Beardsley, 'The Intentional Fallacy,' in William K Wimsatt, Jr, *The Verbal Icon,* University of Kentucky Press, Lexington, 1954, Ch 1.
13 See Carl G Hempel, 'The Function of General Laws in History,' *Aspects of Scientific Explanation and Other Essays in the Philosophy of Science,* Free Press, New York, 1965.
14 See Karl R Popper *The Poverty of Historicism,* 2nd ed, Routledge and Kegan Paul, London, 1960; *Realism and the Aim of Science* (from *Postscript to the Logic of Scientific Discovery*) and *The Open Universe; An Argument for Indeterminism* (from *Postscript to the Logic of Scientific Discovery*), ed W W Bartley, III, Rowman and Littlefield, Totowa NJ, 1983, 1982.
15 See E D Hirsch, Jr, *Validity in Interpretation,* Yale University Press, New Haven, 1967; P D Juhl, *Interpretation; An Essay in the Philosophy of Literary Criticism,* Princeton University Press, Princeton, 1980, and, for a sample of Betti's work, Emilio Betti, 'The Epistemological Problem of Understanding as an Aspect of the General Problem of Knowledge,' trans Susan Noakes, in Gary Shapiro and Alan Sica (eds), *Hermeneutics; Questions and Prospects,* University of Massachusetts, Amherst, 1984.
16 See R G Collingwood, *The Idea of History,* Clarendon, Oxford, 1946; *The Principles of Art,* Oxford University Press, London, 1938; Wilhelm Dilthey, *Pattern and Meaning in History; Thoughts of History and Society,* ed and trans H P Rickman, George Allen and Unwin, London, 1961; *Poetry and Experience (Selected Works,* Vol 5), ed Rudolf A Makkreel and Frithjof Rodi, Princeton University Press, Princeton, 1985.
17 Hans-Georg Gadamer, *Truth and Method,* trans from 2nd ed Garrett Barden and John Cumming, Seabury Press, New York, 1975, pp 253-8.
18 Charles Taylor, 'Philosophy and Its History,' in Richard Rorty, J B Schneewind, and Quentin Skinner (eds) *Philosophy in History; Essays on the Historiography of Philosophy,* Cambridge University Press, Cambridge, 1984; Alasdair MacIntyre, *After Virtue; A Study in Moral Theory,* 2nd ed, Notre Dame University Press, Notre Dame, 1984; and Richard J Bernstein, *Beyond Objectivism and Relativism; Science, Hermeneutics, and Praxis,* University of Pennsylvania Press, Philadelpia, 1983.
19 See Thomas S Kuhn, *The Structure of Scientific Revolutions,* 2nd ed enl, University of Chicago Press, Chicago, 1970.
20 See Jürgen Habermas, 'What Is Universal Pragmatics?' *Communication and the Evolution of Society,* trans Thomas McCarthy, Beacon Press, Boston, 1979; *Reason and the Rationalisation of Society (The Theory of Communicative Action,* Vol 1), trans Thomas McCarthy, Boston: Beacon Press, 1984, Ch. 1; *The Philosophical Discourse of Modernity: Twelve Lectures,* trans Frederick Lawrence, MIT, Cambridge, 1987.
21 Karl-Otto Apel, *Toward a Transformation of Philosophy,* trans Glyn Adey and David Frisby, Routledge and Kegan Paul, London, 1980; *Understanding and Explanation; A Transcendental-Pragmatic Perspective,* trans Georgia Warnke, MIT, Cambridge, 1984; 'The Problem of Philosophical Foundations in Light of a Transcendental Pragmatics of Language,' in Kenneth Bayens, James Bohman, and Thomas McCarthy (eds) *After Philosophy: End or Transformation?,* MIT, Cambridge, 1987.
22 Clement Greenberg, 'Modernist Painting,' in Gregory Battcock (ed), *The New Art: A Critical Anthology,* Dutton, New York, 1966; 'Avant-Garde and Kitsch,' in Clement Greenberg, *Art and Culture; Critical Essays,* Beacon Press, Boston, 1961; *The Notion of 'Post-Modern',* Bloxham and Chambers, Sydney, 1980.
23 Heinrich Klotz, 'Synthesis,' UIA *Journal of Architectural Criticism,* No I, 1988, p83; also, 'Vision of the Modern,' in the same journal. See also, Charles Jencks, 'Late-Modernism vs Post-Modernism: The Two-Party System,' in the same journal; and *Post-Modernism: The New Classicism in Art and Architecture,* Academy, London, 1987.
24 See Richard Wollheim, *Art and Its Objects.* enl ed, Cambridge University Press, Cambridge, 1980, §§ 4-1.
25 See Arthur C Danto, *The Transfiguration of the Commonplace,* Harvard University Press, Cambridge, 1981; *The Philosophical Disenfranchisement of Art,* Columbia University Press, New York, 1986.
26 See G W F Hegel, *Philosophy of Fine Art,* 4 Vols, trans F P B Owaston, G Bell, London, 1920.
27 See G W F Hegel, *Phenomenology of Spirit,* trans A V Miller, Oxford University Press, Oxford, 1977, Preface, §§ 20-28.
28 Habermas, *The Philosophical Discourse of Modernity,* Lecture II, particularly pp 29-31.
29 The best recent characterisation of these alternatives is given in John F Post, *The Faces of Existence; An Essay in Nonreductive Metaphysics,* Cornell University Press, Ithaca, 1987, particularly Ch 4. For a running discussion of Post's theory, see Margolis, *Texts without Referents,* Ch 6.

30 See Jean-François Lyotard, *The Postmodern Condition: A Report on Knowledge*, trans Geoff Bennington and Brian Massumi, University of Minnesota Press, Minneapolis, 1984, Introduction.

31 See Rudolf Carnap, 'Psychology in Physical Language,' trans George Schink, in A J Ayer (ed) *Logical Postitivism*, Free Press, Glencoe, Ill, 1959, p 165.

32 See Adolf Grünbaum, *The Foundations of Psychoanalysis*, University of California Press, Berkeley, 1984, 'Introduction: Critique of the Hermeneutic Conception of Psychoanalytic Theory and Therapy'. For a sustained discussion of Grünbaum's view in this regard, see Joseph Margolis, *Science without Unity: Reconciling the Human and Natural Sciences*, Oxford, Basil Blackwell, 1987, Chs 8, 11.

33 See, for instance, Arthur C Danto, *Analytical Philosophy of Action*, Cambridge University Press, Cambridge, 1973, Chs 2-3; and *Narration and Knowledge*, Columbia University Press, 1985, Ch 14.

34 Arthur C Danto, *The Transfiguration of the Commonplace*, Harvard University Press, Cambridge, New York, 1981, p 5.

35 See Wilfrid Sellars, 'Philosophy and the Scientific Image of Man,' *Science, Perception and Reality*, Routledge and Kegan Paul, London, 1963

36 Danto, *Analytical Philosophy of Action*, p 63

37 Danto, *Narration and Knowledge*, p 311

38 See Danto, *The Philosophical Disenfranchisement of Art*, Ch 5; also, Berel Lang (ed), *The Death of Art*, Haven, New York, 1984.

39 *The Philosophical Disenfranchisement of Art*, pp 83-85.

40 Compare G W F Hegel, *Phenomenolgoy of Spirit*, trans A V Miller, Oxford University Press, Oxford, 1977, Preface, §§ 20-28; and Karl Marx, *Capital: A Crital Political Economy*, Vol II trans Ben Fowkes, Vintage, New York, 1976, Preface to the Second Edition.

41 Danto, *The Philosophical Disenfranchisement of Art*, p 84

42 See, above, note 23

43 A substantial body of evidence for this sort of expectation is unintentionally provided in the special 'Postmodernism' number of *Theory Culture & Society*, V, 1988. See, also, Fredric Jameson, 'Postmodernism, or the Cultural Logic of Late Capitalism', *New Left Review*, for a clear specimen of a line of Marxist optimism that (apart from its own merits) quite plausibly indicates both the possibility of the his tory of art and of the philosophy of history applied to the arts.

44 Arthur C Danto, 'The Artworld,' *Journal of Philosophy*, LXI, 1964.

45 Danto, *The Philosophical Disenfranchisement of Art*, pp 44-46.

46 *ibid*, p 82.

47 This is the point, for instance, of Beardsley's Principle of Autonomy: 'literary works are self-sufficient entities, whose properties are decisive in checking interpretations and judgments,' *The Possibility of Criticism*, p 16. A more flexible stance of the same general sort (opposed of course to Beardsley's own opposition to intentionalism) appears in Hirsch's *Validity in Interpretation*. In fact, Hirsch offers at least one concession toward modernism (which he nevertheless implicitly opposes) when, adhering to the notion of the fixity or boundedness of the recovered meaning of a literary text, he concedes: 'The speaking subject is not . . . identical with the subjectivity of the author as an actual historical person; it corresponds, rather, to a very limited and special aspect of the author's total subjectivity; it is, so to speak, that 'part' of the author which specifies or determines verbal meaning' (pp 242-243). In the same spirit, Hirsch distinguishes between the 'meaning' (pp 242-243). In the same spirit, Hirsch distinguishes between the 'meaning' of a text and its 'significance' to author or reader p 8. This corresponds very closely to Beardsley's thinner contrast between 'interpretation' and 'superimposition' (*op cit*, 43-44).

48 On the notion of incarnation, see Joseph Margolis, *Art and Philosophy: Conceptual Issues in Aesthetics*, Humanities Press, Atlantic Highlands, N J, 1980, Ch 3; *Culture and Cultural Entitie: Toward aNew Unity of Science*, D Reidel, Dordrecht, 1984, Ch 1.

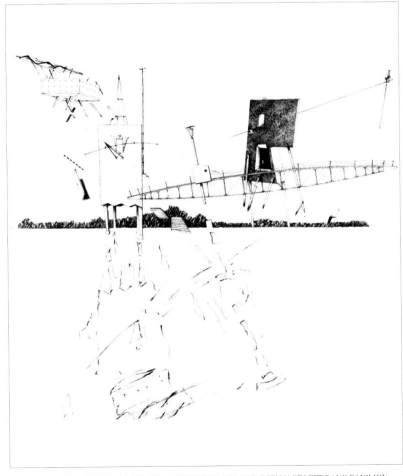

PETER WILSON, PONT DES ARTS, PARIS, EXPLOSION AND REFLECTION OF LEFT BANK PAVILION

VARO, ABOVE: FIG 1, *EMBROIDERING THE TERRESTRIAL CLOAK*; BELOW L TO R: FIG 2, *TO THE TOWER*; FIG 3, *THE ESCAPE* (TRIPTYCH)

WENDY STEINER
Pynchon and Pictures

In this last of meeting places / We grope together / And avoid speech Gathered on this beach of the tumid river / Sightless, unless / The eyes reappear / As the perpetual star / Multifoliate rose / Of death's twilight kingdom / The hope only / Of empty men.

T S Eliot, 'The Hollow Men'

I have recently been interested in the function of the visual arts in the literary romance, particularly as that function relates to narrative.[1] Since the Renaissance, paintings have been taken as archetypally atemporal objects – still, beautiful, made to be contemplated. They are by definition non-narrative, in that they do not relate a continuously unfolding story. More than any other art, painting has acted as an analogue to the beautiful woman of romance – a static object to be loved through the eyes, but whose visual fascination at the same time has the power to enthrall and immobilise the onlooker, to turn him to stone, to divert him from his quest, which is the narrative heart of romance. The transcendent value and concommitant danger of the aesthetic object – picture or woman – are the pressing concerns of the literary romance, a mode intent on discovering identity and value in a world presented as an interpretative nightmare. This essay concerns Thomas Pynchon's use of pictures and other still images, and the importance of these issues to the project of Post-Modern fiction.

Because romances dramatise the search for identity and value, they divide the world into opposites – good and evil, beauty and ugliness, the male and the female. These extremes represent the poles between which identity can be situated and value located. They are what linguists and cyberneticists call binary oppositions, terms alike in all ways but one, with that difference being significant, that is, capable of distinguishing or constituting meaning. Value depends on the existence of polar opposites. To live in a one-term system, a world without contrasts, is to inhabit a world without voice, a redundant universe where everything is the same and meaning is absent. As Gilbert and Sullivan put it in another context, 'When everybody's somebody, then no one's anybody.'[2] This is the state of boredom, in which by definition there can be no adventure or romance.

In one of the many funny songs in the novel *V*, Pynchon criticises Wittgenstein on the grounds that his elimination of opposed, alternate worlds would be the end of romance: 'If the world is all that the case is/That's a pretty discouraging basis/On which to pursue/Any sort of romance.'[3] Romance depends on the projection of alternate, though parallel, worlds, like the Wonderland or Looking-Glass Land of the Alice books, the underground or undersea worlds of fairytales, the enchanted forests or glades or castles or caves that extend from Chaucer to Spenser to Cervantes and beyond. In these alternate worlds, values are starkly polarised, although they often cross over and reverse. The romance hero negotiates the tricky task of self-definition in a world where meaning is both simplistic and riddling.

Pynchon's *V*, is a contemplation of the structure of romance levels – how they come to be projected, maintain their distinctness, and create significance in life. The protagonist, Benny Profane, is a confused '*schlemihl*' who encounters a monomaniacal quester named Stencil. Like a typical romance hero, Stencil has dedicated himself to finding the identity of V, a woman or place or idea that became imprinted on his psyche when he was a young man. For Stencil, everything in the normal world is a potential clue to this realm of value, involving him in myth, legend, international politics, espionage, and the exotic locales of Malta and the imaginary Vheissu.

Benny Profane associates as well with a crowd of decadent artists and hangers-on called the Whole Sick Crew. They are so sunk in re-dundancy that their life is an exercise in repetition. Benny spends his days riding back and forth on the New York subways – yo-yo-ing, as the book terms it – and later, at his job shooting alligators in the labyrinth of sewers below the city. Drawn against his better judgement to the compulsive quester Stencil on the one hand, and to the Whole Sick Crew on the other, to the high excitement of the alligator hunt and the total boredom of subway yo-yo-ing, Benny is a living embodiment of romance oppositions, and what the reader and Benny await is his forging of meaning and a goal in life out of the extremes that surround him.

Thus, as *V* presents it, adventure, love, engagement, and ultimately plot all depend on our constructing a world more complex than what the case is, and this construction is founded on the parallelism of worlds. Without such layering there is no romance, and one ends up like the Whole Sick Crew. Among these beatniks, *schlemihls*, and avant-garde artists, one named Slab is painting a continuing series of *Cheese Danish* canvases. The Whole Sick Crew 'produced nothing but talk and at that not very good talk. A few like Slab actually did what they professed; turned out a tangible product. But again, what? Cheese Danishes. Or this technique for the sake of technique – Catatonic Expressionism. Or parodies of what someone else had already done … This sort of arranging and rearranging was Decadence, but the exhaustion of all possible permutations and combinations was death' (p 277).

Pynchon is referring to Abstract Expressionism and Pop Art here, the exploration of formal means in the absence of a subject or with blatantly trivial subjects, even when these lead to redundancy and repetition. The word 'exhaustion' that he uses to describe this decadence was the operative term in the 60s for the state of art. John Barth wrote an influential essay in 1967 called 'The Literature of Exhaustion', claiming that writers had nothing left to do but contemplate the act of writing itself, since all the possibilities of the novel had been used up. With such statements from him, Leslie Fielder, Susan Sontag, and numerous others,[4] the death of the novel became a cliché. Gore Vidal even had Myra Breckenridge give a little diatribe on the subject. That both life and art could be a mere shuffling of variables, an exhaustion of possibilities, is the spectre haunting Benny Profane. It is this analysis that generates other worlds, allegorical layers, the wish-fulfilment realms of romance.

The trouble with projecting romance levels, however, is that these alternate worlds may themselves prove empty, simple mirrorings of the decadence that generates them. The character Stencil represents this possibility. He has devoted his whole adult life to a search analogous to the most orthodox romance quest. From Malta to New York to the mythical Vheissu, through all the vicissitudes of 20th-century European history, he has looked for clues that begin with the letter V: Queen Victoria, the girl Victoria Wren, a rat named Veronica, Ver Meroving, Helvig Vogelsang, Botticelli's Venus, the Maltese capital Valletta, Vivaldi's lost Kazoo Concerto. And yet, by the end of the book, he is no closer to finding the truth of V. 'Stencil sketched the entire history of V that night and strengthened a long suspicion. That it did add up only to the recurrence of an initial and a few dead objects' (p 419). Trying to stamp all of reality into a meaningful if compulsive pattern – trying to stencil it – to see his 'grand Gothic pile of inferences' cohere (p 209), Stencil must always face the possibility that reality is a mere collocation ', a few dead objects'. The 'scattering' of characters, the literal bodily disassembly of the decadent False Priest, and the removable parts of the character V – feet, eyes – express this ever-present possibility of fragmentation and disorder, of entropy, as Pynchon labels it in his short story of that name and in *The Crying of*

Lot 49. On the one hand, Pynchon gives us the stencilled redundancy of a cookie-cutter mind; on the other, the anarchic fragmentation of a psyche that, as Eliot put it, 'can connect/Nothing with nothing.'[5]

Almost any price is worth paying to avoid confronting a purely entropic universe, or even the tamer version of a mere cause-and-effect world where everything runs by mechanical, inhuman laws. Thus, the narrator informs us that 'No apologia is any more than a romance – half a fiction – in which all the successive identities taken on and rejected by the writer as a function of linear time are treated as separate characters ... So we do sell our souls, paying them away to history in little instalments. It isn't so much to pay for eyes clear enough to see past the fiction of continuity, the fiction of cause and effect, the fiction of a humanised history endowed with "reason"' (p 286).

But if continuity, cause-and-effect, and a humanised history are all fictions to be disdained, romance alterity might equally be a fabrication, in fact, is such by definition. The poet Fausto Maistral specifically connects poetry and artifice to a theory of paired worlds, the street and under the street, the kingdom of death and the kingdom of life. 'How can a poet live without exploring the other kingdom, even if only as a kind of tourist?' (p 304), he asks. But because the poet lives in the world of metaphor, he or she 'is always acutely conscious that metaphor has no value apart from its function; that is as a device, an artifice' (p 305). The assumptions behind reality are all fictions, but so are the romance artifices we build to belie them. Stencil's father finally gives up his quest, relaxes his critical faculties, and opts for blind faith. He ends up in an affair with one Veronica Manganese, sunk in a nostalgia so deep that he becomes totally alienated from time and history, just as the capital of Malta, Valletta, from a distance deteriorates into a mere spectacle and is 'assumed again into the textual stillness of her own history' (p 446). This willed surrender to a fiction – either that of the romance underworld or the matter-of-fact reality in plain sight – is treated as an unfortunate weakness, an abnegation of one's vitality in the game played out between the two worlds. Benny Profane, a *schlemihl* doomed to yo-yo between worlds, comes out to the adventure with the antinomies still intact. When asked, '"The experience, the experience. Haven't you learned"' he promptly replies no, '"offhand I'd say I haven't learned a goddamn thing"' (p 428). To have learned would have been either to fall in with the underworld of metaphor or to accept and pump up normal reality. Either of these strategies involves a flat allegorical consciousness, in Pynchon's view an x = y logic.

Pynchon introduces the issue of allegory through a painting. The Cheese Danish artist, Slab, paints a picture of a device meant to separate him from Catatonic Expressionism and to replace the cross in Western symbolism. It is a painting of a foiled perpetual motion machine: a partridge in a pear tree that will die. The perpetual motion works as follows. The partridge eats the pears and its droppings fertilise the tree, causing the tree to grow taller and produce more pears for the partridge to eat, and hence more droppings and more pears, seemingly *ad infinitum*. Since the Latin *perdix* means partridge, the pear ('*per-*') is in the partridge as much as the partridge is in the pear tree, and a pun – and possibly an obscene pun – runs the machine. However, at the top of the painting Slab has placed a gargoyle with sharp fangs. As the tree grows, the partridge will one day be impaled on the gargoyle's teeth, for, as we are told, the bird has forgotten how to fly. 'I detect allegory in all this,' says a friend of Slab's. '"No," said Slab. "That is on the same intellectual level as doing the *Times* crossword puzzle on Sunday. Phony. Unworthy of you"' (p 263). Allegorical readings reduce complexity, flatten levels, opt mechanically or sentimentally for a simplicity of meaning that is not available.

The partridge as a symbol reinforces Pynchon's point. Ad de Vries speculates in *The Dictionary of Symbols and Imagery* that the 12 days of Christmas (the partridge in the pear tree being the gift given by the lover on the first day) 'often represented the 12 months of the year, [so that] the gifts may refer to those, and "my true love" may be the fertility-sun-god.'[6] Jean Chevalier and Alain Gheerbrant list the fol-

lowing symbolism for the partridge: its song in China is a call of love; its eyes in India are symbols of beauty; its carriage in Iran is taken for that of a haughty and elegant woman; its flesh elsewhere is eaten as a love philtre; in Christianity it has been seen as an incarnation of the devil; and in Greek legend it stood as an Icarus parallel transformed as it fell by Athena's pity into a bird who then looked on with pitiless joy at Icarus' fall. Chevalier and Gheerbrant conclude, 'As we see, the symbolism of the partridge is quite ambiguous,'[7] Pynchon's point precisely.

Slab's painting, arrested at the moment when the perpetual-motion potential of the symbol is still viable -- the pear tree and the partridge mutually flourishing – contains death as a narrative extrapolation. And yet it is a great improvement, the novel would have us believe, over the Cheese Danish series. At the same time, to read it as a pure allegory – perhaps that life itself involves this mutual nourishing with the spectre of death lurking beyond – would be to diminish the experience of the miraculous pun and the hilarious conceit of the work. Or at least from Slab's point of view – the standpoint of the engaged artist – the reading through the painting to this allegorical conclusion would have such an effect. Thus, in order to enable romance and the search for meaning one must proliferate levels, but in order to preserve the distinctness of these levels one must not apply mechanical techniques of allegorical interpretation to them.

Pynchon expresses this paradoxical anti-allegorism through an elaborate theory of mirrors and of voyeurism, culminating in the oddest episode in this extraordinarily odd book – a love affair between the woman V and a 15-year-old dancer named Mélanie. Their relationship is pure decadence: Mélanie on the bed in exotic costume contemplates herself in the mirror with V watching. The narrator describes the scene as follows: 'An adolescent girl whose existence is so visual observes in a mirror her double; the double becomes a voyeur ... She needs, it seems, a real voyeur to complete the illusion that her reflections are, in fact, this audience. With the addition of this other ... comes consummation: for the other is also her own double' (p 385). Voyeurism becomes narcissism, a doubling of the self. It is the construction of a fetish, the text asserts, that serves the kingdom of death (p 386), for it guarantees the correspondence of layers, the mechanical adequacy of illusion to reality. It prevents the honest confusion of a vulgar *schlemihl* like Benny Profane, who, like Kilroy, 'was possibly the only objective onlooker in Valletta that night' (p 410).

Pynchon goes to some trouble to identify Mélanie as a fetish. 'Come, fétiche, inside', one character calls to her, and just in case she does not understand the term, Mélanie is given a definition. 'Do you know what a fetish is? Something of a woman which gives pleasure but is not a woman. A shoe, a locket ... *une jarretière*. You are the same, not real but an object of pleasure' (p 379). Since Mélanie's nickname is '*La jarretière*' (the Garter), she seems indeed to be a Freudian fetish. The forming of fetishes is at the very essence of decadence, like the Cheese Danish works of Slab or the day-to-day existence of the Whole Sick Crew. 'A decadence is a falling away from what is human,' we are told. 'Because we are less human, we foist off the humanity we have on inanimate objects and abstract theories' (p 380).

Given Pynchon's pointed use of the term, we might look at what Freud has to say about the fetish. He explains the fetishist as a boy who is so threatened at the discovery that his mother has no penis (and hence that he might be deprived of his, too) that he constructs a substitute for it in her foot, shoe, garter, etc. His fetish allows him both to give up the belief in her phallus and to retain it, for the fetish is both different from a phallus and a version of it. Moreover, as Freud observes, it 'now inherits the interest which was formerly directed to its predecessor. But this castration has set up a memorial to itself in the creation of this substitute.'[8] Since the fear of castration is tantamount to the fear of death, Pynchon's equation of fetish objects with the servants of the kingdom of death is understandable. The paradoxical thinking surrounding the fetish allows one to deal with absence and death, but also memorialises them.

The imagery surrounding this complex of ideas is intimately associated with mirrors and pictures. The love-scene between V and Mélanie is described as 'a well-composed and ageless still-life of love at one of its many extremes: V on the pouf, watching Mélanie on the bed; Mélanie watching herself in the mirror; the mirror-image perhaps contemplating V from time to time. No movement but a minimum friction' (p 385). By introducing a third term – Mélanie, V, and the mirror image – the disturbing binarism with its hierarchy of dominance and submission has been eliminated. Necessity and death are apparently obviated in such a scheme, for though binarism is a crucial first step for the formation of the fetish (the present phallus discovered to be absent), binarism is also at the very heart of the dilemma. Faced with the unwelcome perception of the woman's absent phallus and the wish that she had not been so dismembered, the boy evades an either/or understanding of the situation by positing yet another possibility – the fetish, with its simultaneous absence/presence. Likewise with the romance, one must first forge oppositions, but to live in a world of unresolved contraries is very disorienting. One needs a symbol – a Grail or girdle or beautiful princess – to merge or organise the violent oppositions that beset one.

But Pynchon will not allow this solution to work. V's and Mélanie's love continues quite nicely until the première of Mélanie's ballet, in which she is to play a Chinese princess who is first ravaged and then impaled – something like Slab's partridge – on a spear: what amounts to a huge metal penis. Having forgotten the chastity belt device that was to protect her, Mélanie dies and V flees. The death suggests the impossibility of replacing the missing penis in the fetishistic theatre of art. Even the ballet, the ultimate banisher of contraries (note Yeats' epitome of high Modernist fulfilment: 'How can we know the dancer from the dance?') cannot overcome the artificiality of the solution to binarism. As one Freudian commentator, Homi K Bhabha, has stated, 'in that form of substitution and fixation that is fetishism there is always the trace of loss, absence. To put it succinctly, the recognition and disavowal of "difference" is always disturbed by the question of its re-presentation or construction.'[9]

Now, the binarism of presence and loss is not the problem of sexual fetishists alone, for it it were we would be hard-pressed to understand why Pynchon would spend so much space on such a subject when the whole thrust of *V* is to undermine decadence. The reason that Freud's work has had such a revival in recent years is that the trauma of real or imaginary loss is exemplary of the Post-Modern state. Jacques Derrida characterises all of culture through its belief in the 'Western metaphysics of presence', the assumption of an originary moment in which wholeness, fulfilment, and reciprocity prevailed, only to be lost through a fall into adulthood, sin, difference or any of the various names for separation. Whereas before there was unity, now the world divides into subject and object, self and other, presence and absence, meaning and difference. This binary universe is the site of frustration and bewilderment, for the elements of the pairs are unstable, oscillating in value, but inevitably returning to the same deep structure of p and ~p. In a world without God, faith, or some anchor of belief, binarism, though a necessary precondition to value, is impossible to transcend, and produces nothing but boredom and redundancy.

During the past 15 years, virtually every aspect of reality has been analysed in these terms, including the situation of women. Eugénie Lemoine-Luccioni, a follower of Jacques Lacan, claims that woman 'truly lives under the sign of abandonment: mother, father, child, husband, penis, the entire world deserts her.'[10] This abandonment produces the need, she argues, for woman to complete herself, and thus to treat herself as both subject and object. Consequently, woman is 'always divided, always deprived of half of herself, narcissistically divided between subject and object, an orphan in every way. In a word, narcissistic by structure and dedicated to a destiny of partition' (p170). The literary romance memorialises this set of connections among femininity, narcissism and loss. As Donald Barthelme writes in his camp-Heideggerian update of the fairytale *Snow White*: '*The psychol-ogy of Snow White*: What does she hope for? "Someday my prince will come." By this Snow White means that she lives her own being as incomplete, pending the arrival of one who will "complete her". That is, she lives her own being as "not-with.".... The incompleteness is an ache capable of subduing all other data presented by consciousness.'[11] Psychoanalysis and literature explain not only the romance's treatment of woman as fetishes, but women's treatment of *themselves* in this fashion.

Following this logic, Pynchon's second novel, *The Crying of Lot 49*, begins with a female protagonist, Oedipa Maas, who must be propelled out of a state of boredom into, initially, a narcissistic splitting of the self. Oedipa's quest for knowledge thus starts as self-concern. Made the executor of her dead lover's will, she drives to a town called San Narciso and stays in a motel called the Echo Courts. While there she attends a performance of a revenge tragedy which opens with the good duke fatally kissing the poisoned feet of a statue of Saint Narcissus. Self-exploration is perilous (and ludicrous, too), but Pynchon implies that it is better to take this trip than to stay at home. Only then can one execute a will, and the fact that the framer of the will is called Pierce Inverarity suggests that narcissism is prerequisite to piercing into the truth, or possibly the untruth, of things. (Pierce, of course, is also the perennial name of romance heroes, such as Piers Ploughman.)

Oedipa's narcissism is supported by symbolism linking her to philosophical solipsism. The radical relativism of knowledge is a central theme of the literary romance as a whole, its maidens locked in towers serving as ready symbols of the self-enclosed solipsist who must be released into a world of others. Oedipa remembers a time when she saw herself as Rapunzel locked in a tower, waiting for a knight to release her. The tragedy of solipsism is thus shifted to the latency of the romance innocent, whose tower, with its 'conchlike stairs'[12] becomes an image of the head with its ear spirals through which the lover's words may enter. When her lover, Pierce Inverarity, finally does release her, before the action of the book begins, they go off to Mexico, where Oedipa sees a painting of maidens locked within a tower embroidering a tapestry that flows out of the window and fills the world outside, becoming that world (fig 1). Oedipa then realises that the ground 'she stood on had only been woven together a couple thousand miles away in her own tower, was only by accident known as Mexico, and so Pierce had taken her away from nothing, there'd been no escape' (pp 10-11). And what she had been trying to escape, we are told, is the unknowable force that locked her in the tower in the first place and gave the tower the shape it has.

There is hardly a more explicit image of the solipsistic dilemma to be found in literature: the paradox that all knowledge is limited to the self, but that that self cannot be known as another, objectively, accurately, historically. Even after Oedipa has been drawn through the extraordinary discoveries of the novel, she is left absolutely ignorant of the tower's source. As she puts it to herself, 'Either you have stumbled ... onto a secret richness and concealed intensity of dream ... Or you are hallucinating it. Or a plot has been mounted against you ... so labyrinthine that it must have meaning beyond just a practical joke. Or you are fantasying some such plot, in which case you are a nut, Oedipa, out of your skull' (p 128). No interpretation is grounded, and all quests for knowledge threaten to become like Oedipa's first view of the philatelist Gengis Cohen 'framed in a long succession or train of doorways, room after room receding in the general direction of Santa Monica, all soaked in rain-light' (p 68).

Given a radically undecidable world, a world of twinned hypotheses each as viable as the other, Oedipa's response to the painting had been to give up and sink into anomie, an undifferentiated world without opposition and hence without value. She drops Pierce Inverarity, marries a disc jockey, and settles down in the suburbs into a life of lasagna and Tupperware parties where each day is the same as the one before. When she is roused from this state by the challenge of Pierce's will, her investigation still turns up no other possibilities. She is left with nothing but the binarism with which she started: 'it was now like walking among matrices of a great digital computer, the zeros and ones twinned above, hanging like balanced mobiles left and right, ahead, think, maybe endless. Behind the hieroglyphic streets there would either be a transcendent meaning, or only the earth ... Ones and zeros. So did the couples arrange themselves' (p 136). However, though this binary world is mechanistically repetitive and seemingly inescapable, Oedipa's response to it at *this* point is not to focus on the redundancy but to ignore it and proceed to the next clue in the quest, to see where that leads. Likewise, in *V*, Benny Profane kept yo-yo-ing between worlds in order to maintain his honesty and intellectual respectability, for romance depends on the possibility of imagining an alternative to 'what the case is'. Pynchon is thus insisting on the forming of binary oppositions, paired alternatives, and at the same time, through his critique of the fetish, refusing his reader the luxury of a structure of belief that would accommodate that binarism comfortably. As we have seen, 'the articulation of multiple-belief that Freud proposes in the essay "Fetishism" is a non-repressive form of knowledge that allows for the possibility of simultaneously embracing two contradictory beliefs, one official and one secret, one archaic and one progressive, one that allows the myth of origins, the other that articulates difference and division. Its knowledge-value ... provides ... the lasting matrix, the effective prototype of all those splittings of belief which man will henceforth be capable of in the most varied domains, of all the infinitely complex unconscious and occasionally conscious interactions which he will allow himself between believing and not-believing"' (Bhabha, quoting Metz, p 168).

Nevertheless, Pynchon characterises the fetish as a prop of the kingdom of death that must be destroyed. Oedipa Maas starts out her quest with a trip to San Narciso, symbolically splitting and fetishing herself. In a hilarious episode, she watches herself in the bathroom mirror as she puts on layer upon layer of clothing in preparation for playing strip Botticelli with her future lover. In doing so, she is multiplying allegorical layers and obscuring truth in a fashion normative for romance, with its veiled Unas. But as she dresses herself in San Narciso in the Echo Courts Motel, she tips over a can of hairspray, which careers wildly about the room, breaking the huge bathroom mirror. Narcissism is denied in the progress of this symbolism.

Similarly, when Oedipa goes backstage after the performance of *The Courier's Tragedy* to talk to the director, Driblette, she passes through a 'region of brightly-lit mirrors'. Here she asks Driblette for the original manuscript of the play, but he disappears into a shower, from the mists of which he tells her that her request misses the point. The text of the play is nothing but words: '"You know where that play exists ..." – a hand emerged from the veil of shower-steam to indicate his suspended head –" in here. That's what I'm for. To give the spirit flesh ... the reality is in *this* head. Mine. I'm the projector at the planetarium, all the closed little universe visible in the circle of that stage is coming out of my mouth, eyes, sometimes other orifices also"' (p 56). In this episode, Oedipa travels through a mirror world to discover another solipsistic vision, one which in many respects mimics the tower maidens in the painting she had seen in Mexico. For Driblette's theory of meaning makes him a projector, an embroiderer, of the world. The life of art is not in the literal text but in the interaction with the perceiver, who ends not as a passive recipient of an aesthetic fact but the active maker of the text. And here 'embroidery' and solipsism are given a new meaning, for in transmitting his vision to Oedipa, Driblette gives her the impetus to action as well, supplying clues to the Trystero and an offer of love. Aesthetic experience is a narcissism that is transformed into engagement with the world and a precious generosity toward other people.

In all the treatment of mirrors, Pynchon pushes us toward binarism and the fetish and then destroys or invalidates them, as if it were necessary to have the binary world acknowledged and in place in order for a new stage of interpretation to occur. The question then is, why is the fetish as a structure not the way to deal with loss? Why should the

quest for value *not* end in the establishment of a substitute that both is and is not what we lack? In other words, what is the matter with metaphor, allegory, and ultimately art as a solution to loss?

The analogy between fetish and artwork that I am drawing is not gratuitous. Narcissus' image in the pool is a perennial symbol of painting. Leon Battista Alberti, for one, makes the connection in his treatise *On Painting*.[13] Moreover, the fetish-value of all art is pronounced. It is an institutionised splitting of belief, since its truth-status is so paradoxical. A work of art both represents the world and bears no responsibility for the accuracy of that representation; it does not lie, but neither does it tell the truth. What art does, and what the romance does most markedly, is to allow us to have our cake and eat it too, to experience loss in a form so full and so satisfying that, to reverse Eliot's phrase, it gives with the famishing. But aestheticism, necessary to the romance quest, cannot be its end, for like any determinate end it can lead only to repetition, redundancy and the kingdom of death. To fixate on art for its own sake is to replay the decadent scenario of the late 19th century. Rather than allowing aestheticism to stand as the final reaction to loss and incommensurability, Pynchon proposes a different strategy of response, and interestingly he does this by giving the reader a research assignment that turns the static painting by Remedios Varo into an open-ended narrative sequence exactly analogous to the plot structure of *The Crying of Lot 49*.

Oedipa's initial lesson in solipsism, we recall, was Remedios Varo's painting, and paintings in general function as romance archetypes of atemporality, self-enclosure and noncontingent value. Like so many details in this novel, the picture that Oedipa saw, *Bordando el manto terrestre* (*Embroidering the Terrestrial Cloak*) is an actual work. It was painted in 1961-2 and quite possibly seen by Pynchon on one of his trips to Mexico. The painter, Remedios Varo, was a Spanish woman married to the poet Benjamin Peret and living in Paris from 1937 to 1942 at the centre of the Surrealists. Her name is almost too good to be true, with its suggestions of remedying the truth or perhaps remedying variety. The name signifies the scores of true modifications of truth in the novel.

Oedipa takes the painting as a lesson in the inescapability of solipsistic self-enclosure. But quite a different lesson is available from it. *Embroidering the Terrestrial Cloak* is the second painting in an annotated narrative triptych of Varo's, representing a woman's escape from a world of regimented sameness into romance adventure. The first canvas, *Hacia la torre* (*To the Tower*) (fig 2) shows a group of identical young women riding identical bicycles, emerging from a building with many identical towers that Varo's note calls a beehive. The girls are led by a dour nun and a bearded male figure and, as Varo notes, 'guarded by the birds so that none of them can run away. They have a hypnotised gaze and they carry their embroidery hooks like bicycle handles. Only the girl in front resists the hypnosis.' We have here an archetypal romance situation: the repression of individual identity into repetition (as with Oedipa Maas in her initial boredom) with a figure trying to break loose into self assertion.

In the central triptych panel (fig 1), the one Pynchon describes, the girls sit in a tower like Oedipa's. Varo's note states that 'under the orders of the great master they embroider the terrestrial cloak, seas, mountains, and living things.' They produce a curious Breugelesque landscape, an intricate microcosm of reality with buildings, fields, seas, animals, boats and trees spilling out of slots in the tower. The gold of the woven land and the blue of the sea exactly match the golden hair and blue dresses of the girls within the tower who weave them. The world they make is merely their self-projection.

But one girl, Varo's note informs us, no doubt the one who had evaded the hypnosis in the first canvas, 'has embroidered a trap in which one can see her together with her lover.' The lovers appear upside down on the right border of the cloth to the left of the tower. The girl on the front left has woven them into her design so that she can escape the tower into the world outside. The third canvas, entitled *La huida* (*The Escape*) (fig 3) takes us outside the tower into a world not pictured in the woven landscape. Varo writes that 'As a consequence of the trap she manages to escape with her lover. And they are setting out in a special vehicle through a desert toward a grotto.' They are launched, like proper lovers, journeying over a dangerous landscape toward a grotto, the bower of archetypal romance. From this vantage point, however, the grotto looks dark and rather forbidding, so that the ending of this quest is suspended between the possibilities of danger and fulfilment.

Pynchon does not allude to the first and third canvases in his novel, but as soon as we seek out the second panel we discover these other two. Just as Oedipa's quest involves her tracking down the sources and variants of a revenge tragedy, the whole point of the novel is to transform us from passive consumers of art into active constitutors of its meaning, as we saw already in the case of Driblette. Like Oedipa, we must learn how to do research, for otherwise we shall be sunk in the very anomie that she experienced. Or else, fetishising the artwork, we shall be embracing a sentimental, self-deluding solution to what is an insoluble problem. If instead we dwell on the traps woven into art, the omissions or hints at hidden richness in it, we shall come up with new complications and new ways to escape its intricate weave into a heightened reality. Virtually every aspect of the triptych – for example, the name of its painter, Remedios Varo – repays the investigator with new insights. Oedipa – and the reader – must take the trouble to view Varo's painting, which leads to the other canvases in the triptych and Varo's crucial annotations. One must go *outside* the text. One must violate the atemporal self-sufficiency of the middle canvas to produce a narrative that has interest, meaning and relation to life.

To take the process one step further, then, we might look at Varo's life. We learn that she, like the rebellious girl in the triptych, had a repressive childhood and was unable to adjust to the bourgeois forms that were imposed upon her. Except for her dark hair, the girls' faces in the picture are modelled on her own face, with its huge eyes and heart shape, 'wide at the brow, narrow at the chin, soft in contour – with a straight nose and a relatively small mouth.'[14] Varo's own life and appearance thus become a subtext for the triptych. And so, we might expect, does her death in 1963, a year after finishing the triptych and a year before the exhibition at which Pynchon would likely have seen the painting.

Here, then, is the sequence of connections. Varo (Pynchon's *V*?) projected her own image into a bored heroine who embroiders a trap to allow herself and her lover to escape the tower. This painting teaches the equivocal lessons of attempting that escape, and Pynchon is one of those enlightened, though his teacher Varo is by then dead. Pynchon then creates the figure of Pierce Inverarity, whose name contains 'Varo' within it and who posthumously effects the release of *his* lover Oedipa Maas from her tower. Oedipa did not learn the painting's whole lesson when she saw it on her trip to Mexico with Inverarity. Instead, she read the tower as inevitable and the escape as pure delusion, and concluded that the attempt to escape was impossible.

'She had looked down at her feet and known, then, because of a painting, that … there'd been no escape' (pp10-11). But when Inverarity names her as his executrix, her understanding grows deeper. What Pynchon does is to make Oedipa proceed *through* the triptych rather than stop at a single work, and so transform that painting into part of a narrative. Of course, because the trap is as much a product of the girl as the rest of the world she projects, and because traps are notoriously tricky, it may be that the escape is a delusion. The third canvas might be only a disguised version of the first, with the 'special vehicle' in the third only a dream image of the bicycle in the first, the two lovers only variants of the nun and bearded carrier of embroidery stuffs, and the grotto merely a romantic vision of the tower toward which the bicycles are headed. Certainly triptychs have functioned this way, with the pendants on left and right, simultaneous comments on the central panel. But the passage through the triptych is just as likely a real narrative: a first, and a then, and a now. Oedipa's quest will be to explore these two pictorial possibilities and to discover the conditions for meaning and value in each. The book, in a sense, is about the psychology and ethics of turning picture into story, or fetish into vital adventure.

In other words, instead of treating the central picture as a fetish, a beautiful, enticing compensation for the loss it chronicles, Pynchon wants us to see it as an opening into other possibilities, new discoveries, such as who Remedios Varo is and what the escape in the third canvas might mean. The interpretative strategies we should cultivate are not the formalist techniques of closure that aesthetic training in the late 1960s inculcated in both art historians and literary critics, but instead a kind of quirky text-philology, a tracking-down of clues and inferences wherever they lead, to produce a new, expanded interpreter. (We should recall that Oedipa's nickname is Oed – *OED* – and that she shares her surname with the famous philologist Paul Maas.) Hence the inexhaustibility of Pynchon's work, and at the same time the uncompromising honesty of the vision that instructs in the temptations of fetishism and the techniques for avoiding it.

If any Post-Modern work can de defined as a fetish warning against its fetishisation, then Pynchon's novels contain the theory of that dilemma and, as such, spell out the normative state of Post Modern writing. For the problem now is how to create a body of literature, a canon, that does not reinstitute the elitism, hermeneutic closure, and aesthetic distancing that defined the previous attitude toward it. Narcissism, solipsism, binarism, the fetish, woman, and art are all bound together in Modernism, and Post Modernism must forge a style of reading and interpretation that does not simply reinstitute the attitudes of awe, unacknowledged prurience and willed forgetting that characterise our aesthetic legacy. The reader must instead search out the traps, or build them into the text to start with. It is that never-ending involvement with the artwork – not a failed closure but a continuous opening out – that allows it to be meaningful at this time.

Notes

1 See *Pictures of Romance: Form Against Context in Painting and Literature*, University of Chicago Press, Chicago 1988.
2 'There Was a King' from W S Gilbert and Sir Arthur Sullivan, *The Gondoliers*.
3 Thomas Pynchon, *V*, Bantam, New York 1963, p 239.
4 John Barth, 'The Literature of Exhaustion,' *Atlantic Monthly* vol 220 August 1967 pp 29-34; Leslie Fielder, 'The New Mutants', *Partisan Review*, XXXII, Fall 1965; Richard Poirier, 'The Literature of Waste', *The New Republic*, May 20 1967. For a summary, see Jerome Klinkowitz, *Literary Disruptions: The Making of a Post-Contemporary American Fiction*, University of Illinois Press, Urbana 1975, pp 3-8.
5 T S Eliot, *The Waste Land* in *Selected Poems*, Harcourt Brace Jovanovich, New York 1936, ll. 301-02.
6 Ad de Vries, *Dictionary of Symbols and Imagery* North Holland Publishing, Amsterdam 1974, p 359.
7 Jean Chevalier and Alain Gheerbrant, *Dictionnaire des symboles*, Editions Jupiter, Paris 1982, p 740 (my translation).
8 Sigmund Freud, 'Fetishism,' *Standard Edition of the Complete Psychologiccal Works of Sigmund Freud*, ed James Strachey, Hogarth Press, London 1964, p 154.
9 Homi K Bhabha, 'The Other Question: Difference, Discrimination, and the Discourse of Colonialism', *Literature, Politics, and Theory*, ed Francis Barker *et al*, Methuen, London 1986, p 169.
10 Quoted in Alice Jardine, *Gynesis*, Cornell University Press, New York 1985, p 169.
11 Donald Barthelme, *Snow White*, Atheneum, New York 1967, p 70.
12 Thomas Pynchon, *The Crying of Lot 49*, Bantam, New York 1966, p 10.
13 'Narcissus who was changed into a flower, according to the poets, was the inventor of painting. Since painting is already the flower of every art, the story of Narcissus is most to the point. What else can you call painting but a similar embracing with art of what is presented on the surface of the water in the fountain?' Leon Battista Alberti, *On Painting*, tr John R Spencer Yale University Press, New Haven 1956, p 64.
14 Estella Lauter, *Women as Mythmakers*, Indiana University Press, Bloomington 1984, p 83.

JACKSON POLLOCK, *THE BLUE UNCONSCIOUS*, 1946, OIL

JULIA KRISTEVA
Jackson Pollock's Milky Way: 1912-1956

Il est de forts parfums pour qui toute matière
Est poreuse. On dirait qu'ils pénètrent le verre.

Baudelaire, *Le Flaçon*

Scent, 1955, is, together with *Search*, 1955, Pollock's last great painting. The almost joyous sensuality of the brush (this is not a 'drip' and so synthetic pigments were used) that traces the daring but controlled arabesques from which no figure emerges, leads me to see – or to feel? or to penetrate? – not a *surface*, but the intense fibrousness of an unknown and opaque substance which resists me. We might call it *matter*, and the artist's gesture, even the artist himself, is now inseparable from it.

Looking at *Scent* mobilises all the senses: it is not so much a vision as an experience. The retina is pulverised, becomes porous. The body is atomised, as though by a bomb or a spray.

I associate the impact of *Scent* with the famous images from Hans Namuth's film about Pollock. In it we see the painter splashing paint over a floor of glass which has become a transparent arena for a theatre of cruelty; but is it inside or outside? (*Number Twenty-Nine*, 1950). Drunkenly, majestically, Pollock dances, sculpts, organises-disorganises a body and a space, like the Japanese calligrapher who inscribed a book on Zen art with the character meaning *Void* for me at the gates of Rioanji in Kyoto. He later placed this carefully splattered sheet of glass outside the door to his East Hampton studio, so that he could watch the landscape throught it . . .

The Brownian movement of the masterly interpenetration-diffusion-dissemination which dominates Pollock's style between 1948 and 1950 is now seen as one of the outcomes of the tradition of pictorial research that stretches from the old masters of Baroque drapery to the Impressionists. But is it a logical outcome, or a challenge to the tradition? The now-conventional term *action painting* was coined by Harold Rosenberg, and it emphasises a physical movement which defies representation. For Rosenberg, action painting does away with the need to represent states, and foregrounds the enacting of physical movement. Action on the canvas becomes its own representation.

From the Gnostics to Baudelaire and beyond

Pollock himself told Rosenberg that the act of painting was a supreme source of magic. But when I look at *Blue Unconscious*, 1946, *Eyes in the Heat I*, 1946, *Eyes in the Heat II*, 1947, *Shimmering Substances*, 1946, *Full Fathom Five*, 1947, *Lavender Mist*, 1950, *Echo*, 1951, *Moon Vibrations*, 1953, *Scent*, 1955, or at the still more abstract and vibrant *Numbers* (*One*, *Seven*, *Ten*, *Twenty-Nine*, etc), I have the feeling that this 'action' has nothing to do with the physical or voluntarist activism in which we can so easily recognise a whole tradition within American ideology. In reality, it would seem out of place for this man to perform any gymnastic *act*; his biographers tell us that his sole display of social activism was the protest he organised in the Manual Arts High School's Department of Physical Education in Los Angeles when he was 15 or 16. He was expelled for his pains, and began to attend Communist Party meetings. There is something sculptural about his pictorial 'action', and he did dabble in sculpture as an adolescent, but its main feature is an almost vibrant swimming movement (*Full Fathom, Five Moon Vibrations*), and a sombre and delightfully Baudelairean mistiness (*Lavender Mist*).

His action can be seen as the speaking being's sublime attempt to tear itself away from separation and to melt discreetly, by which I mean with a sense of destiny, not into an other, but into an infinite whole. Pollock told Hans Hoffman that he was nature. It was Hoffman who discovered the drip technique, but he did not turn it into a general method. Pollock's subjectivist declaration of faith also signals the immersion of inside in outside, the part in the whole, the spirit in matter. Baudelaire's metaphor of perfume seems to me to be emblematic of the *sublimation* that is at work here, much more so than the word 'action'. I use sublimation in its most literal sense: a solid body is super-heated (*Eye in the Heat*) and transformed into vapour, into a subtle flux, a gaseous movement, a mist, a wave, a vibration. And as it is purified, contraries merge, opposites meet and become infinite. . .

Malevich said that he wanted to turn his subjective impulses into new signs. More so than anyone else, Pollock paints a space which is neither internal nor external. He moves through the image and finds a sign for the pneumatic body, for the sublime body of which the Gnostics dreamed. American critics usually try to place Pollock in the history of art (the Baroque, Impressionism, Expressionism, Cubism) so as to give him letters of nobility. His violence and his use of foreign matter, on the other hand, tend to be explained in terms of the influence of the Navajo Indians (sandpainting, textile designs, etc). His 'all-over' and 'drip' techniques are said to relate essentially to the immensity of American space (The Grand Canyon, the West) and to express the deep religiosity of *Homo Americanus*. In such arguments, space and religion appear to be beyond analysis, to be the raw materials of the pictorial experience. But what space? What religion?

A total lack of public understanding meant that Pollock spent a brief season in hell, and it is thanks to the early support he received from Rosenberg, Greenberg and Peggy Guggenheim, who organised his first one-man show in 1943, that we can now see his uniqueness. Those who are willing to break free of the shackles of clean imagery [*image propre*] and of the Prim Image [*Image Propre*], who are willing to be dissolved in the fragrances of Pollock's chromatic atomism, encounter a subtle, perfumed, feeling of airy universality in his incongruous work. But it must never be forgotten that Pollock's experience is one of violence and death.

The image and the destruction of the image.

'Thus the fact that good European moderns are now here is very important, for they bring with them an understanding of the problems of modern painting. I am particularly impressed with their concept of the source of art being the unconscious. This idea interests me more than these specific painters do, for the two artists I admire most, Picasso and Miro, are still abroad.'

Jackson Pollock, *Arts and Architecture*, February 1944

With the exception of the 'classic Pollock' period of 1948-1950, Pollock's whole experience is one of a battle with the image. From 1935 onwards, Picasso becomes the dominant influence, and drowns out the impact of Benton. Pollock studied under Benton from 1930 to 1934, but was influenced by him to only a limited extent, the sole legacy of his regionalism being a theatrical taste for movement.

JACKSON POLLOCK, *NIGHT MIST*, c1944, OIL.

Pollock carefully studied the Picasso reproductions published in the Surrealist journal *Minotaure*, and he must have been struck by the ferocity and the sexual violence with which this 'Cubist Goya' handles the female figure in particular. His early notebooks and juvenalia clearly show that the young painter was fascinated by Picasso: breaks inflicted on space and on figures which can never be separated from one another. Picasso's characteristic fragmentation is clearly visible in *Guardians of the Secret*, 1943, (as is that of Klee and Miro, though they are more explicitly endebted to China and Japan).

And yet at the same time, a less figurative tendency, which is closer to Monet's vibrant colourism, can also be seen in the play between chiaroscuro and radiant luminosity that characterises *Seascape*, 1934, and *The Flame*, 1937. The merging of the two gestures seems to be the trajectory which will lead to Pollock's unique and autonomous style. The Picasso-like fragmented image is gradually veiled, and finally vanishes into the flow of dripping paint. And 'veiling' was in fact the term Pollock used when he described his handling of imagery to Lee Krasner.

Birth (which is closely related to the *Masked Image* of 1938) might have been a product of Picasso's 'studio'. But thanks to an interplay between erasure and veiling, whose logic is more easily followed in the sketches of 1939, this 'masked birth' topples over into the luminous meanders of the rose window of *Gothic*, 1944, and is then pulverised even further in *Cathedral*, 1947. If we turn to *Cathedral* after looking at *Birth* and *Gothic*, we can see Pollock's stroke of inspiration: the style of a new master has found its first mature expression.

A masterly series spiralled out of this simultaneous absorption and concealment of the image, which does not really seem to have been liquidated, but to have been concealed, to have been dazzled by the silvery ground of a canvas splashed with dark greys and subtly toned pastels. *Full Fathom Five*, 1947, *Number One*, 1949, *Lavender Mist*, 1950, *Number Twenty Eight*, 1950, etc. No brush and no instrument, apart from the curves and volutes of a gesture which evokes swimming, music, the infinitesimal and truly mathematical discretion of an infinite web in which inside and outside, instrument and gesture merge and are redistributed. Enamel, oils and synthetic Duco combine to produce the effect of a shimmering whirl in which the image drowns. And yet the image does show through in more indentifiable form in

Blue Poles, 1953, where we seem to see the dark blue outline of totem-poles or crosses tearing apart the fibrous silvery texture; it also shows through in *Out of the Web*, 1949, where the amoeba-fish stand out against their hirsute mother.

A semiotic space.

Usually however, no image is visible in the pulverised texture of these canvases, even though there is something to suggest its enigmatic disappearance. Images are suspended, symbols avoided. And nor is the resultant *space* a symbolic space; it does not depend upon geometry or on geometric forms which derive, as has been said so often, from the articulations of human *speech*. Pollock's space is infra- and supra-formal, infra- and supra-linguistic, infra- and supra-symbolic. I call it semiotic, to use a term I once related to Plato's *chora* so as to evoke a maternal receptacle, a crushing, dancing receptacle (the Greek term refers to both the womb and a popular dance performed in the open squares of the city).[1]

The veiling of the image seems to dominate the drip paintings done between roughly 1948 and 1950, the period in which he gave up drinking. But the battle with representation begins anew in 1951 (*Black and White* series), and reappears in drastic form in *Portrait and a Dream*, 1953, where the two approaches – the fragmentation of representation – and exhalations of chromatic atoms – are once again dissociated and made to occupy the right- and left-hand areas of the canvas respectively.

The similarity between Pollock's drip technique and Siquieros' paint-splattered floor and use of spray guns is purely superficial: Pollock's gesture is very different; it is not instrumental, but an encounter with chance. A throw of the dice instead of the decorative energeticism of the Mexican, a sign of the 'counting' of the *Numbers* series (for example, *Number One*). Similarly, when Pollock embeds fragments of broken Coca-Cola bottles into the clouds that veil the imagery (*Full Fathom Five* and *Blue Poles*) one thinks, not of the Dadaists, but of Schwitters and Max Ernst, and of their cult of ugly objects, of the rocks that punctuate the sand in a Zen garden; the edges of representation, holes in representation.

An analytic experiment: Jung 'analysed' by Picasso.

I'm very representational some of the time, and a little all of the time.

But when you're painting out of your unconscious, figures are bound to emerge.
Jackson Pollock, June 1956, in Selden Rodman, *Conversations with Artists*, New York, 1957, p 82.
Even though early works like *Seascape*, 1934, do outline the programme for the later pulverisation of the image, it seems that it was only from 1940 onwards that Pollock really turned to abstraction. He had just spent a year in analysis with Dr Joseph Henderson, a New York Jungian.

In 1934, the artist's mental state began to deteriorate, and in 1937 he went into a detoxication programme for eight months. He was hospitalised again in 1938, but in 1939 he was introduced to Dr Henderson by their mutual friend Helen Marot, who taught at the City and County School where Pollock had been working as a janitor since 1934. Helen Marot seems to have been something of an adoptive mother to the young painter. It was also in 1939, or in other words while he was still in analysis, that Pollock met the painter Lee Krasner, who was later to become his wife. Although he later went into analysis on a number of other occasions, Pollock was deeply impressed by his conversations with Henderson. Three months before his death, he admitted : 'I've been a Jungian for a long time'.

Whilst it did not block his creative urge, as many artists fear it may do, analysis does not appear to have 'cured' Pollock of his symptoms either as, apart from one brief interlude of sobriety, he remained an alcoholic until the day he died. Even so, his analyst's counter-transference, and Henderson did have the courageous modesty to admit to its existence, does seem to have helped Pollock in his masterly progress through the image. Henderson confesses to asking himself why he did not attempt to cure Pollock of his alcoholism, adding that the drawings that came out of his patients unconscious resulted in a counter-transference on to the symbolic material he was producing. His urge to follow the movement of the symbolism was as irresistible as Pollock's urge to produce it.[2]

According to this Jungian analysis, the unconscious is, then, *visible*. Indeed, if we read both his text and those of Jung, it becomes apparent that, in the depths of the visible, in the hidden depths of things themselves, we find 'the all-giving mother'. Jung transforms this impenetrable remembrance, this screen memory of the archaic Mother who is feared and loathed by the wounded narcissist, into a bedrock.

Jung erects a representation, he *positivises* at the very point where the border-line patient fears that he will fall into a hole and be destroyed, and therefore negativises. Hence the mutual fascination, which is visible even when Jung's detractors counter his claims with the *image* of a fearsome and paranoically destructive Mother.

And so Pollock does all he can to please the analyst, just as one might try to please one's mother. He draws embryos, powerful, horrible mothers, births, ambivalent figures belonging to different orders (horse and bull, man and woman). And he asks Henderson to comment on them. And Henderson obviously finds a meaning in them. But not the meaning that torments the artist. What is worse, it also torments the other, who *speaks* and falls into the trap set for him by these gift-symbols in which the fantasy, far from being shaken off, tightens its oppressive, unshakeable grip. Pollock did, however, finally free himself from it ... when his analyst left New York in 1940. Helen Marot died that same year.

Mother-Earth trampled underfoot.
Look carefully at *Psychoanalytic Drawing No 57*: it clearly depicts a fantasy aspect of the androgenous fusion that was so dear to Jung's heart. A composite body-breast-thorax-bull clings to another body which is no more than a rump seen from behind. This fusion, this embrace centres upon a cloacal act of coitus in which the penis merges with the 'anal penis'; similarly, penetration towards the outside becomes an inward thrust. The invisible mouth seems to have been replaced by the hands which clumsily clasp the bust. Henderson symbolically *(discreetly)* interprets this obscene condensation of erogenous zones and of ambiguous sexual identities as a primitive representation of the *axis mundi* , and as a manifestation of 'ego strength'. Whilst it is true that an extraordinary phallic-anal solidity is visible, and that it does allow the subject to maintain a certain stability in the turbulence of this stormy embrace, the fact remains that this economy is based upon oral-anal aggression.

The only surface on which the artist can paint-write is the body of mother-earth, and he tramples it underfoot in an exquisite act of profanation. In order to do so, he has to free himself from his veneration of the sacred image, of its consistency and its meaning; he must 'smash its face'. The fantasy in sketch 5 (to take only one example among many) is no doubt still the fantasy of a *hidden space*,

37

JACKSON POLLOCK, *SEA CHANGE*, 1947, COLLAGE OF OIL AND SMALL PEBBLES ON CANVAS

or even of the secret behind the drip technique. But it will be concealed, veiled, erased, displaced and, therefore, literally perverted in a transposition which, like a vortex, emerges from within it but no longer has anything to do with it. In Pollock's later paintings, which were not done for his analyst, but for others, that is to say for no one, nothing remains of this fantasy: those paintings are its sublimation.

The painter's ally in this dissolution of the tragic obsession which torments him is . . . Picasso's destructive brush.

Another transference occurs during the analysis and, by means which remain invisible to a symbolist analyst, it fragments images and delivers Pollock from his mother's grip. It is Jackson's love for Picasso. Although Pollock was interested in the automatic writing of the Surrealists, Picasso was initially more important to him than symbols, and put an end to his depiction of embryos, child-mothers and primal scenes. The primordial devouring mother will be devoured[3] by the very space of representation that was crushed by Picasso. At a later stage, Pollock will have to free himself from his liberator. Picasso helps to liquidate Jungian symbolism, and action painting will allow Pollock to get over his worship of Picasso as abstraction absorbs the figure. And then Picasso's 'son' will be able to assert his sovereignty in his own name: Pollock.

In the course of the trajectory that leads to the advent of the abstraction which we described earlier (*Birth – Gothic – Cathedral*), Pollock's gesture tears itself away from the symbolism of *birth* and of the *bestiality of female desire*. Both the titles, of *Male and Female*, 1942, *She-Wolf*, 1943, *Pasiphae*, 1943, originally entitled 'Moby Dick', and rebaptised *Pasiphae* by JJ (Sweeney) and *The Moon Woman Cuts the Circle*, 1944-5, (and Pollock appears to have attached great importance to their titles), and their space, which is borrowed from Picasso, are a clear indication that his representation of even a fragmented body is still an act of worship dedicated to the eternal fetish: the female body. The aim of the later paroxysm is to pulverize it. The point is not that pulverising her makes the other invisible, or represses her. No, the point is that it makes *mater*, or matter, easier to penetrate. As Baudelaire might have put it, she/it becomes porous, gaseous and vibrant. And so, they can merge, she and him, him and her, neither nor, in a counting process.

The pneumatic body
When I am in my painting, I'm not aware of what I'm doing. It's only after a sort of 'getting acquainted' period that I see what I have been about . . . It is only when I lose contact with the painting that the result is a mess. Otherwise there is pure harmony.
Jackson Pollock, in *Possibilities*,[1] Winter 1947-8.
Pollock paints against the unconscious. He lightens his burden by means of a free and highly controlled discharge. His semiotic galaxies lie beyond symbolism; they are not pre-symbolic.

Jackson was the name of the family who adopted the father of Paul Jackson: Leroy McCoy, who came originally from Iowa and who lost both his parents within the space of a year. It was in a sense an assumed name, and Leroy McCoy never changed it. It is as though he wanted to acknowledge some symbolic debt. He was part Scots and part Irish, a retiring farmer, the father of five children, and completely dominated by his wife Stella McClure, an Irishwoman who also came from Iowa. She was devoutly religious and domineering, and, inspired by God alone what impulse, she forced her tribe to live a nomadic life. They moved house nine times in six years, criss-crossing both Arizona and California in the years following the birth of the last Paul Jackson in 1912. Apparently a typical American matriarch, she seems to have

wanted to become an artist . . .

A dead father, a real family name that died out when a man defeated by the Depression was buried; the all-powerful desires of an Irish mother who was religious and nomadic . . . There ought to be enough there to nourish a psychotic body.

The alcoholic is a starving man, always eager for a bull-like embrace with his Pasiphae, his sacred cow. But he is also afraid of her, loathes her, so much so that the only *jouissance* he wants is total, complete oblivion. Without any risk of being deprived of anything. But he does lose consciousness as his body and his mind drown in the bottomless seas of drunkenness.

For him, the pleasure of incest is beyond representation. Left speechless, without a sign, the ultimate appeal is a call to plunge to his death. No third party, no imaginary father is there to make reparation.[4]

The artist, however, never stops way-marking a mother-space that has no boundaries. Diving, marking the way. An imaginary Son, an imaginary Father. Alcohol or opium are the accomplices who calm him as he drowns in an artificial paradise. Or drive him into a paroxysm.

The 'mystical secret', the silent, unnameable underside of religions, of which the alcoholic body is a morbid symptom, has both its devotees (drug addicts) and its guardians (theologians).

Pollock's galaxies are like the stained-glass windows of a cathedral, and they allow us to see-feel-penetrate the very space of the exquisite pulverisation that springs from the incestuous embrace. Neither hole nor phallus. 'I am nature'. I disperse myself in nature. 'We' interpenetrate one another. I 'is', love I can get drunk without wine, without drugs. I am the powerful arabesque of a *jouissance*: my diffusion in the other, the diffusion of the other in me. A chromatic disappearance . . .

The artist is like a frogman; he explores the marine depths of the mother, Thanks to him, the unnameable explodes in our faces, and is at last represented. Is this the end of art? The pulverisation of the maternal secrets of religions? We can at least detect in it the incandescent underside, the violently tragic but jubilatory underside of the Western individual when he transcends his search for his own image, an image which is always entwined with that of his mother.

The male body that Pollock paints in his youth, and especially in the psychoanalytic drawings, is Christ crucified. And the body of Christ crucified suffers because it cannot disperse itself to the four cardinal points of space assigned to it by the cross. The passion of Christ crucified is the answer given in male terms by the women who were shattered by having intercourse with Picasso. Abandoned by the Father, exposed to the bestial Mother-Woman (*She-wolf*). Is man the artist an image of suffering? Pollock's galaxies transform this passion into a gentle vertigo, into the silvery glimmer of a vaporous, perfumed harmony. *Scent, Lavender Mist* and *Blue Poles*, 1953, transpose the Cross into a visible burst of glory which can never become an object. Yet there are points at which the cross tears apart this successful incest; its presence can be read in the sculptural projections of *Blue Poles*.

Am I doing anything more than reproduce Pollock's own conflicts, torn as he was between the image and its destruction, between sense and nonsense? What if these totem-poles, these crosses, had no meaning? What if they were simply rocks in a Zen garden, with traces of sand, traces of the void, swirling around them? How can we ward off the demon of interpretation and, ultimately, the demon of symbolism? Why should we fight them off? They act as a foil to the whirlwind, and they permit the advent of a name that owed a symbolic debt, but which is now the name of a master: JACKSON POLLOCK.

Notes

1 Julia Kristeva, 'Noms de lieu', in *Polylogue*, Editions du Seuil, Paris, 1977; *La Révolution du langages poétique*, 1974.
2 'A Psychological Commentary', in C L Wysuph, *Jackson Pollock: Psychoanalytic Drawings*, Horizon Press, New York, 1970.
3 *ibid*, plates 76, 77, 79.
4 *cf* Julia Kristeva, 'Abjet d'amour', *Confrontation*, Autumn, 1981.

JOHANNES VERMEER, *WOMAN IN BLUE*, c1662-4, OIL

CLIVE DILNOT AND MARUJA GARCIA-PADILLA
The Difference of Allegory

A painting

The woman in a pale blue smock and the long mustard-coloured skirt is reading a letter. We see her in profile, facing left from where we stand, somehow not far from her. Both her hands holding the paper, she is lost in her reading, her head slightly inclined, her lips not completely closed. Most of her hair is pulled back, but a small part falls to the side of her head to cover her cheek. Her face and arms are slim. Her body seems somewhat too heavy in comparison. Is she pregnant?

Behind and slightly above her a large map hangs on a white wall, though we can only see part of it. In front of her, to our left, one of its sides very close to us, there is a table covered with a dark bluish cloth; lying on it are several objects: a brown cloth – which falls off the nearest edge of the table and seems the one small moment of disorder in the scene – some pearls, a box, perhaps an envelope . . . It's hard to tell from here. Behind the table, facing us, its back a few inches from the wall, a chair projects its shadow against the white surface. Two dark wood lion heads decorate its back. Strange how the blue upholstery is attached by alternating small and large golden tacks . . . To the woman's left, at her back, a similar chair stands very close to us, almost in the way between her and us. Though we cannot see it, there must be a window on the left. Its light falls on the objects on the table, on her face and hands, on the front of her jacket, on the letter. She seems completely focused on herself and her reading. Oblivious to anything else. Oblivious to us. Being.

Being, being present, being there. Because she and her world are so present. Vermeer's *Woman in Blue* tempts us to allow ourselves to look at it as *world* before we look at it as *painting*. Almost unaccountably, for the moment of this first perception steals clearer thought, mimesis compels us towards narrative. Explanations begin, in spite of our reluctant realisation that the action that here presents itself is of the most minimal kind. Our contemplation of the solitary image engenders an illusion of compensatory presence in the image. The intensity of the absorption depicted, imitative at once of our own transitory state before the picture and of our deeper desire for equivalent self-absorption, pushes us to project our own presence into the picture, which appears at once to evoke, recognise and embody these desires, and to lay them out for our contemplation. In turn, our sentience and presence acknowledged, we gratefully dissolve the fact of representation for the fiction of presence. *Tableau*, in part recognised as such (no perfect illusions: for then the game would not work), gives way to *portrait*; absence and fictive configuration, to presence, to the depiction of a desired 'real', with all the double ambiguities which this implies. What is not, but has nonetheless now inescapably been granted an identity (though of precisely what kind?), here asserts its demands. It demands that we ask where we are, where we fall with regards to that presence. All illusion of presence works in something like this manner: a double recognition of figure and self prompts an exchange of identities, a lending of being to that which has no being. The paradox of the illusion of absorption is precisely one mechanism whereby this exchange is achieved.

In the spirit of old *ekphrastic* descriptions, the first moment of the description above acknowledged no gaps between the thing and the mark, the sign and the signified, the world and its representation. But, rather than a description of the image, ours is already the description, or better, the projection, of an imagined world, of the world we desire to be denoted by the image. At the centre of Vermeer's image there would seem to be an extraordinary effort to prevent the world from dissolving into paint. The painting can be seen as an act of representational work designed to assert, to exemplify, to bring into being, a secular trinitarian unity, where being, world and representation are worked as one, fused around a double moment: that of the achieved fiction of the *moment* depicted, and that of the *extended* moment of depiction. We know that in actuality this achieved fiction is fugitive: *is not*, but is only constantly remade in every act of looking and wilful suspension of disbelief. Nonetheless it is in this double moment that the illusion of presence and the presence of illusion are achieved.

But the painting nonetheless embodies a tension. The relationship within which the illusion of presence is achieved is not, in actuality, marked by unity. On the contrary, between the represented moment (however this is projected) and its representation, is an unbridgeable abyss. There is an interesting paradox here; as illusion, as figure, as fiction, no gap between image and illusory referent need be projected. But, precisely as the illusory presence of the referent is given status, as the image is *made real*, so a gap, a difference, must necessarily be opened between the image and 'the moment depicted', however this is conceived and in whatever way this is thought of as belonging to the 'real'. In other words, the difference between the projection of a 'real' that is more 'real' than the picture itself (and to which it then refers) and 'the picture itself' opens the chasm of reference. The representation could be thought of as a trace of existent moment *only* if we could conceive of the impossible task of defining what in fact that represented moment is itself. Since we already know this task is impossible, the difference that was opened to make the image a more or less contiguous representation of a 'real' is closed.

The application at this point of the characteristic distinction between metaphor and metonymy, between a signifying practice founded on relations of similarity in difference, and one based on relations of contiguity between image and referent, is not so much disabled by a failure to define the image as such, as it is by the difficulty of determining what it is we could take to be that that with regards to which the image stands in one or the other type of symbolic relationship. This question above all requires some kind of answer. If we grant the potential verisimilitude of the image (at least within a certain set of conventions and standards) the problem of what it is verisimilar to revolves wholly around the issue of its referential status. Yet, even as we begin to think about the problem, we realise that no answers of any certainty can emerge from this question. We can, for example, ask whether the correspondence between the image and figural narratives we can project into the picture is one of reality or of fiction. Is it 'portrait' – with, therefore, an extra-imagistic referent, a referent we must try to grasp? Or is it 'tableau' – without a specific referent, an 'artificial' configuration which we must read? It is of no help to reformulate the questions. Thus, if we ask whether the model for the figure does (or could) exist outside Vermeer's rendition of 'her', we realise the question already defies answer. Outside the language in which 'she' is presented to us, the *fact* of the model's existence or non-existence could tell us little about *this* figure who is not, of course, a *figure* at all, but only and necessarily a figural construct. Already in this projection of a referent, a figure, the very question presumes a tacit separability of the figure from its field of representation (just as so often a character in a novel is pulled out of the narrative and words wherein he or she is evoked). But to sunder figural construct from its representational ground in this way is already to perform a violence to the image. It is to wilfully deny the way in which the image we read cannot in actuality be so disfigured if we are to preserve its internal integrity. In other words, the original question is unanswerable, and is so at base, whether we attempt to posit an alternative referent concept as global as 'a fragment of a world for which it metonymically stands', or as mundane as 'the mimesis of an action'. For in each case we have to ask which 'world', which 'action' and which 'gesture'. None of the worlds, actions or gestures that might be posited here are so; they are not actions, gestures or the like, but rhetorical figures, constructs that open precisely the same problems of reference we are facing here. Nor of course can we satisfactorily pose as the image's primary referent some metaphorical reference to our own presence, our own being. We are certainly addressed by the picture; in a powerful way the picture does not exist outside us, its viewers. But we are not therefore what the painting is 'about', even if we are that in relation to which the image stands.

This problem should give us pause for thought. For we also know that in a sense a more subtle game is being played here, that in practice a third concept is interpolated between the alternatives of 'portrait' and 'tableau'. As De Man points out in relation to a comparable problem in Rousseau's *Julie*,[1] the conflicts of fiction and experience (and of truth to experience) can be abrogated through a reference to 'universal' experience. The conceptual figure 'experience' (which always translates into ' "man" and his experience of the world') now stands as that which translates and demarcates between the world of experience, 'our world', and the fictive world. Common experience, referred to through this overarching idea into which all possible experiences are subsumed, unproblematically allows us to negotiate between and to provide a court of last (and first) resort for settling disputes between real and figural worlds; in particular, disputes as to the essential validity of the latter for bearing on the life, thought and ethics of the former.

Have we then solved our problem? Not at all. The reference to universal experience, although it explains what was in any case obvious, our relatively unproblematic perceptual seduction into the 'real' *suggested* by the image, merely refers to an equally unstable figure – 'experience'. Just how unstable this idea is we can grasp the moment we remember that its figural/conceptual counterparts are 'man' and 'woman'. Far from being universal and unproblematically related to our core of common experience, and far from the figure possessing 'the common traits shared by all men', it is precisely 'woman' that reveals that no reference to universal experience is valid. For we simply ask – who's experience, from what basis? – to discover again a shifting and uncertain field. If we here follow Rousseau in his scepticism as to whether such a concept can indeed have stable or even useful reference, we can say that what 'experience' in an existential sense, and 'man' and 'woman' in a more figural and immediately evocative manner, do, is to confer an 'illusion of proper meaning (on) to a suspended, open semantic structure'[2]

Yet, if we consider that all such figures (metaphors) reflect, and are driven by, our desires to give stable frames to experience, to name things, what this idea does refer us to is that this drive, and these figures, these would-be frames of reference, are inevitably images themselves. Rousseau's comments on the figure 'love' appear wholly apt for all of Vermeer's painting: 'it fashions, so to speak, another universe for itself; it surrounds itself with objects that do not exist . . . and since it states all its feelings by means of images, its language is always figural'.[3] In other words, desire replaces the absence of identity, not with a concept that makes connection with the 'real', for

it almost confesses the impossibility of so doing, but with a figure that compensates: hence, desire projects a figural world. But exactly this ensures its success. Thus, despite its actually problematic status, the figural metaphors of 'experience' work in a pragmatic sense – the figure of absorption, for instance, reflects, embodies and brings to mind our own desires for absorption. Identity is enabled. Indeed precisely because of this distinguishing feature of our reading practice, 'all' that the figure has to do to be recognised and *read* , or taken up into our world, is to be articulated in such a way that desire is indeed evoked. In that moment the absence of the 'real' figure is irrelevant. On seeing Vermeer's picture we instantly populate the universe that he provides and, charmed by the ability to exercise our desire and contemplation in this way, thank Vermeer profoundly for having so provided for our experience. Since, in addition, Vermeer does us the inestimable service of rendering *his* figure with the maximum of evocative naturalism, he minimises the pathos of desire, the fact that it is figural and not referential. Indeed, in contemplating the painting, we scarcely recognise desire; it is evoked but is almost below a threshold of consciousness. In this stillness, an apparently 'pure' contemplation intervenes; gratifyingly we accept the exchange.

But this still does not solve our problem. We still have secured no referent for our picture that lies outside, or is exterior to, the picture itself. In fact, the best that we can say at the moment is that the painting is in large part exemplificatory of itself: a representation of the processes of configuration and representation (even though representation is not its ostensible subject matter). But the assertion is not entirely valueless: in drawing attention to the double moment of the picture (represented moment represented), it reminds us firmly that the latter is a double configuration brought together in a single plane. On the one hand, there is the configuration as construct of a represented moment. In other words, and crudely, Vermeer's decision to paint, in a certain manner, representations of a defined and chosen inventory of objects brought together in a deliberate 'constellation' of evocative and figurative-representational meaning. Thus, Vermeer selects a number of objects, relatively meaningless in themselves, possessing only their 'own' meaning: he organises them conceptually to constitute a significant group, a 'world'; to represent, in Benjamin's terms, an 'idea'. On the other hand, brought together in a particular conceptual but emotionally motivated configuration, they are now visually organised in such a way as to evoke a particular kind of experienced space, and articulated in a manner that will evoke a certain mood or feeling. The two moments are fused on the plane of the picture itself. This is not to say either that the second of these moments is wholly secondary to the first, chronologically or in terms of a hierarchy of intended meaning – rather, the first moment of the configurational process may equally be said to be the result or the product of the second – or that the picture thereby gains a mythic unity of identity. On the contrary, the one moment of necessary identity in the picture, the moment of configuration, is differentiated on a number of levels. We have already pointed to the fact that, if Vermeer is to create an illusion of the represented (depicted) moment, the one plane of identity – the fused double moment of configuration – is precisely *that which must be repressed in the picture* in the service of displacing the illusion of identity from the configured moment to the depicted moment – from the figure as a configured figure (fiction), to the illusion of figure as portrait of a referent. This is why, after all, we were induced to evoke the effects of Vermeer's work on his audience and to make the kind of description we first made of this picture. But if we were equally led to undermine this description and the illusion of presence, it is because Vermeer's painting embodies a tension between the reprinted moment and its representation, with the illusion of the first appearing to deny the gap between a perception and its recording, and attempting to carry us over the rift between experience and representation.

But the first of these moments will not hold. It is riven by an inescapable paradox. The attempt to assert the unity of the pictorial sign demands an intentional consciousness about the act of representation which rests on the prioritisation of that same process and effort which it is designed to deny. The theoretical and critical vocabulary which is linked to the different forms of realism in Western art overflows with expressions exemplifying this effort: from the term 'realism' itself, to 'mirror-like', 'window-on-the-world' 'un-mediated', 'photographic' – all expressions which focus on the achievement, on the creation, the making 'real', of what is, however, on the other hand conceived and presented as natural. To assert the unity between perceived reality and its representation, that is, to propose the unmediated nature of representation, we must unavoidably focus conscious effort on the closing of that gap, the *negation* of whose very existence is a prerequisite for our assertion. But the gap, its denial, and the fluctuating tension between them, are a trait of the process of representation itself. They cannot be wished away, though they can, as we have seen, be all but sublimated.

Even more importantly, and inseparable from the positions taken by the artist or image-maker regarding this condition, are positions of 'being'. Every stance towards representation is in fact a stance towards a concept of 'being', and towards the means whereby 'being' is known, structured and represented. This stance is consciously or unconsciously exemplified in the formal choices made by an artist or image-maker. One can read Vermeer's work as a whole, for example, from within the Dutch tradition of *being-in-appearance*, and one can watch it fluctuate and evolve in exploration of the representational tensions we have described: first following and perfecting the rules of realistic representation of appearance as a mirror of 'being-in-appearance', in the early period; then taking them to their limits, inverting, undermining, subverting and dissolving them, in the allegories and the other late works, where the whole structure of representation and 'being' is placed into question. As a whole then, Vermeer's work is a simultaneous process of reflection upon the act of representation, upon the definition of 'being' and 'being in the world', and *thus on the gap existing between being-in-appearance and the manner in which that appearance can be defined and represented.*

This last point is fundamental. If we posit this gap between 'signifier' and 'signified' as a condition of representation, and thus simultaneously posit the impossibility of unmediated representation, the nature of that unavoidable mediation becomes a fundamental epistemological, aesthetic, political and ethical issue. Nothing so exemplifies this problem as the extreme point which defines itself in opposition to the illusion of unmediated representation, namely allegory.

Thinking about allegory

Allegory is an overtly mediated, interested and intentional mode of representation. As a mode of representation it is, in effect, a mode of writing in the Derridean sense, a 'solution' to the problem of dealing with the dichotomy of presence and absence in representation. Allegory is defined, not through its proximity to the idea of presentation, but by its frank awareness and incorporation of the gap that must occur in representation. Far from the orderly essential totality of the symbol, with its confidence in its own, and the world's, unshakeable permanence, allegory incarnates and exemplifies an essential absence. In refusing the idea of unity, allegorical configurations proffer a sustained tension and play between the illusion of presence given and representation or language, the essential absence of the referred-to object, and the 'presence' and revelation in representation of a deeper multi-levelled 'real'; that which the allegory postulates to be veiled, but true. This gap, or play, can be formulated alternatively as that between signifier and signified, or that between intended presence and the absence that necessarily accompanies, and in fact determines, the construct or production of 'presence'. More concretely, allegory can be seen as embodying or underscoring the play between the illusory and uncanny presence of the represented thing in the image (as in Vermeer) and the absence of meaning from that image which in turn necessitates assigned, and not 'natural' meaning, and which hence erodes representation's pretence to present the 'things themselves'.

Thus both in its conceptual formulation and in the formal configuration in which that formulation is embedded, the allegorical mode manifests itself as the expression of what Benjamin described as a deep-rooted intuition of the problematic character of the representational truth of art.

The traditional definitions of allegory, marked as they are in most cases by the dispute around the romantic aesthetics of the symbol, are not wholly satisfactory. Nonetheless, they reveal certain features of the mode. Ruskin's definition for example, read carefully, indicates some important features of the genre:

> [D]epriving the subject of material and bodily shape, and regarding such of its qualities only as it chooses for a particular purpose, it forges these qualities together in such groups and forms as it desires, and gives to their abstract being consistency and reality by striking them as it were with a die of an image belonging to another matter, which stroke having once received, they pass current at once in the peculiar conjunction and for the particular value desired.[4]

Certain points emerge from Ruskin's formulation: allegory is intentional, it intends meaning, and refuses to be held to establishing identities between the desired meaning and the thing used for depiction. Allegory breaks the natural linkage which still subsists for us between a thing and the meanings that accrue to it. Instead, it *takes meaning from elsewhere* than the vehicle it deploys, and stamps it on to the vehicles it selects, takes up things and uses them to stand for other meanings. Allegory is semantic, then, in that it translates things into signs.

All of this is at once true, but, as we shall see, not wholly what allegory is, nor how it works. Above all, allegory is by no means fundamentally confined (as tradition has it) to issues of content (interpretation). It is a means of *speaking other*, but that *other* involves reflection on the formal and the structural, on the configurational and the representational processes, as much as it does on the content of what is spoken. To be sure, allegory's thematics have essentially to do with a stance on the world – which is why allegory is irredeemably ethical at core. And it is obviously true that a decisive aspect in allegory is the 'disjunction between the phenomenal appearance of the sign (world) and the value which the sign (world) possesses'. But we shall see that this claim, like so many others that accrue to the allegorical, can also be seen to be true in part for other modes of representation. We can, for example, take two further commonplaces that 'define' the allegorical: the fact that in allegory 'the relation between the sensory features of the sign and its meanings is arbitrary', and the idea that 'the aesthetic value of an allegorical sign cannot be generated by reference to the natural object that the sign resembles'[5] Both of these features are also, in part at least, replicated in a number of other representational forms. The decisive feature of the allegorical then lies not in a listing of its features, but in grasping the way in which, as a mode, it accepts or utilises the condition we have laid out above, and, indeed, uses it for cognitive or emotive effect. Hence, the 'features' of allegory are no more than the particular structural forms that allegory uses. The decisive point in the allegorical system is to be found in the refusal of presence and in the structural devices that allegory uses to declare and exploit absence rather than presence.

In speaking of an allegorical system, we should perhaps differentiate between the concept of an allegory (or an allegory presented at the conceptual level) and an allegory bodied forth, or, better, necessarily translated into, an allegorical image. Clearly, these are not identical, though they are inevitably spoken of together. The allegorical representation embodies or exemplifies the allegory; but, precisely because the allegory concerns a difference – that between the object and what it stands for, between a thing (image) and its significance – allegorical representation is impelled to reflect on this peculiar concept. For, if the allegorical painting simply reflects – or unproblematically depicts – the allegory, it denies at the level of its own representation what allegory claims as the state of the world. Hence the acute consciousness regarding issues of language and representation to be met with in allegorical works. And hence too the problems that they face. For allegorical representations are doubled in peculiar ways. The fact of the allegory coming to 'presence' in a representation must involve the construction of a web of signifying traces which, in the end, evades the presence of (semantic) 'meaning', undermines the alleged programme of the work, defeats its intentionality, and potentially causes allegory to be itself doubled and destroyed. Thus allegory, as bodied forth in an image, is also necessarily defined as an impossible tension between a represented moment – which lacks presence, yet construes an illusory, seductive identity, a would-be presence – and the programme, the intended signification, the allegorical 'content' – which however is never reached, is always subverted (at least in part) by the conditions of the translation of programme into image, by the making of an illusion which to 'carry' the message exceeds it. But the doubling does not stop here, for in turn the allegory once again subverts this subversion. Precisely because allegory refuses the identity, the fusion, the belief in presence that characterises symbolist aesthetics, it also refuses to allow the illusion of presence to hold, to sustain itself. Indeed, we find the allegory deliberately disfiguring the representational illusion, even as it exploits naturalistic effects.

Allegory is, thus, a mode of representation that utilises the *double* (or even treble) character of representation. Hence, allegory operates between two worlds: that of aesthetics and that of language. In the former it stands either under the heading of condemnation (by symbolist aesthetics) or of appreciation (by Post-Modern theory). In either case it stands as that which is placed against the aesthetic, understood in the Kantian sense. In relation to language (and thus also to aesthetics, since allegory refuses this distinction), it stands for that displacement which both disdains and refuses the direct possibilities of speech, preferring instead to 'write', to speak obliquely, to stand at the side of expressive discourse and comment on it, to refuse identity and, in distance from the speaking voice, speak through echoing and doubling the acts of speaking and writing. In its scepticism with regard to 'speaking directly', allegory embodies that necessary understanding which perceives that, at certain moments, in certain conditions, certain things can only be said by speaking obliquely. Always understood here to be referring to content – as when most clearly, we speak of political allegories, attempting to speak round or through the barriers of censorship – this understanding is in actuality just as often perception about the conditions of speaking and about the problems of how languages refer and how they are read, and represent an acute understanding of the relationship between conditions of speaking and conditions of reading and comprehending. Allegory, as De Man has extensively explored, is a sophisticated response to the conditions of reading; a perception of what, in particular circumstances, language might evoke, or might refer to. As such, allegory is once again a response to the fundamental 'unreliability' and uncertainty of reference and meaning. Behind it lies a determination to disclose the truth of this condition, whether seen in terms of language, reference and reading – and the bodying forth of the dislocated textual truth of this condition (Rousseau, Derrida) – or as the attempted recovery of meaning from a linguistically dislocated world (Benjamin).

But for this very reason the familiar idea that the allegorical and the aesthetic are necessarily in opposition is quite wrong, a reflection of the constructed opposition between allegory and symbol in Romantic aesthetics. (An opposition that was scarcely known in Wincklemann's day, for example.) On the contrary, the dichotomy between the allegorical and the aesthetic is so only for an aesthetics conceived of as in effect refusing or down-playing both the ethical and configurational moments. Allegory understands the linkage between representation and truth, and therefore can neither tolerate an aesthetic that is merely so (formalism), nor an aesthetic that will not comprehend that it *configures* the grounds of its representations but, rather, believes that it depicts the *things themselves* (as, most obviously, in the ideology, though not necessarily the practice, of Romantic aesthetics).

The allegorical is configurational in the extreme. It *configures* the world of objects/signs that it represents. It considers this configuration, and its representation (in the depiction of signs) and exemplification (in the structural parallels allegory constructs between 'the world', the *constellation* it configures and the configuration through which it embodies and secretly makes evident this world), in relation to both aesthetic and representational questions. The world that the allegorical evokes and makes reference to is therefore simultaneously representational, configurational and aesthetic. Hence allegory can be thought of as a 'hinge' concept between these moments. The fact that as such, allegory necessarily also opens this conjunction of fields to questions of ethics – for we might say the ethics of representation are its subject matter – in part explains allegory's central (but not wholly understood) place in Post-Modern thought.[6]

Although the characteristic of allegory is to exemplify these problems, the issues that it deals with, and, more importantly perhaps in the long run, *opens to be able to speak about*, are generalised within and across representation in general, in precisely the same way that the problems of writing and *différance* that Derrida identifies cross all limits of discursive boundaries and simply address conditions of speaking in general.[7] Now, if it is possible to claim or posit that the allegorical can, in a similar way, stand as a metaphor for, or as indicative of, a necessary condition of representation in general, this does not mean that all representation *is* allegorical. On the contrary, allegory is fought against as much as, if not more than, it is articulated. Allegory implies consciousness – to some extent the ironic consciousness of reflective distance – and, being distanced from its desired meaning, it turns and reflects on the conditions of meaning and representation. Thus, it becomes doubly antithetical to those modes of representation whose aim is to construe, and incarnate, presence. But since we can claim that the allegorical condition, at least as a moment, *inhabits* representation in general (that, in other words, there is no representation without at least a trace of the allegorical), we can claim that all representation deals, in some way, with the allegorical problem – even if it is most notably the repression of the conditions of identity and difference that describes this process. One way of reading the history of art and representation, particularly in the post-Baroque world, is to see it in the light of the suppression of the allegorical within aesthetics, and the outright refusal and repression of allegorical theory, as a struggle with this condition, a condition which, precisely because of this history, cannot yet be adequately spoken of.

In modernity, the explicit denial of the inevitability of the gap between sign and meaning, and the subsequent goal of eradicating that gap, has its origin in the myth of a unified non-arbitrary prelapsarian language (whose 'loss' is at the same time the result and the index of human fall from grace), and in the project of reviving that unmediated relationship between language and experience. Thus, the Romantic aesthetic stance constitutes a wider Utopian project of redemption and reconciliation, which transcends the sphere of art, but which places the aesthetic in an exemplificational, generative and reconciliatory role. The desire for the suppression of the fissure of meaning, world and experience is a defining trait of Romantic aesthetics and of the theoretical definition of Romantic poetry. In Friedrich Schlegel's words, the latter can:

> more than any other form hover between the portrayed and the portrayer, free of all real and ideal self-interest, on the wings of poetic reflection, and can raise that reflection again and again to a higher power, can multiply it in an endless succession of mirrors.[8]

Schlegel's phrase contains its own irony, of course; he was, in any case, particularly aware of the limitations of Romantic theory. Nonetheless De Man's prescient summary of Gadamer's statement on (and critique of) Romantic aesthetics, as that which 'refuses to distinguish between experience and the representation of this experience' captures exactly the Romantic condition. De Man continues:

The poetic language of genius is capable of transcending this distinction and can thus transform all individual experiences directly into general truth. The subjectivity of experience is preserved when it is translated into language; the world is then no longer seen as a configuration of entities that designate a plurality of distinct and isolated meanings, but as a configuration of symbols ultimately leading to a total, single, and universal meaning.[9]

The paradox of this quotation, an indication of the complexity of relations involved here between the symbolic and the allegorical, is that only the first two sentences apply wholly to the symbolic. The last sentence, providing perhaps that we substitute 'symbols' with 'signs', applies to both: the difference between the symbolic and the allegorical here is the stance they take on this identical premise, which is to say the stance they take towards two different types of signifying practices essentially distinguished by the purported existence of either 'natural' or 'rational' relations between signifier and signified. In this context, symbolic representation is understood to stand in a natural, immediate, spontaneous relationship to that which is symbolised by it. In contrast, according to this account, allegory presupposes a clear distinction and independence between sign and thing, the connection established by means of a conceptual mediation which displaces or shifts the meaning of one term superimposing it on the other. The production and interpretation of allegorical objects are thus conceived as 'rational', 'intellectual' processes. This is how Coleridge sees allegory, as a translation of a non-aesthetic structure, of an abstract idea, into an image:

> Now, an allegory is but a translation of abstract notions into a picture-language, which is itself nothing but an abstraction from objects of the senses: the principal being more worthless even than its phantom proxy, both alike unsubstantial and the former shapeless to boot. On the other hand, a symbol . . . is characterised by a translucence of the special in the individual, or of the general in the special, or of the universal in the general; above all by the translucence of the eternal through and in the temporal. It always partakes of the reality which it renders intelligible; and while it enunciates the whole, abodes itself as a living part in that unity of which it is the representation. The others are but empty echoes which the fancy arbitrarily associates with apparitions of matter, less beautiful but not less shadowy than the sloping orchard or hill-side pasture seen in the transparent lake below.[10]

Underlying Coleridge's classic statement of this opposition is his distinction between mechanic and organic form, whereby in the former 'on any given material we impress a pre-determined form, not necessarily arising out of the properties of the material', while the latter 'is innate: it shapes, as it develops, itself from within, and the fullness of its development is one and the same with the perfection of its outward form. Such as the life is, such is the form.'[11] This conception of form can then be returned to the distinction between allegory and symbols in which the symbol is defined as being 'always itself a part of that, of the whole of which it is representative'.[12]

Implicit in this opposition between symbolism and allegory (and essential to it) is a wider system of differences on the basis of which the limits of the modern have been articulated. Radically calling into question the definitions of the terms of oppositions such as emotion and intellect, intuition and reason, natural and artificial, perception and interpretation, mediated and unmediated, science and aesthetics, art and non-art, would undermine the foundations of the allegory/symbol dichotomy. Indeed, one can suggest that it is precisely the erosion of these oppositions in the Post-Modern which has enabled a space to be created wherein the allegorical can once again be thought. Conversely, the critique of symbolist aesthetics and the rehabilitation of the allegorical poses a direct threat to the structure of Kantian aesthetics and hence to the presuppositions of post-Kantian versions of the modern. This issue was most clearly understood in Gadamer's critique of the limits of Kantian 'subjectivist' aesthetics, given in the first part of *Truth and Method*.[13]

Historically, the opening of the question of the aesthetic in the Post-Modern sense, which is often retrospectively assigned, in terms of artistic practice to the work of Johns, Rauschenberg and others in the late 1950s, (and conveniently linked to Rauschenberg's paintings of 1959-60 titled *Allegories*), finds its perhaps surprising philosophical parallel in Gadamer's *Truth and Method*, first published in 1960. Gadamer's attempt at establishing a foundation for an adequate hermeneutic practice is based on an exploration of the 'question of truth as it emerges in the experience of art'. Yet in an opening gesture, whose radicality is quite belied by the tone and thrust of Gadamer's writing, he insists not on the comprehension of the necessarily limited model of truth contained in the experience of art as it is given to us through Kantian aesthetics, but on the truth model of art *as it might hypothetically be reconstructed* from a *critique of* the 'subjectivisation' of Kantian aesthetics. Thus Part One of *Truth and Method* begins as a sustained examination of the presuppositions of Kantian aesthetic thought, and as a critique of the subjectivisation of the aesthetic which this entailed. Most unusually at this date, it includes, as a key moment, a critique of the valorisation of the symbol and of symbolic thinking in modern theory, together with a parallel schematic *rehabilitation* of allegory. Moreover, this critique is arguably the key moment of the argumentative scheme, for, among the elements of the Kantian aesthetic that Gadamer deals with (and he ranges widely over the constitutive notions of Kant's aesthetics), it is the critique of the symbol and the rehabilitation of allegory which most strongly provoke his doubts concerning the adequacy of modern aesthetic thinking. As if to confirm this, it is from this point in his argument that Gadamer can launch his attack on the 'abstraction' of aesthetic consciousness and can then go on to attempt his own re-structuring of the 'ontology' of the work of art. In relativising the opposition between allegory and symbol (in making an allegedly universal relation merely one of contingency), Gadamer finds himself revealing, and then calling into question, not only the structure by which Kantian aesthetics is in part secured, the valorisation of the aesthetics of the symbol and the repression of the allegorical, but the adequacy of the aesthetic as an explanatory, and even practical category. His conclusions to this critique are worth recording in full:

> From this survey of the linguistic history of 'symbol' and 'allegory' I draw a factual inference. The fixed quality of the contrast between the two concepts of the symbol that has emerged 'organically' and the cold, rational allegory, becomes less certain when we see its connection with the aesthetics of genius and of experience. If the rediscovery of the art of the Baroque . . . has led to a certain reinstatement of allegory, we can now see the theoretical reason for this. The foundation of 19th-century aesthetics was the freedom of the symbol-making activity of the mind. But is that a sufficient foundation? Is this symbol-making activity not also in fact limited by the continued existence of a mythical allegorical tradition? If this is recognised, however, the contrast between symbol and allegory again becomes relative, whereas the prejudice of the aesthetics of experience made it appear absolute. Equally, the difference of the aesthetic consciousness from the mythical can hardly be considered as absolute.

> The raising of such questions involved a thorough revision of the fundamental concepts of aesthetics. Obviously we are concerned here with more than a change in taste and aesthetic evaluation. Rather, the idea of aesthetic consciousness itself becomes doubtful and thus the standpoint of art to which it belongs. Is the aesthetic attitude to a work of art the appropriate one? Or is what we call 'aesthetic consciousness' an abstraction? The new estimation of allegory of which we have spoken indicated that there is, in aesthetic consciousness too, a dogmatic element. And if the difference between the mythical and the aesthetic consciousness is not absolute does not the concept of art itself become questionable; for is it, as we have seen, a

produce of aesthetic consciousness? At any rate, it cannot be doubted that the great ages in the history of man are those in which people without any aesthetic conciousness and without our concept of 'art' surrounded themselves with creations whose religious or secular life-functions could be understood by everyone and which to no one gave solely aesthetic pleasure. Can the idea of aesthetic existence be applied to these without reducing their true being?[14]

An allegory of faith

Unlike nature, where difference is easily conceptualised into a dichotomy of subject and object, the work of art exists as a non-dialectical configuration of sameness and otherness, sufficiently uncanny to be called god-like . . .

(De Man, *Allegories of Reading*, p 177)

If a misapprehension can be said to lie at the foundations of the weaknesses of the traditional critique of allegory, it could be described as its deeply anaestheticising conception of art. Underlying this critique and, indeed, most writing on allegory, is a surprisingly unquestioned (though outwardly denied) assumption about the *divisibility* of form and content whereby, paradoxically, 'form', though exalted, is to a great extent deprived of its meaning; while 'content', though often exiled and despised, is, nevertheless, granted an almost totally autonomous capacity for bearing a meaning independently from its configuration. As a result of this, the ever-present tension between the two levels, the manner in which they simultaneously strengthen and subvert each other, and indeed, the essential ambiguity, multi-levelledness and contextuality of meaning itself, can be consistently obscured and denied. Benjamin has most strenuously developed this last point. One of his major critiques of symbolism runs as follows:

> The most remarkable thing about the popular use of the term is that a concept which, as it were categorically, insists on the indivisible unity of form and content, should nevertheless serve the philosophical extenuation of that impotence which, because of the absence of dialectical rigour, fails to do justice to content in formal analysis and to form in the aesthetics of content. For this abuse occurs wherever in the work of art the 'manifestation' of an 'idea' is declared a symbol, is distorted into a relationship between appearance and essence. The introduction of this distorted conception of the symbol into aesthetics was a romantic and destructive extravagance which preceded the desolation of modern art criticism.[15]

The importance of formal issues and awareness, on the one hand, of the irreducible embeddedness of all levels of meaning within formal configurations; and, on the other, of the irrevocably signifying charge of every formal choice, becomes, therefore, an essential premise for the reconsideration of allegory and of the dichotomy in which it was placed by Romantic theory, as well as for the manner in which it is capable of illuminating aspects of representation in general.

Representation works by operating with a tacit concept of the referential mode of what is figured. De Man notes that the satisfactory reading of a representation presupposes three conditions or propositions. Firstly, the proposition that representation is fundamentally referential. Secondly, the condition that the status of the representational mode we are faced with is unambiguous in itself. Thirdly, that on any given occasion we possess sufficient information to decide what mode of representation is being offered to us. What the precise mode of representation is becomes here less important than the fact that we can assign it a specific place amongst our repertoire of representational modes.

To briefly develop these propositions, we can say that the first point presupposes reference in general as the originating condition of representation. And hence the further understood proposition that figural or non-referential languages are a special exception, are declared as such and are in any case, formed in relation to this primary referentiality. The second point stresses that it is not the case, there-

fore, that we can only read referential language: on the contrary, we have no problems with reading figural or abstract languages, providing that we understand them to be such. As De Man points out, we are scarcely helpless when confronted with *figures* of speech: 'as long as we can distinguish between the literal and the figural meaning we can translate the figure back to its proper referent.'[16] But that distinguishing knowledge is a key factor, for reading can scarcely take place outside of assuming 'a possible knowledge of the rhetorical status of what has been written.'[17] Thus it is not, at least at this level, the *form* of pictorial or linguistic representation that necessarily causes problems to our understanding. Even if we presume reference, or use referential meaning as a kind of base assumption of what representation is, as long as we can make an *informed* decision about the referential status of a representational language, reading can take place.

By opening the paper with a discussion of Vermeer's *Woman in Blue*, and by pointing, in effect, to the 'allegorical' structure of that picture, or at least to the structure of absences that underlies its extraordinary illusion of presence, the implicit, complementary image from Vermeer's later paintings with which that work was being compared was the *Allegory of Faith*, his last known picture. Painted around 1672, no work by Vermeer is more clearly and deliberately allegorical, and no work is more critically condemned.[18] The almost unanimous conclusion of those who have written on Vermeer is that the work appears as an aberration amongst his paintings. But, in contradiction to this notion, it is possible to see the *Allegory* rather as the culmination of a distinct project; or perhaps less strongly, as a quite logical conclusion to certain tendencies and ideas about representation that were developing in Vermeer's work as early as 1664-5. Vermeer produces, in this period, pictures that are some of the most extraordinary (and rightfully popular) instances of the rendition of absorbed or engaging presence in Western art. Yet at the same time Vermeer quietly but firmly dissolves the simple representation of presence. Thus what appears, in these pictures, as the rendition of the illusion of presence can also be read, in this light, as a complex meditation on, and exemplification of, the conditions of representation; a deconstruction of the figural structures of representation that takes the form of precisely indicating the ultimately figural nature of all representation and thus of the instantiation of doubt as to what it is that these images refer to. To use De Man's terms, we would say that in these paintings Vermeer gradually shows as rhetorical what, in the earlier paintings, is made to pass as the logic and grammar of representation. In other words, what appeared to be a document, an image of almost photographic veracity becomes revealed, and explicitly so, not as a depicted, but as a configured, scene: as a construct; a tableau whose 'objectivity' is then inverted and whose simple reading is put in doubt.

It is immediately evident, even to the most casual viewer, that the *Allegory of Faith* denies all three claims, and does so by steadily refusing the conditions on which the satisfactory reading of a representation is dependent. First, it refuses us access to the information required to 'complete' the scene – for the more we ask what is laid out here, or what scene this represents, the less satisfactory are the answers. The evident and astonishing naturalism (in the painting of the curtain, or the rendering of the transparent globe) seems immediately undercut both by the theatricality of the space and, more seriously, by the rhetorical gesture of the figure of 'Faith'. Second, and again evident at first glance, the picture instantiates a deep ambiguity as to the referential or representational mode in play here. By effecting a play between both figural rhetoric and its representation, *and* the logical grammar of pictorial naturalism, the picture takes each moment to its limit, and then, through a kind of excess, inverts it, deploying the moment against itself in the sense of displacing the 'normal' assigned roles of pictorial elements. The three most obvious instances of this are the painting of the transparent globe, the empty pathos and gesture of the figure of 'Faith', and the choice and manner of rendering the foreground curtain. Each at once deploys a moment logical to it, but then, through the deliberately 'excessive' manner of that deployment, puts into question not only itself as an item in the painting, but the apparently naturalist logic of the painting as a whole. In turn, as these items lose their place in the logical schema of things, so that schema is rendered as undone or as provisional or uncertain, and the picture ceases to cohere. But thirdly, in establishing this uncertainty in the very act of first looking at the picture, the painting can be said to put into question the referential moment as a whole. It does so not simply by opposing other figural languages which begin from a referential moment – even if construed in opposition to reference – but by more fundamentally casting doubt on reference itself, by the very act of evidencing astonishing capacity for referential illusion.

As a consequence of this process, the picture lays itself open to five levels of immediate criticism. In the first place, it seems un-pictorial in the specific sense of seemingly wishing to deny the kind of pleasures that Vermeer's pictures normally offer. The motifs and spatial structure are comparable to those in the earlier pictures, but even the sumptuous painting of the curtain on the left cannot free the picture from a sense that within it, aesthetically speaking, everything remains the same (ie repeats Vermeer's aesthetic) and yet at the same time, everything changes. (The figure is clearly a key point here, and we shall presently return to it.) Secondly, whereas nearly all other Vermeer pictures are seen in terms of the achievement of an extraordinary and seemingly unproblematic pictorial harmony, wholly consonant with the apparently harmonious domestic scene presented to us, the *Allegory of Faith* upsets this model. In the earlier pictures there is an interaction between the logical, grammatical-syntactical and rhetorical moments in the picture, such that each is both subjected to the constraints of pictorial harmony, and yet made to work to reinforce the satisfaction of a design and the depiction of a moment. In *Allegory of Faith* this is at once reproduced and denied. Superficially reproduced, the viewer cannot help but notice that the spatial and emotive organisation of the scene now no longer coincide. The violence of the figure's gesture breaks the delicate relation that usually exists in Vermeer's work between the understated presences of his figures and the understated manner of his painting. This sundering of the harmony between the rhetorical and syntactical, and rhetorical and logical or naturalistic languages displays them, disconcertingly, as at once themselves and as inverted images of themselves. But this opens a third level of criticism. Naturalism thus deployed is also clearly figured: made rhetorical – if in nothing else than in the bravura of the painting of the curtain which stands as deliberately 'excessive', as declarative, and thus while standing as almost exemplificational of the abilities to render objects in the world naturalistically, also undermines the conventional representational logic of naturalistic painting. Since the latter generally demands that objects in the rendered world are depicted within representational hierarchies that give maximum respect to images of sentience, Vermeer's deliberate flouting of this rule, whereby figure is inverted to a quasi-grammatical moment and a grammatical or largely syntactical element is given rhetorical purpose, upsets the logic of 'expression' and thus the logic of naturalism. In turn, finally, the disjunction undoes the unity of the 'world' created by the picture. Instead of one world, here we have four or five: a naturalistic space, itself made unmistakably theatrical, so that even this naturalism comes into doubt: within this space, the sense of a stage, of drama, of an acting out of a narrative – although the space is clearly not a stage in any literal sense. Then two other 'spaces' opening within the picture – that belonging to, or referred to, or opened by, the curtain, and that belonging to, or referred to, by the crucifixion. And together with all these, the world of the text: the one apparent fixed world in the picture, which, however, is of course not 'in the picture' at all. Nonetheless, as the only certain referent for the painting this instills its own anxiety. For, in saying that the referent is only this, we are very close to Nietzsche's world, where, as Deleuze puts it:

   . . . the world becomes fable, the world as such is only fable. A fable is something which is told, having no existence outside the tale. The world is something which is told, an event which is narrated. It is therefore an interpretation. Religion, art, science, history are so many diverse interpretations of the world. Or rather, so many variants of the fable.[19]

The fear of the fabularity of the world is intensified by the fact that Vermeer is now upturning his 'photographic' rendition of the world's materiality, and substituting for it the products of a subjective and configurative Vermeer, who is no longer depicting, but disconcertingly weaving, a world whose origin lies not in the real but in a text, a 'world' composed of chimerial images which resist any final attempt to force them to cohere into a unity, into something we can comfortably recognise. That 'unity', in any case refused, cannot even be reconstructed and is not, therefore, that of a natural, perceptually discovered and revealed world, the world disclosed to sight, but of one that is contrived, arbitrary and thereby denied. Yet it is a world, and as such, naturalistically rendered, it makes some claim to be a depiction of our world. In that sense it claims us.

This contrived world, and its claim on us, in turn points to a further problem: that of recognising the extent to which Vermeer's picture threatens to undo his own world, not only because of the allegorical limits of the meaning of the image, but precisely because the picture is essentially unstable and 'contradictory' at core. On the one hand it lacks all 'natural probability', its intention appears simple and the freedom granted the viewer for its interpretation very limited. But this conceptual fixedness, the determination of a truth of the known but hidden order revealed by the allegory, subverts the reliability of the representation of the visual experience. At the same time, however, the conscious stress on a skilful and carefully crafted illusion of life in the description of appearance in turn subverts the fixedness of the allegorical exegesis.

The problem is embodied in the figure of 'Faith'. Vermeer's pictures usually centre on a single figure, nearly always a woman. These women are painted such that one of their main traits is their pervading *sense* of being and presence. Yet in this picture, this 'realism' is almost violently shattered by the figure of 'Faith'. To the developed eye of the Vermeer spectator, she lacks all visual consistency and proportion, all sense of what Alpers calls, in describing Vermeer's *View of Delft*, 'just being there for the looking'.[20] Neither her body nor her stance are designed to bear witness to her presence in the world of crafted, visible objects. The artifice is so evident that it offends both on aesthetic and theological grounds. The transparency of faith seems rendered here on the edge of caricature. Yet, conversely, the figure is nothing but faith – a *figure* of faith, a construct, a device which, by the standards of Vermeer's earlier work, makes relatively little attempt to try to convince us of its quality as a human portrait.

As we have already noted, a reversal of norms is taking place in Vermeer's picture. The pictorial logic of naturalism is on two levels rendered as a figural conceit, embodied at once in Vermeer's bravura naturalistic painting – which here pushes towards the notion of a demonstration the very limits of whose success point to the artificiality of the exercise – and in the refusal of the illusion of 'portrait' to the figure of 'Faith'. But in fact this refusal of 'portraiture' goes even further. For, systematised, and placed in reference to other Vermeer paintings, the figural and the rhetorical now participate in a schematic logic that threatens to turn figure into syntactic moment. Already figure is made grammatical: its gestures replicate stock-in-trade gestures and pronouncements. The figure of 'Faith' here becomes a kind of parody of the injunction regarding the rendering of the human so as to appeal to human experience that Rousseau attacked. As Rousseau put it (with regard to the appeal that, via the concept of 'universal human experience', the figure makes its representation) provided that every human figure (in the tableau) possesses the 'common traits shared by all men', the fiction will be readable, the picture graspable and representation essentially unproblematic. In *Allegory of Faith* this principle is observed almost to the letter, but, in so rhetorical a manner that the existence of figure, as only figure, only motif, cannot be in doubt. But as only figure, the figure becomes merely a 'stock-in-trade', a rhetorical motif, but one that is now brought out and used grammatically as well as rhetorically.

The same thing occurs in reverse with the choice and rendering of the curtain. Here is a deliberate exaggeration and development of a motif, traceable of course by precedent to other uses of the same motif in the late paintings where it already seems to play a complex role (although the motif is nowhere as familiar in Vermeer's work as we tend to think; indeed in this form it belongs exclusively to the *Allegory of Painting* and two or three other late paintings). But in the *Allegory of Faith* the motif attains an unprecedented splendour. Perceptually it functions to engage the spectator and draw the beholder closer to the picture surface. In the two allegories, the close focus and luminosity of the curtains produces a psychological nearness that counters the 'distancing' tendencies of each picture. At the same time, in both of these pictures, and in *The Love Letter* and *Lady Sitting at the Virginals*, the curtain functions also to break the rigidity of the frame and to stand, as chairs so often do in early Vermeer, between beholder and scene, mediating the beholders' presence. But this motif has also figural purposes. A drawn curtain in this context intimates of disclosure. A *painted* drawn curtain suggests two things. First, reference to the act of disclosure and, hence, metaphorically, to the act of painting (which is why the curtain is so appropriate a motif in *Allegory of Painting*: 'I, the painter, draw back the veil so that you may see'). Second, both drawn curtain and its rendition suggest metaphors of the act of *looking*, particularly of looking on to and into the scene displayed, a scene that exists, this metaphor suggests, outside and in spite of our looking. At no point then does the curtain play only a plastic or scenographic role. But in the *Allegory of Faith* the sumptuousness of the curtain, its brilliance and luminosity, is enhanced by the curtain's carrying of a figural image. Depicted in a manner that leaves no doubt of intent, no possibility of Vermeer's 'accidental' or 'merely depictive' rendition of the curtain, the additional rhetorical-figural significance with which it is now endowed threatens to overwhelm the ostensible disclosative function (which is in any case reduced to only a nominal reference in the picture). In other words, despite the literalness of the rendering, literal is the least of what the curtain is. To put this another way, here is a literal image, of no ostensible meaning, and of no theoretical allegorical meaning, which must also be read as not-literal: not as curtain but as a semi-ironic comment on the gesture of disclosure. Once so granted, it is possible to see the curtain as deployed in this way in large part against the nominal allegory of the picture. Although we cannot go into this here the further development of this point would be that what in fact lies within the *Allegory of Faith* is a doubled allegory, a 'redemption' of the picture from its own ostensible theme and subject matter.

Two themes are being played out here. On the one hand, in a development that can easily be traced in the paintings of the late 1660s, is the giving of rhetorical force to the so-called incidental elements of the picture. In these earlier pictures those elements included tapestries, fabrics, the marbled sides of virginals, bands that run through hair: abstract formal elements that are crystalised into effective metaphoric signatures of Vermeer's presence. Endowed with rhetoricity through a mark, essentially the mark of being constituted in and as paint, they become the sign of presence and they register, not always ironically, the gap between the mark and the mechanisms of depiction.

On the other hand, the reverse of this is the grammaticisation of the figural moments and, hence, the reduction of figure and the figural, to precisely, figure. This latter theme undoes, directly, that which the former only indirectly puts in doubt. Both mark an insertion of Vermeer 'into' the picture, such that at the point at which, naturalistically, he appears to write himself out of the picture, he appears, as a doubled signature, a mark or trace of presence, of he who configured, continued, worked the picture. This doubled mark or trace suffices to establish the presence of the picture not only as presence as *picture* but also as *absence* as picture *of*.

The demonstration painting of this process is probably the Amsterdam *Love Letter* of c1670. In this picture, in comparison to the *Woman in Blue*, the disintegration of the painting as harmonic unity has developed almost to the point where the spatial logic of the picture begins to break down (despite the precise way that exactly this logic is registered and noted in the image). The very formality of the picture addresses and compels the beholder to become engaged not in the illusion created but in the creation or configuration of the illusion itself. Is there a reason for this development? Almost no-one has pushed presence and unity to the point which Vermeer achieves, as *illusion*, in *Woman in Blue*. The temptation is, as we have said, to read this pretension of totality back into the world (as a representation *of*), rather than to acknowledge the *Woman in Blue* as an extraordinary representation defined not by its symbolic unity with being but precisely by its difference: by its projection as a moment of desire; as a representation not of what is but of what, precisely, is not. But here representation reaches a kind of high-water mark. On the one hand, an achieved illusion of compelling force: on the other, only illusion, a 'figure' who can be reached only through other figures, who has no 'existence' outside a web of other figural images and relations of representation. From this moment on, a 'loss of faith' in the generative, pygmalion-like power of representation was almost bound to set in. It is worth recalling here that the unity that *Woman in Blue* seems to achieve is threefold – with a desired projection of being; with a model or illusion of presence; and, less acknowledged, but powerfully evident, an imaged embodiment of co-presencing between ourselves and our world – metonymically defined in Vermeer's painting in general by the intensity of the figural and representational interactions between figure and space and objects. These relations of reciprocity, of projection and response, of recognition and reflected sentience, are figured in the extraordinary tautness of relations between figure and objects. But once pushed to the point of *The Woman in Blue* these depicted relations of projection and response begin to break asunder, to dissolve from figural relations to grammatical relations, to move in other words, from the seduction of presence to the seduction of script: from subject-object relations to relations of representativity – of formal grammar formally acknowledged and displayed.

Yet the figure cannot easily be disturbed. In the late 1660s Vermeer came close to dissolving the formal grammar of his painting and, at the same time, he pushed towards – but not quite to – the point where a comparable dissolution of the figure as such falls into the simply and deliberately figural. What the *Allegory of Faith* exemplifies is this move. Vermeer may well have considered it necessary. We spoke earlier, in relation to *Woman in Blue*, of the thesis that the referent to which that painting can most easily, and is most usually attached, is that mode of referent that classically serves to reconcile fiction and truth in reading; that is, the notion of *'universal experience'* of *'man'* (or *'woman'*; with all the marked differences that this implies). The appeal to the concept, and through it to experience, resolves our worries about the determinacy and status of the referents and enable us, in Rousseau/De Man's sceptical words, to use the notion as a metaphor 'that confers the illusion of proper meaning'[21] on to the activities of the characters we read about.

Now, De Man/Rousseau are sceptical of this move on two levels. In the first place, conferring the illusion of (a) meaning on to what is actually a suspended, and therefore uncertain and *open*, text, allows the possibility of a premature closure of meaning (worse, one legitimated by appeal to 'commonsense' experience). Secondly, the move gives status to what is in any case a problematic concept. Rousseau is particularly sceptical of the weakness of this concept, for a concept implies a referent; a truth outside itself to which it points. But for Rousseau the concept 'man' is not a concept at all, rather it is metaphoric, and thus figural, and hence its referent is wholly problematic. For his, the figural 'man' is like the concept – actually figures of thought and feeling – of 'love' (or 'faith'). It is an illusion, a figural construct that *disfigures*. Once put into discourse, it fashions another (figural) world for itself, a world that communicates now not in concepts but in images and figures. But how then does one refer in language? How can language work (refer) in such circumstances? Reference itself, the path of making language 'mean', transparently, will not do. For even if the intention is critical, sceptical and deconstructive, the terms of the language will once again be taken up and read referentially – but that is to say figuratively. The only move Rousseau can make is to declare language figural and not representative, to deconstruct the concept of referential language, to prevent (false) meaning from coming into being as such. But now how we think of language itself shifts: as necessarily figural it must needs declare itself so, it cannot ride out in non-figural guise. But at the same time, figured, it must necessarily also turn its back on simple figuration, take its distance in language, acquire an ironic or doubled moment.

In this, a critical language is helped by two other possibilities that are now opened. On the one hand, in place of simply either reference or deconstruction we have a figuration of pathos: what replaces the loss of identity and reference is not just absence but the presence of desire, the pathos of unsatisfied yearnings for an impossible referentiality. (De Man adds in his commentary at this point that the more fictional the text becomes 'the more it becomes the representation of its pathos'.[22]) The figure now means by making it 'mean' the pathos of its own undoing. But at this point, the figure is no longer a figure but a substance. It has a referent, it is self-referential (it refers to this desire) without thereby appealing to an illusory figure 'outside' itself. On the contrary its referent is to its own history as a figure. Now as such, the text that describes it and figures it, need no longer be regarded as 'tableau', as fiction. The text, the image, can now be a 'portrait' of this substance, (in Rousseau's case, though it will do perfectly for Vermeer) 'of the deconstructive passions of a subject'.[23] We now have a new referential system based on the 'pathos of temporal predicament in which man's self-definition is forever deferred'.[24] On the other hand, as a figural world, the refusal of simple figuration necessitates a transformation of the figural process. The necessary relation now becomes one of reaching concepts through the figural. In Vermeer, this move, anticipated in the paintings of the 1660s occurs in the *Allegory of Faith*. The *Allegory of Faith*, read in this way, can be seen as a structural attempt to escape the impossibility of figural reference.

Structures, ideas, constellations

The discussion of Vermeer's *Allegory of Faith* was intended to further stress the necessity of considering allegory structurally. While Benjamin is often ascribed an obsession with the thematics of Baroque allegory, in fact, his major contribution to allegorical thinking is finally through the analysis he initiates of the structural, configurational and organisational character of allegory, and in the implicit and explicit thrusts that he gives to a linked cognitive and political-ethical reading of the allegorical. It is Benamin's theory of the allegorical that can allow us to make further sense of allegorical representation.

But to follow the theoretical road that his critique of Romanticism/symbolism implied, Benjamin needs to propose certain philosophical premises whose initial importance for allegory lies in the terms of his critique of the Romantic opposition between allegory as representation of concepts and symbolism as representation of ideas.[25] As opposed to the Romantic position, Benjamin's formulation involves a redefinition of concepts and ideas, and of the relationship between them. Far from conceiving them as two different processes of representation, he posits their inseparability and affirms the mediating role of concepts for an otherwise impossible representation of ideas. Ideas, according to this argument, 'are to objects as constellations are to stars'.[26] They can only be represented through empirical reality, but physical phenomena need to be redeemed from the actual crudeness of their empirical state, to arrive, unhampered by appearances, at their basic elements. 'They are divested of their false unity, so that thus

divided, they might partake of the genuine unity of truth.'[27] Concepts have in this context an organisational task, for it is by their means that the categorisation of the constituent elements of phenomena is effected. 'It is the function of concepts to group phenomena together',[28] whereas 'the idea, the objective interpretation of phenomena – or rather their elements – determines their relationship to each other.'[29] The role of concepts is, thus, to make phenomena fit for the representation of ideas, since the latter 'are not represented in themselves but solely and exclusively in an arrangement of concrete elements in the concept: as the configuration of these elements.'[30] As a result of this manner of conceiving the problem, what Benjamin calls 'the distinguishing power of the intellect' has two important and inseparable effects: 'the salvation of phenomena and the representation of ideas.'[31] This concept is linked to Benjamin's distinction between factual knowledge, *Erkenntnis*, and truth, *Warheit*. The aim of knowledge is possession , the possibility of acquiring and presenting its object. Truth, on the other hand, belongs to an entirely different realm. It can only be grasped through and in the process of immersion into the different levels of meaning which result from the examination of an object. It does not lie in an object but in an activity, in a process; it does not take a certain form, it *is* that form. Thus, rather than *presentation*, its mode, and its method is *representation*, outside or prior to which it lacks any existence. Hence, truth finds in representation both its dwelling place and the activity of its pursuit, and, for Benjamin, this representation, as we have seen above, is characterised by the manner in which it achieves and embodies, through the conceptual distinction of the basic elements of phenomena, 'the discontinuous structure of the world of ideas.'[32]

The terms of the Romantic opposition between allegory and symbol dissolve in this formulation, demanding and laying the ground for a reconsideration of the nature of allegory. As Bernard Cowan points out:

> The affirmation of the existence of truth, then, is the first precondition for allegory: the second is the recognition of its *absence*. Allegory could not exist if truth were accessible: as a mode of expression it arises in perpetual response to the human condition of being exiled from the truth that it would embrace.[33]

And it is precisely in the context of this search for a truth which can only be 'bodied forth in the dance of represented ideas'[34] that the nature of the distinction between the two modes can be redefined. The space of the symbol is that of the fallacy of the immediacy of the availability of truth, of the illusive faith in the possibility of unmediated representation of phenomena, in the truth value of their unity. Thus, the symbol arises from the intolerable awareness of, and the desire to bridge, the gap between ideas and phenomena. But this tension is, as Cowan points out, a characteristic of human life. The definition of the symbol is based, not on the experience and exemplification of the tension, but on the ever unfulfilled desire for the absent unity. In contrast, allegory results from the awareness of the gap between representation and phenomena, from the tortuous search for a truth embedded in the configuration of the basic elements of phenomena, as they have been divested of their 'false unity' by the concept. It is the formal representation of relationships and processes rather than of unicity and momentariness.

Transforming things into signs, says Cowan, 'is both what allegory does – its technique – and what it is about – its content.'[35] But, in fact, it is in the *organising principle* through which those signs are related among themselves that the essential signifying function of the mode is embedded. Allegory defines itself through structure. Its structure is its meaning. It is illuminating to consider in this respect that, far from being limited to the sphere of artistic representation, the allegorising impulse, both in its productive and its interpretative manifestations, is extremely widespread in everyday life: from proverbs and informal conversation, to advertising , education and political discourse. In all these instances, the allegorical mode is immediately and almost unconsciously acknowledged by all involved, as unfolding a cognitive process which enables both the understanding of the nature of the suggested connections and their extrapolation into a wider context. In other words it directs itself to an analogising drive functioning on the complex level of structural relations, rather than on the more immediate level of isolated or individual analogy. As such it constitutes itself into a manner of looking at the world, of seeking to disinter the layers of meaning which lay hidden beyond the level of immediate appearance. It becomes, even if problematically, both an epistemological instrument and a method of interpretation.

From the intuition of the essential transience of the world, 'from the apprehension of the world as no longer permanent,'[36] arises the allegorical willingness to destroy the appearance of reality in fragmentation. The 'false appearance of totality' is broken so that phenomena can be the object of intellectual selection, synthesis and reconfiguration. It is through this fragmentation, through this dispersal of the false unity of the world, which rejects certain aspects and chooses others for their reorganisation into a representational scheme, that the allegorical intention transforms things into a form of expression, into a mode of writing.

The isolation of the traditional allegorical emblem, or indeed, of any allegorical fragment, is an essential trait of the mode which, however, does not only manifest itself in spatial terms within the composition of the image. The visual clarity of the 'dry rebuses which remain'[38] is, as Fletcher has pointed out, like 'the hyperdefinite sight that a drug such as mescaline induces'.[39] It could be likened to the re-assembled fragmentations of Memphis furniture, whose description, given here in the instructional terminology of the museum catalogue, reads:

The objects are characterised by unexpected juxtapositions of materials, shapes, colours and a diversity of surface decoration. Industrial materials, such as plastic laminate and sheet metals are often mixed with traditional materials like marble and wood, poking fun at conventional taste and the hierarchies of Western society. The various elements that make up Memphis design are never subordinated to a whole but read as assemblages of parts, providing 'a milkshake of possibilities'. The forms are bizarre and quirky, frequently incorporating busy decorative patterns which reflect the hyperactivity of the modern electronic world.[40]

The manner in which this fragmentation is theorised by Ettore Sottsass at once sheds light on certain general traits of allegory and underscore some aspects of the characteristics of the Post-Modern 'allegorical impulse'. In Memphis, the fragmented, isolated element, the ornament, the *part*, is not conceived as alien to the basic structure of the design. In a similar fashion, surface is not opposed to structure, rather 'structure is decoration. Structure and decoration are one thing.'[41] What matters is not, therefore, that the fragment is so; as in the fragmented allegorical image, it is in the *manner* in which the fragments come together that both the work's organising principle, and that which exemplifies the objects' conceptual formulation, are embedded. The fact that, for Memphis, design is conceived as 'a series of accidents that come together by chance . . . a possible sum, not an inevitable story,'[42] should not be read as implying any kind of simple nihilism or a denial of design (though it may be a denial of Design). What is actually given here is more complex. On one level Memphis rework the notion of object – through playful rhetorisation and self-referencing of the *terms* and *structural grammar* of 'object', 'product' and 'sign'. In a parallel fashion, Memphis 'objects' are deconstructive of the assumed rhetorical and logical *relations* between objects (permanence), products (consumption and obsolescence), and sign (transience). In turn, these re-mapped relations form the thematic content of the allegories that Memphis construct. Thus the organising principle of the allegory itself lacks – and as in Sottsass' theories indeed happily refuses – any enduring essential quality. 'If a society plans obsolescence, the only possible enduring design is one that deals with that obsolescence . . .'[43] However, the opposition is not simply so. It is not obsolescence placed against permanence in some dialectical struggle. Rather, Memphis doubles itself by simultaneously finding

no difficulty in accommodating the desire both to dissolve and yet to make objects. In this it follows the traditional allegorical desire to grasp and in some manner – even while bearing witness to it – to halt transience. Benjamin's analogies of allegories as ruins are so familiar that the point scarcely needs reference, but it is perfectly logical to read Memphis objects in these terms, the more so that, ironically placed within the immediacy of consumer culture, Memphis objects are now increasingly shown in their rightful home – the Museum. And, if the very flippancy of the 'language' of Memphis embodies and exemplifies that absence and denial of the transcendental, this is, nevertheless, not far from Benajmin's formulation of the 'heart of the allegorical way of seeing':

Whereas in the symbol destruction is idealised and the transfigured face of nature is fleetingly revealed in the light of redemption, in allegory the observer is confronted with the *facies hippocratica* of history as a petrified, primordial landscape. Everything about history that, from the very beginning, has been untimely, sorrowful, unsuccessful, is expressed in a face – or rather in a death's head. And although such a thing lacks all 'symbolic' freedom of expression, all Classical proportion, all humanity – nevertheless, this is the form is which man's subjection to nature is most obvious and it significantly gives rise not to the enigmatic question of the nature of human existence as such, but also of the biographical historicity of the individual. This is the heart of the allegorical way of seeing.[44]

The Milanese *death's head* is the solitary commodity, spot-lit in the galleria, exercising, in pristine beauty, that peculiar quality that only commodities and angels know of – the refusal of the passing of time. So thought, Memphis is scarcely the trivialisation of the theocratic allegory one might have thought. What Memphis take their distance on and that on which they ironically comment, is the complex contemporary allegorisation of commodities, an allegorisation that is paired, inevitably, with the legitimising denial of its own condition.

Memphis construct an ironic mirror for the subjects of their commentary, and, thus, like all exemplifications of irony and allegory, at that moment condemn themselves either to a symbiotic existence with the subject of their critique, or lay themselves open to misunderstanding and misapprehension – for allegories and ironies are far less robust than is commonly imagined. But even so, it is worth considering how, as critical tool, the concept of allegory can lay bare certain aspects of those same moments of contemporary culture with which Memphis deals. Political allegory tells us that allegory can work both by subverting the versions of the past embedded in preserved traces and, by proposing alternative, hitherto silenced versions. This is the case with its use in feminist art and in much work of artists from historically oppressed cultures. In both cases the question of the construction of 'being' through representation comes to the forefront. The redefinition of the subject takes form in the subversion of the naturalised, legitimised, 'objective' Western versions of history and language, and in the dissolution of this monological voice into a complex, multi-levelled dialectic of voices of difference and otherness, a complex which allows other moments to be thought, other voices to be heard. By exposing the rhetorical quality which conceals itself beneath the constructed literality of practice, and by uncovering the allegorical quality of commodity culture, we deprive it of its claims to naturalness and immanence, and expose its historicity, its actuality as an ethical stance, its character as a rhetorical instrument proposing an interpretation of the world and forcing submission to it.

The commodity is of interest as an object of critical attention because of its capacity to refuse that attention from the usual means of criticism. This structural refusal to be enclosed and differentiated by thought might indicate a particularly efficacious cultural practice, in as much as its very role as that which operates underneath thought, guarantees, so to speak, the enormous breadth of its cultural work. The commodity is such a practice. All the more surprising in one sense since the commodity is, at the same time, a *rhetorical instrument proposing an interpretation of the world and forcing submission to it.* But the question is, how is it so? And how does it evade thought?

Consider, for instance, the form of the 1956 Necchi sewing machine. As a designed object it seeks to define itself visually as functional, as lacking appended elements which deviate from the requirements of the practical role it is intended to fulfil. It appears to deny that fragmentation which is inherent to allegory, and which the Memphis objects so explicitly stress; its smooth outlines, the simplicity of its form, the absence of decoration, all insist on its unity and harmony as object. It addresses nothing beyond itself; its form, we are made to feel, results intrinsically and unmediatedly from its essence as an object to be used. Considered visually it seems to exhibit – if such a thing can be said of a practical object – an almost Kantian disinterest in anything but itself and its function. To this extent, the design of the machine places itself before us as symbolic, as a formal construct embodying a set of qualities which bear a metonymic relationship to the machine itself.

This self-representation as a symbolic entity, which is a fundamental trait of Modernist design, is, of course, not adopted in isolation but in opposition to a previous mode, to the overt '*allegoricity*', the exemplified '*difference*', of the Victorian model. Far from a sense of coherence and harmony, the latter is marked by its multi-layered, fractured condition. The design of the machine displays itself as the explicitly and unresolvedly problematic layering of the aesthetic over the functional. With 'alien' ornaments superimposed on the machine itself, it mirrors, almost in caricature, the scheme of allegory as it has been traditionally understood. The fragmented, isolated, decorative elements seek to point away from, but paradoxically to underscore, the functionality of the machine. It is, in this sense, very close to the cosmic device of allegory. Fletcher quotes Lane Cooper on this subject: 'The very *kosmein* is explained as a process of likening the object you wish to praise (and have accepted) to a better object with a fine name'; and then adds: 'Notice that there is nothing neutral about the process: to adorn, in the rhetorical sense of *kosmein*, means to elevate a lower rank to a higher one'.[45]

By the very process of ornament, the design makes explicit acknowledgement of the divorce between the spheres of production and private life, underscoring the aesthetic inferiority in which the industrial object is placed, its purportedly natural exile from the world of beauty, and its necessary but still awkward incorporation into the domestic world. But in spite of its overlaid decoration, the visibility of its actual functional parts is not at all denied. Much of the machine is neither hidden nor decorated: through the visible structure it is still possible to discern direct correspondences between the notational elements of the machines and the function they are meant to fulfil within the complex structure of the mechanism.

In the same way that allegory was, as Benjamin points out, adapted by Romantic aesthetics to fit the symbol/allegory dichotomy 'so as to provide the dark background against which the world of the symbol might stand out',[46] the new design is defined in terms of difference from, and value above, the previous model, which becomes the 'dark background' against which the new model identifies itself. Thus the object presents itself not as two but as one, not as machine and aesthetic but as machine-aesthetic, not as functional and domestic but as industrially-functionally-domestically-desirable. But this very background is in fact the dark mirror in which we are allowed to glimpse the new design's hidden allegoricity, its nature as an arbitrary sign; for, in the case of the apparently literally and unmediatedly functional object that now lies in front of us, all visual trace of the elements on which that functionality actually rests have been erased and replaced by an emblem, a layer which, lacking itself almost any functional quality (save that of desire), nevertheless stands as a *sign of that functionality* which is emblematic, even exemplificational, in its visible *economy*. One might almost be encouraged to say that we have here a *pure form*. This form is allegedly not representational, it is exemplificational. But of what? Of the purity of the machine, of the

perfect balance of economy, effort and functionality that is embedded in the product. The form is desirable for itself, it is a form of desiring and desirable use-value. Aesthetics is here welded to the machine, the seamless unity of modern culture is evoked, and brought into the home. Modernity is announced as being in residence.

But here we are no longer exemplificational. Here, we are already making reference, evoking states of desire. Moving the object outwards into the world, where it becomes less an example, or a sample, and more an emblem: a *hieroglyph*. As such, it points, rather than specifically at something it is, at a wider conceptual formulation, at the Modernist ethics of history for example, and, above all, at its melancholic desire for a primeval formal-functional coherence (for the real and imagined coherence of the simple tool: symbol *par excellence*, as Heidegger shows, of the desire for a 'lost' way of working). As an emblem the form is, of course, abstractedly simple. But that simplicity is emblematically functional in a number of ways: not only does it reinforce the notion of 'unity' (for how can something this simple be not unified?), but this simplicity and abstraction refutes thought, it cannot be criticised, it cannot be 'opened' to challenge. The form refuses the intellection that might wonder about its existence. Of course that abstraction presents itself as marking precisely that which is not allegorical. The form refutes difference and hence refutes the allegorical. Only, of course, it does not. Not only is all form opened to difference, but the abstract, posited so often as the exemplification of the symbolic, can equally be read (must be read) as fundamentally allegorical. Read critically, we can say that abstraction reflects one of the conditions of the allegorical, for :

> . . . allegory is much more profoundly abstract than in the mere use of animated philosophic terms. It is abstract in Whitehead's sense, when he says that abstraction is 'the omission of part of the truth'. It is abstract in the sense of suppressing part of the conditions relevant to its subjects and objects.[47]

Here abstraction serves to practice an omission of difference: the Necchi sewing machine, transfigured as it is by its immaculate shroud into a transcendental object, represses its dark moment, its obligation to perform as a commodity. Through the unity of pleasure (form) and function (use) – a unity which is not a unity – and through the presence which is not a presence, the commodity is, in actuality, riven by difference, yet turns and presents a smooth and abstract face to its public.

Yet we know that the commodity is not a happy object. In this too it confers with the allegorical project. For the commodity is an allegory precisely to the extent that, just as, in Joel Fineman's words, 'the structurality of the text [of the allegory] holds out a promise of meaning that it will perpetually defer',[48] so too the commodity is precisely a sign of deferred happiness, but is of course by no means that which realises happiness. Its condition evokes the double condition of allegory, one that Fineman only partly understands by his notion of deferral. On the one hand, he is right when he says, extending the note above, that deferral is the:

> . . . formal destiny of every allegory in so far as allegory is definable as a continued metaphor. Distanced at the beginning from its source, allegory will set out on an increasingly futile search for a signifier with which to recuperate the fracture of and at its source, and with each successive signifier the fracture and the search begin again: a structure of continual yearning, the insatiable desire of the allegory.[49]

But is this the destiny of the *allegory*, that is, for instance, of Ripa's *Iconology*, or is it the destiny of the allegorical *representation* or *configuration*, of the *Allegory of Faith*? Fineman's point suggests, acutely, the limits, even the impossibility of the allegorical; it suggests that sense in which, just as at best the allegorical disperses the false unity of the world and chooses certain aspects and rejects others for their reorganisation into a representational scheme, so too it is confined to that scheme, in the end to naming. Naming is at once the most powerful and weakest of activities. Its power, if the act is granted, is not subjective (will) but intersubjective (collective force or consent). Recall the case of Borges' Fumes the Memorious, who:

> ... in 1886 invented ... an original system of numbering ... in place of seven thousand thirteen, he would say (for example) *Maximo Pérez*: in place of seven thousand fourteen, *The Railroad*; other numbers were *Luis Melián Lafinur, Olimar, sulphur, the reins, the whale, the gas, the cauldron* ... in place of five hundred he would say *nine*. Each word had a particular sign, a kind of mark; the last in the series were very complicated ... I tried to explain to him that this rhapsody of incoherent terms was precisely the opposite of a system of numbers ... Fumes did not understand me or refused to understand me.[50]

Recall too Benjamin's sense that the power of allegory, to convert objects into signs, was a double-edged sword, whose power was mediated by the 'sadness' that significance and naming bring into the world. The perpetual danger of allegory, Benjamin recognises, is that 'objects could not retain their own identity; they were in perpetual danger of being summoned to appear in allegorical reference to something else. And it was this disrespect for objects that caused grief.'[51] In other words, on two counts – that of the dissolution of the world of things, and that of the hyper-subjectivity of, and hence solipsistic quality of – the allegorical insight the allegorist may be convicted of playing an impossible, even reprehensible game. For the counter of an inescapable subjectivism (since in the modern world, no text can be thought of as the word of God: all texts are fallen in that sense) is that, in parallel, and *not* in this case in opposition to, the subjectivism of Romanticism, the allegorist, out of desire to convert the loneliness of subject insight into objective fact, falls towards an authoritarianism of meaning.

Now, if it is true that allegory is authoritarian, in as much as the allegorist proposes an interpretation of the world, and presents what he is positing as a truth about it; it is also true that allegory is explicit in its interpretational stance, does not lay claim to naturalness or objectivity, and defines itself as commentary. Here we begin to re-draw, yet again, that distinction between the allegory and its representation or its deployment in critique. The allegory is necessarily authoritarian: it proposes its truth, and that truth is not open to dispute. It is an instance of willed identity thinking which *forces* the relation between sign and meaning. Thus, even though the allegory contains non-identity, this can never be acknowledged or the allegory collapses. Yet, in critique, or in commentary, in representation and realisation, it can never *not* be instanced. There is, therefore, in allegory as representation or critique, implicitly acknowledged space for dissidence and difference. Allegory (a word whose Greek etymological origin, from *allos* and *agorevein*, can be directly translated as the 'discourse of the Other'), necessarily gives weight to alterity. The symbolic, by contrast, in declaring itself natural and immanent, in denying its own condition as interpretation, also negates the freedom it supposedly embodies. Anti-allegorical positions seek to free the image from the constraints of a defined, pre-established, imposed, and, hence, authoritarian meaning. However, the very denial of meaning which defines itself as unmediated and intrinsic – and therefore defines meaning as its 'other' – thereby naturalises its own equally authoritarian interpretative stance.

But however enlightening, liberating or repressive the versions of the world represented by allegorical means, they are not the dwelling-place of the fundamental redemptive force of allegory. Its power lies elsewhere. And in two places. First, in its capacity to remind us that the world is no longer (and thus never was, or never is) permanent; that the illusion of neutrality, of objectivity, of the *natural*, is but a fallacy; and that being in the world necessarily involves positioning ourselves within it. By its very nature as a mode of representation, allegory underscores the human capacity for, and indeed our embeddedness in, judgement. It reminds us that the 'false appearance of totality' is only that. Secondly, in so doing, it restores to us, even while it may try to stifle it, our consciousness of ourselves as potentially active beings. The allegorical willingness to destroy representation bodied forth as identity opens the world so that phenomena can be the object of conscious selection, synthesis and reconfiguration. This is the core of allegory's essential value as an ethical stance. Thus the allegorical, with its potential for alternative structures of organisation and interpretation of experience and with its intrinsic tension between isolation and aggregation, multiplicity and unity, randomness and meaning, is capable of representing, and also of exemplifying, within this layered configurational discourse, Benjamin's notion of 'truth bodied forth in the dance of represented ideas'.

Notes

1 Paul de Man, *Allegories of Reading*, Yale University Press, New Haven, 1979, p 197.
2 *ibid*, p 198.
3 *ibid*.
4 Quoted by Michael Sprinker, *Imaginary Relations*, Verso, London, 1987, p 25.
5 *ibid*.
6 The interest of the Post-Modern sensibility in allegory is articulated in a series of essays published in the early 1980s, largely in the journal *October*. Extensively reprinted, these now constitute the foundations for the structure of contemporary discourse on the allegorical, supported by the translation of Walter Benjamin's *Origin of German Tragic Drama* (and attendant scholarship) and De Man's provocative thinking on allegory in *Allegories of Reading*. The *October* essays are: Douglas Crimp, 'Pictures', no 8, Spring 1979, pp 75-88; and 'On the Museum's Ruins', no 13, Summer 1980, pp 41-57; Joel Fineman, 'The Structure of Allegorical Desire', no 12, Spring 1980, pp 47-66; Craig Owens, 'Towards a Theory of Postmodernism', no 12, Spring 1980, pp 67-86 and no 13, Summer 1980, pp 61-80; Stephen Melville, 'Notes on the Re-emergence of Allegory', no 19, Winter 1981.
7 The question of the relation of allegory to the issues that Derrida raises is potentially both a fascinating topic for comparative exegesis and probably the most useful way of opening Deconstruction to the visual. Notions of 'supplement', 'difference', and so on, appear so close to moments of the allegorical process, that comparative work should yield some important ways of thinking representation and configuration. The work of Raymond Gasche, *The Tain of the Mirror* Harvard University Press, Cambridge, Mass, indicates how this comparison might be grounded in a rigorous manner.
8 Friedrich Schiegel, Fragment 116 of 'Athenaeum' quoted by Charles Rosen and Henri Zerner in *Romanticism and Realism. The Mythology of 19th-Century Art*, Norton, New York and London, 1984, p 17.
9 Paul De Man, *Blindness and Insight*, University of Minnesota Press, Minneapolis, 1983, p 188.
10 S T Coleridge, *The Stateman's Manual, (Complete Works)*, ed by W G T Shedd, New York, 1875, pp 437-8. Quoted in Angus Fletcher, *Allegory. The Theory of a Symbolic Mode*, Cornell University Press, Ithaca, 1964, p 16 no 29.
11 S T Coleridge, *Essays and Lectures on Shakespeare and Some Other Old Poets and Dramatists*, London, 1907, p 46, quoted in Fletcher, *op cit*, p 15, no 28.
12 S T Coleridge, *Miscellaneous Criticism*, ed by T M Rayssor, London, 1936, p 29, quoted in Fletcher, *op cit*, p 17, no 30.
13 H G Gadamer, *Truth and Method*, Sheen and Ward, London, 1975.
14 *ibid*, pp 72-3.
15 Walter Benjamin, *The Origin of the German Tragic Drama*, trans from German by John Osborne, introduction by George Steiner, Verso, London, 1977, p 160.
16 *ibid*.
17 *ibid*.
18 *Allegory of Faith*, Metropolitan Museum, New York, the problems that the painting causes for Vermeer criticism, and the more general problem of the confusion between the allegory and allegorical representations, are illustrated even in the relatively innocuous entries for the painting in Vermeer catalogues. The entry reproduced below is typical of this criticism in respect of the confusion and the problems that result from a viewpoint trying to account for the painting in terms of a comparison to Ripa's *Iconology*. This in turn illustrates the acute problems that criticism has in reading allegorical pictures as pictures: the textual comparison on which criticism becomes hooked prevents their comprehension not as one thing but as two, or even three, things – an allegory and a picture; a narrative of signification and a doubled narrative of representation.
    A J Barnouw first recognised the literary source of the composition of this *Allegory of Faith*, which is found in C Ripa's *Iconology*, which first appeared in 1603 and which was translated into Dutch in 1644. The relevant passage reads: 'Faith is represented by a seated lady... with a chalice in her right hand, her left hand being posed on a book which rests on a firm cornerstone – that is, Christ – and her

feet resting on Earth. She is dressed in blue silk with a carmine overdress. Under the cornerstone lie a crushed serpent and Death with his arrows broken: nearby an apple represents Sin. Behind the woman, hanging on a nail is a crown of thorns which needs no explanation. In the background is a representation of Abraham on the point of sacrificing his son'. The painting does not carry out Ripa's text to the letter: the chalice and Bible together with a crucifix, are on the table not on a cornerstone, though this is the solid block that is crushing the serpent near the symbolic apple. Behind the figure is not a Sacrifice of Abraham but a Crucifixion next to a leather panel decorated with a gilded motif. There is also the curtain which is found as a motif in most of Vermeer's later works. . . and the empty chair, found in the works of his youth: the purpose of these features is plastic and scenographic rather than symbolic. Also missing from Ripa's description is the crystal sphere seen here suspended from the ceiling by a blue ribbon. E de Jongh has shown that for this feature and for the Crucifixion Vermeer was apparently inspired by the allegorical representation of Faith contained in *Emblemata Sacra de Fide, Spe Charitate*, (1636) by the Jesuit W Hesius, in which a crucifix and a sphere appear. The commentary accompanying this plate explains that man's idea of God is as limited as the reflection of the whole universe in a sphere. One should however recall Paul Claudel's interpretation of Vermeer's allegory: 'And as for the symbolism of the triple sphere, of that globe which the Church, seized by her high ideal, tramples under foot, of that culpable fruit, which she has rejected, scarcely tasted, and of that perfect And transparent truth which her desire contemplates – what could be simpler to interpret?' (*Introduction à la peinture Hollandaise*, RDP, 1935). . . Recent critics generally agree about its authenticity and hold almost unanimously adverse opinions about its quality; Only Paul Claudel thinks highly of the work. . . Veth found that the woman's expression was merely that of a 'tearful actress'. . . Goldschneider (finds) the model fat, the size of her hands and feet is large, her head looks like an easter egg: dressed for a party she is posing almost indecently (like a drunken woman by Jan Steen) and certainly uncomfortably (even if – as Goldschneider admits – her position is not very different from that of Bernini's *Truth* . . . De Vries sees a total lack of imagination in it; and Bloch more specifically states that this defect and the smoothness of the painting are not compensated for by the wonderful treatment of the curtain'. This description is slightly adapted and edited from that in *Vermeer*, introduction by John Jacob, Notes and Catalogue by Piero Bianconi, first published Rizzoli, 1967. English version, Penguin, Harmondsworth, 1987, p 97.

19 Quoted in Vincent Descombes, *Modern French Philosophy*, Cambridge University Press, Cambridge, 1980, p 184.
20 Svetlana Alpers, *The Art of Describing: Dutch Art in the 17th Century*, University of Chicago Press, Chicago, 1983, p 27.
21 De Man, *Allegories*, p 198.
22 *ibid*.
23 *ibid*.
24 *ibid*, p 199.
25 This opposition is stated most clearly by Coleridge in the following terms:

'Allegory changes a phenomenon into a concept, a concept into an image, but in such a way that the concept is still limited and completely kept and held in the image and expressed by it (whereas symbolism) changes the phenomenon into the idea, the idea into the Image, in such a way that the idea remains always infinitely active and unapproachable in the image, and will remain inexpressible even though expressed in all languages.' (Quoted by Fletcher, *op cit*, p 17, n 30.)
26 Walter Benjamin, *The Origin of the German Tragic Drama*, trans from German by John Osborne; introduction by George Steiner, Verso, New Left Books, London, 1977/1985, p 34.
27 *ibid*, p 33.
28 *ibid*, p 35.
29 *ibid*, p 34.
30 *ibid*.
31 *ibid*, p 35.
32 *ibid*, p 33.
33 Bernard Cowan, 'Walter Benjamin's Theory of Allegory', *New German Critique*, No 17, p 114.
34 Benjamin, *op cit*, pp 29-30.
35 Cowan, *op cit*, p 110.
36 *ibid*.
37 Benjamin, *op cit*, p 176.
38 *ibid*.
39 Fletcher, *op cit*, p 102.
40 *Memphis Design* exhibition, Boston Museum of Fine Arts, August-October, 1988.
41 Ettore Sottsass, *ibid*.
42 *ibid*.
43 *ibid*.
44 Benjamin, *op cit*, p 166.
45 Fletcher, *op cit*, p 118. Cooper's quote is from 'The Verbal Ornament' in *Aristotelian Papers*, Ithaca, 1939.
46 Benjamin, *op cit*, p 161.
47 Fletcher, *op cit*, p 29, no 8.
48 Joel Fineman, 'The Structure of Allegorical Desire' in Stephen Greenblatt (ed), *Allegory and Representation*, John Hopkins University Press, Baltimore, 1981, p 44.
49 *ibid*, pp 44-5.
50 J L Borges, 'Funes the Memorious', in *Labyrinths*, New Directions, New York, 1982, 1964-5. Borges is one of the great allegorists of the 20th century. The fact that he denies it is illuminated by a reference on p 27 of *Labyrinths* in the story of the 'Garden of the Forking Paths'. Borges, speaking now as the tragic assassin and spy Dr Yu Tsun recounts a conversation with the sinologist Dr Stephen Albert during which at one point Albert asks Tsun: '"in a riddle whose answer is chess, what is the only prohibited word?" I thought for a moment and replied, "The word *chess*"'
51 Julian Roberts, *Walter Benjamin*, Polity Press, Cambridge, pp 145-6.

JOHANNES VERMEER, *ALLEGORY OF FAITH*, c1670, DETAIL, OIL.

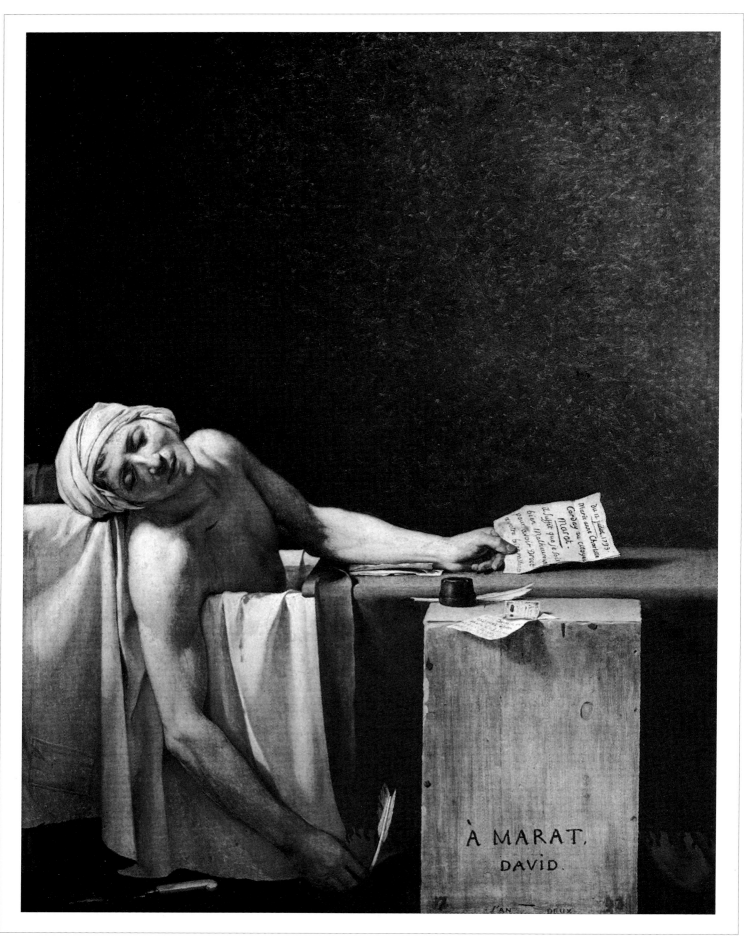

JACQUES LOUIS DAVID, *THE DEATH OF MARAT*, 1793, OIL

PAUL CROWTHER
Violence in Painting

That he with energy and art/Can picture evil and its sequel/Proves the beauty of his heart.
(Baudelaire on Daumier, *Fleurs du Mal* No LXI trans Alan Conder)

The representation of violence is a source of enduring pleasure and fascination in our culture. Why is this? A familiar answer is one which characterises the approach of many feminist art historians. This view seeks to link pleasurable responses to violence in painting to the way male sexuality is 'constructed' in a patriarchal society – the violent work is found pleasurable because it reflects, and thereby consolidates, male fantasies of virility, power and control. It feeds, in other words, upon socially negative attitudes, especially towards women, which are deeply embedded in patriarchal ideology. Unfortunately the current debate about violence in painting seems to be conducted *entirely* in terms of this sexocentric approach. This places the female viewer in an impossible position. For if she should respond positively to a violent image, then, from the sexocentric viewpoint, she is implicitly identifying with the conditions of her gender's oppression. The sexocentric approach is, however, radically incomplete, in so far as it takes no account of the way in which responses to violence in painting can be restructured and redirected by properties and effects arising from both the medium itself and the semantic conventions in terms of which it is read. The sexocentric view, in other words, fails to engage with the ontological and semantic specificity of the medium itself. If, however, full due is given to this specificity, the question of our response to violence in painting becomes, accordingly, much more complex. In this paper, therefore, I shall, in part I, outline the three major categories of violent painting and, in turn, elaborate three factors which can mediate our reading of violence in such works. In part II, I will then consider the question of what cognitive competences are logically presupposed in order for such categories and mediating factors to be brought into play. With these considerations in mind I will, in part III, finally be able to offer a detailed explanation of some of the different kinds of positive response which we enjoy in relation to violent painting and the relation of these to aesthetic experience.

I

Let me first briefly outline the three major categories of painting which might be described as violent. The most obvious kind are those figurative works, such as Artemisia Gentileschi's *Judith and Holofernes* (Capodimonte, Naples); which depict violent events, or the immediate aftermath of such events. The second category consists in those figurative or semi-figurative works, such as Jackson Pollock's *Man With a Dagger* (Tate Gallery), which distort or disfigure some recognisable subject-matter to a wildly exaggerated degree. The final category can apply to either figurative or wholly abstract works. It consists of those cases, for example, Jackson Pollock's *Number 3: Tiger* (Hirschhorn Museum, Washington), which embody and manifest violent painterly means – such as hyper-vivid colouring, nervous and agitated handling, broken brushstrokes and heavy impasto. It is

of course possible for some works to involve several or even all three categories (Pollock's *Man With a Dagger*, for example, might be seen in this light), but even if a work falls under only one of the categories, there is at least a *prima facie* case for describing it as violent. However, our willingness to describe a work in these terms must also take account of the fact that our reading of violence in painting is often mediated by three crucial factors. I shall now outline these in some detail.

The first factor to be considered is that of *narrative-function* (using this term in a very broad sense). In Pollaiuolo's *Martyrdom of St Sebastian* (National Gallery, London), for example, we do not simply find an act of violence depicted. Rather this particular act embodies a recurrent and recognisable signifying motif. It nominally suggests that the Christian believer can transcend his or her finitude by accepting all earthly suffering – even unto death – in the expectation of ultimate redemption. The act of violence, in other words, signifies an imperative. It is to be recognised not in its own right – as a murder, but as a vehicle for some theological-moral message. Consider also, Emile Nolde's 'Head' (National Gallery of Modern Art, Edinburgh). Here the exaggerated distortion of the central motif and the reduction to basic shape and colour serves a narrative function beyond the demands of mere formal unity. It takes up an insistent stand against the traditions and values of Eurocentric academic art by seeking a more 'primitive' and thence more direct communication between artist and viewer. In other words, the putative violence of the technical and formal means should not be seen just in those terms – as an act of pure aggression – it signifies, rather, a particularly insistent rejection and reformulation of the rigidified relation between painter and viewer. I am arguing, then, that a dimension of violence in terms of the subject-matter or medium of painting often serves a broader narrative function bound up with the affirmation of prevailing sets of moral or cultural values, or with the rejection of such values.

Let me now consider a second way in which violence in painting might be modified. This is bound up with its *expressive function*. Consider, for example, Goya's *The Executions of the Third of May* (Prado, Madrid). In a work such as this, the artist is not presenting violence as an object of enjoyment in its own right, nor is he making it the vehicle of a partisan narrative about the rights and wrongs of the Peninsular War. Goya presents us, rather, with a vision of the sheer callousness and barbarity of the execution. The image is manifestly addressed to our tragic sense of life, to feelings of pity for the victims, and to our outrage at the continuing barbarity of the human species. We might also consider here, David's *Death of Marat* (Royal Museum, Brussels). At one level this is clearly a monumentalisation and celebration of French revolutionary idealism. At the same time, however, the work solicits our awareness at a more universal level of feeling. The ultimate isolation and inescapable destiny of the finite embodied being are both set forth in the starkest and most uncompromising terms. I would suggest, then, that in some works the violent dimension is articulated not for its own sake, but in a way that invites a specific range of affective responses from the viewer.

The final modifying feature which I shall consider is *aesthetic function*. Pollaiuolo's *Martyrdom of St Sebastian* interprets the violent event as much in terms of its utility as a compositional device, as it does in terms of its religious narrative function. This means that the violence is wholly subsumed within the demands of formal pictorial unity. We may even feel that the St Sebastian motif is simply an excuse for Pollaiuolo to produce a visually interesting composition. A rather more complex and profound work in this broad category is Delacroix's *Death of Sardanapolus* (Louvre, Paris). Here the violent subject-matter and its episodic distributions provide material which could easily disrupt the formal unity of the work. However, Delacroix integrates this material within a sophisticated composition, wherein the episodic violence is organised in relation to firm diagonals and finds a psychological point of convergence in Sardanapolus' gaze. I would suggest, then, that in some works our reading of violence is orientated towards its formal and aesthetic function. (This aesthetic level of significance can, indeed, reach beyond issues of formal unity alone – as I shall argue in part III of this paper.)

Now it should be clear that the three factors which I have here described as modifying our reading of violence are not mutually exclusive. They can coexist in the same work and, indeed, it will sometimes be very difficult to separate them. The works by Goya and David, for example, might be characterised as complex expressions of moral indignation, ie as involving both normative *and* affective responses in an inseparable combination. This actually shows the complexity of the whole relation between violence and painting. Sometimes we will feel that a work quite clearly satisfies one or more of the three criteria by which it might be described as violent, other works however might seem more ambiguous. Likewise, we might feel that in some paintings (such as Pollaiuolo's *Martyrdom of St Sebastian*) the violence is so modified by other functions that it would be misleading to describe it as violent at all. But again, in other works the role of the mediating functions might seem highly ambiguous, or even completely overridden by the violent aspects. To determine, therefore, whether a painting can be described as violent, and whether (or to what degree) it is modified by other functions, involves some complex cognitive discriminations on the viewer's part. I turn now to the question of what competences are logically presupposed in order to make such discriminations.

II

If we are to recognise that painting *x* is a depiction of some violent act, this logically presupposes only that we have learned the basic code of pictorial representation itself, ie that we can recognise what *kind* of thing the picture is 'of'. However, to call a painting violent on the basis of its disfiguration of form or its roughness of handling, or indeed to see it in terms of mediated violence, presupposes another competence besides. For in order to recognise these aspects, we must not only have assimilated different ways in which the resemblance between paintings and violent acts can be instantiated. Let me illustrate this. Suppose that by some fluke, there is a culture wherein all painters represent in exactly the same style, ie they depict what can be recognised as different kinds of subject-matter, but the *way* in which they depict is entirely uniform. In such a culture there could indeed be depiction of violent scenes, but there could not be 'violent' disfigurations of form or handling, or the narrative, expressive and aesthetic mediation of violence, because we can only describe words in terms such as these when there is a

discrepancy between different individual styles of *manipulating* paint. We characterise a work as violently handled, for example, because it differs and contrasts with the handling we find in other works. We say that this act of violence is mediated by its narrative function because it is clear that (on the basis of a contrast with other works) the violence is being manipulated in the direction of a message rather than skimpily presented in its own right. On these terms, to recognise a painting as violent or to recognise the way in which the violence is modified, logically presupposes both a basic literacy in the code of pictorial representation as such *and* the capacity to recognise different styles and conventions in terms of which this code can be articulated. In practice, this latter condition means that we must have a comparative knowledge of painting, ie a familiarity with many different instances of the medium.

It is, however, important to note that 'comparative knowledge' is not here synonymous with highly specialised iconographical art-historical knowledge. It should be construed rather as a much more basic competence. In *childhood*, for example, we learn to read pictures as being 'of' things. Indeed, through our broader immersion in cultural life we acquire the ability to read pictures as narrative – especially, of course, in terms of familiar moral and religious messages. Likewise, we learn to associate cheering shapes, colours and qualities of paint with certain kinds of emotion. On these terms, then, we acquire what might be called *proto*-iconographic literacy in relation to painting, on the basis of a familiarity with both the code of pictorial representation as such, and with the broad cultural conversions which surround it. It is, I would suggest, at this level of the proto-iconographic – ie at the level of *immediate* legibility – that painting finds its major audience and takes on its general cultural significance. Art historians, of course, may be able to read the work in terms of much more complex and less immediately apparent levels of signification, but this level of literacy does not determine the conditions of painting's general cultural reception. (Art, in other words, is not created *for* the purposes of art history.)

The full importance of the proto-iconographic level of literacy only becomes clear if we now consider some features which are not logically presupposed in order to recognise violence or the mediation of violence in painting. These features consist in a physical acquaintance with the arts, knowledge of the context in which a work was produced, and knowledge of biographical details of his or her life. (By biographical details here I mean both events in the artist's life, *and* those elusive impulses which are sometimes called the 'artist's intentions'.) The reason why these features are only contingently involved in our readings of violence and its various mediations is because when a painting is finished, it becomes physically independent of its creator and, indeed, of the immediate causal context of production. This destiny, of course, is known by the artist at the very outset. If he or she is to find an audience for a work, then it must also use generally familiar formal, narrative and expressive *conventions* which enable it to be read in a more closely focused way. Now of course from the viewpoint of art history as a discipline we are not only concerned with comparing and contradicting paintings, we want also to be able to explain the causal origins of the picture, ie why the artist produced it, what sort of audience he or she intended it for and how it discloses the artist's broader relation to prevailing ideologies and societal conditions. In terms of art historical understanding, in other words, a knowledge of the artist's biography and the work's context of production is indispensable. However from the viewpoint of the painting's general cultural reception, ie its life as a proto-iconographic mode of distinctively *visual* communication, such details are *of necessity* irrelevant. Suppose, for example, that an artist paints a work in the knowledge that it contains a reference which will only be recognised if the viewer has access to biographical data. This means that the work is now directly tied to the physical existence of its creator or, at least, to the traces of the creator's existence beyond the painting itself. What makes this so self-defeating is not only the fact that it is at odds with pictorial representation's status as an immediately 'legible' proto-iconographic mode of visual communication, but also the fact that such private meaning will tend to be overlooked by the viewer. The audience will orientate itself instead towards these levels of signification which do not require distracting re-searches into the artist's life or historical circumstances in order to become intelligible. That there are such levels is shown by the very fact that in creating a painting, an artist – whether he or she intends it or not – is taking up a position in relation to the tradition and history of the medium. The artist will employ technical, formal and narrative motifs, which have general historical and cultural connotations and which a viewer will read on the basis of his or her own knowledge of the medium and cultural experience. In other words, even if the intended private reference remains unrecognised, the work's contract with and similarity to other works will enable it to be read aesthetically or expressively or even, perhaps, in terms of alternative narratives dependent on the culture which artist and viewer share, rather than upon what the artist consciously intends.

I have argued, then, that we describe a painting as violent, or as involving the mediation of violence, on the basis of a knowledge of pictorial representation as a code and by compari-son and contrast with other paintings. We do *not* require any biographical details of the artist's life or the work's context of production. The reason why I have given these latter points such emphasis is because they are crucial to the understanding of a number of our responses to violence in painting – and most especially to the aesthetic ones. It is to the question of viewer-responses that I now turn.

III

I want to begin with those cases where a violent picture is experienced fundamentally in terms of its violence as such. That it is experienced in these terms may hinge upon three facts: a) the absence or minimalisation of mediating factors in the work itself; b) an inability on the viewer's part to recognise the presence of mediating factors; c) a sheer indifference to mediat-ing factors (ie the viewer is interested *only* in the violence). Let us suppose, that for one of these three reasons a viewer is able to respond directly to the violence of the painting. How do we explain the fact that his or her response can be pleasurable? One way of accounting for it would be to take the approach noted at the beginning of the paper – namely that the violence reflects and consolidates male fantasies of power and control. Now in relation to many male (and some female) viewers this will constitute an adequate basis for explaining the pleasurable response. It is, however, by no means exhaustive, for the fact that the viewer is here engaging with a violent *painting*, rather than a *real* scene of violence, can restructure the response in a signifi-cant way.

Consider, for example, the following situation. We witness an act of violence from a position in which we ourselves are not in any danger. Now although the event may be fascinating, and although we may be powerless to intervene, most people will feel that they ought to take some action – even if only that of expressing disapproval. To simply contemplate real violence normally leads to bouts of conscience and guilt at our inability to intervene. To contemplate violence in painting, however, brings no such psychological pressure. For the distance between what is real and what is here known to be imaginary, serves to (at least partially) eliminate the moral constraints which conscience

places upon our response to violence. There is, indeed, another dimension of elimination to be considered. Again let us suppose that we witness some actual event of violence. Here the build up to the event, its development and outcome, and its aftermath, are all entirely independent of us. We are unable to intervene. If, in contrast, we contemplate violence in a painting we are dealing with one single moment from an imaginary event. Indeed, even if the work depicts some event which actually took place, or is a work which is violent in terms of disfiguring its content or in terms of handling, then because the painting is physically discontinuous from the depicted event (in the former case) and from the state of mind of the creator (in both cases), we can in such examples respond imaginatively to the painting without being constrained by reality. We can construct the build up, development and aftermath to the depicted violence or the violence of the painting itself *at will* – using the work only as a vehicle or focus for our own fantasies of control and power.

Whereas the contemplation of violence in real life is inhibited by a sense of conscience and a sense of the independent reality of the events taking place, in painting these constraints are re-moved. The viewer can achieve a complete appropriation of the violence in terms of his or her personal fantasies and interests. Now this structuring of the response again *may* simply embody patriarchal attitudes to sexuality. But it need not be analysable solely in these terms. Many individual men and women crave power and control over others in contexts and for reasons other than sexual ones. Indeed, it does not take a repressed or incipient megalomaniac to fantasise about what it would be like to exercise power and control freed from moral, institutional and physical constraints. The desire to transgress such limits at will is, I would suggest, one of the major sources which our positive response to violence in painting draws upon. Now against this, the sexocentric might reply that whilst such fantasies as these may not involve an overtly sexual dimension the fact that they exist at all is ultimately a reflection of patriarchal ideology. However, in retort to this one might say, that even if – in a matriarchal society – the violent aspects of male sexuality were eliminated, what would not be eliminated is the *finitude* of the individual embodied being and of the species itself. Indeed, if our world-view is materialist, a sense of finitude – with all its anxieties, challenges and desperation – must be paramount. It is here, I would suggest, that we must look for the *ultimate* origin of that desire for violent transgression which painting sometimes draws upon.

Let me now consider our response to violence when it is mediated by narrative, expressive or aesthetic functions. To read violence in terms of the first two functions can involve intellec-tual or affective responses which are, logically speaking, of the same sort we experience in the continuum of everyday life. We recognise, for example, the moral message of the work, and respond to it – either negatively or positively in much the same way as we would respond to an ordinary moral statement, situation or argument. Or again, we may find ourselves moved by the plight of the victim of violence in the picture, in much the same way as we might be moved by an encounter with such suffering in real life. In these cases, in other words, we read the violence fundamentally in terms of its relevance to, or contact with, the interests and values of everyday life. In the case of violence's aesthetic function in painting, however, matters are rather different. Here the violence and any of its narrative and expressive meanings are judged fundamentally in terms of their contribution to the painting's formal unity. It is in this sense that our appreciation of the violence and its significance is *disinterested*. There is, indeed, a further possible level of aesthetic significance here. If, for example, a work is highly original, we may find that its formal organisation of the violence and its narrative and expressive functions serve to delineate a highly individual yet shareable vision of the world. This, I would suggest, is one of the profoundest – perhaps the most profound – and valuable experiences that we can enjoy in relation to art.

To illustrate this in more detail, I shall consider Delacroix's *Death of Sardanapolus*. Now if, as art historians, we are familiar with the play by Byron which furnished the idea for the painting, we may read the work in terms of Sardanapolus' melancholia – on his death, the despot (willing or not) is required by custom to put his slaves to death. This specialist knowledge, however, will not characterise the more general cultural reception of the work. For what the painting invokes at the proto-iconographic level of immediate appearance is a vision of barbarity and tragedy. The relations of brute force and cruelty on which despotic power (however noble the despot) is ultimately founded, are laid bare in the most uncompromising terms. Now to aesthetically empathise or identify with an artistic vision is not simply to *agree* in some sense with the narrative presented by the particular painting under consideration. It is also to delight in the visual means whereby the narrative has been realised. Delacroix's painting is colouristic, opulent and formally sophisticated, and thence runs the risk of *merely* presenting violence as a glamorous spectacle. But it can be argued that the work does not fall into this trap. The artist wins his narrative even though his visual means are so risky in relation to it. Indeed it is precisely this dimension of risk which gives the *Sardanapolus* its verve, panache and existential depth. Delacroix is not simply making a statement about despotic barbarity, he is setting this notion forth in an original sensuous configuration. We find a distinctive and complementary balancing of rational understanding with sensuous embodiment – the two features which are fundamental to the human condition itself. The viewer may, therefore, feel able to identify with this risky and stylish way of articulating despotic power. Now those who prefer their moral truths *uncluttered,* of course will not be able to identify with the work at all. But it is this very dimension of ambiguity in the *Sardanapulos* which gives a further reason for empathising with its style of articulating violence. For since the viewer is here invited to wrestle with the issue of whether the work celebrates violence or should be seen rather as a tragic revelation of it, this means that his or her own interpretative autonomy is respected. The viewer is engaged, in other words, at the level of exercising free, active choice, as opposed to merely passive receptivity.

I am arguing, then, that if the narrative, expressive and formal aspects of a 'work' cohere in a strikingly original way, the work can present a style of engaging with the visual world that leads us to identify and empathise with it. The question now arises as to why this mode of empathy should be regarded as *aesthetic*. Do we not, for example, empathise with people in everyday life, ie identify with their opinions and values, their way of holding these, the total image they project to the world, all in all their sheer style of being? It is, of course, true that we empathise in this way; however, there is a crucial logical difference between this and the aesthetic empathy we enjoy in relation to art. For to empathise with a person's style in the ordinary course of things presupposes that we are directly acquainted with that person or have at least fairly detailed biographical knowledge about them. We have, in other words, an *interest* in the real existence of that person. To empathise with the personal style of engaging with the world which is embodied in an artwork, however, is *disinterested* in the sense that it does *not* presuppose any acquaintance with the artist or any knowledge of biographical details concerning his or her life. As I showed earlier, to read the narrative, expressive and aesthetic functions of a painting, and to recognise its originality, presupposes only comparative knowledge. This comparative knowledge in conjunction with our basic fluency in the code of pictorial representation enables us both to read the painting in terms of its various signifying functions *and* to discriminate unusual and striking articulations of the code, ie those paintings which in comparison with the other works present a distinctive style of engaging with the world. On these terms to empathise with an artwork is not to seek any mystical communion with the artist's life, or soul, or intentions; it is rather to identify with the painting's own special way of *deviating* from established norms and clichés of narrative, expressive and formal signification.

This interpretation of aesthetic empathy raises several questions. First, even if such empathy does not logically presuppose any knowledge of or interest in the real existence of the artist, it is nevertheless true that we often *do* have such knowledge. How, then, does this affect our response? In this respect it should be noted that secondary details about the artist's source material can often enhance our empathy with a work. If, for example, we know that the Byron text which is the source for Delacroix's *Sardanapolus* does not contain any description of the massacre, but that the artist has, rather, harmoniously supplemented the ideas provided by the source text with scenes of carnage derived from engravings of Etruscan reliefs, then this can make us enjoy the originality of *Sardanapolus* the *painting* all the more. But equally, such knowledge might take us in the opposite direction. We might become preoccupied with iconographical analyses and, in consequence, treat the painting as an object of historical discourse alone. I am arguing, then, that biographical or genealogical details can enhance our aesthetic empathy, but that equally they can distract from it. Logically speaking biographical issues are entirely contingent in relation to aesthetic empathy.

There is, however, another rather more serious question. It is simply this. Even if we admit that everyday empathy presupposes acquaintance or detailed knowledge of the person with whom we are identifying, but that to empathise with paintings we need know nothing about the person who created the work; what really hangs on this difference? I would suggest that, in fact, quite a lot hangs on it. When we empathise with a person in ordinary life our empathy is generally *tied* to the actual existence of that person. We may like their style – the way they look or speak; the views they hold, the way they express them; the totality of values which seem to inform their outlook on the world. But, of course, all might not be what it seems to be. On the basis of deeper acquaintance or acquired knowledge, we may decide that the person in question is *just* projecting an image. We may decide that at heart they are insincere; or that they hold views of which we had not previously been aware, and which (in their unacceptability) outweigh all the features we can identify with.

Indeed, we must also remember that the other person's individual style of being is *ultimately* theirs. If we are neither acquainted with them nor know a great deal of information about them, the sheer presence or force of their personality may lead us away from empathy. Instead of a felt identity with and sharing of their style, we may be pushed in the direction of blind admiration and ultimately mere hero or heroine worship, or we may find that their style becomes so intimate and dear to us, that our identifying with them is not sharing, but rather a total absorption in the other's style of being. In the case of empathy experienced in relation to other persons *as such*, in other words, our sharing of their style is subject to various psychological pressures which may tend to inhibit or modify the experience. One might contrast this with our empathy with style in painting. In the case of Delacroix's *Sardanapolus*, for example, the artist has not just provided us with a report of his own private interests and attitudes in relation to violence. Rather he has worked these out in accordance with the formal, expressive and narrative demands of a medium informed by a tradition, and aimed at a much broader audience than that of other artists or (indeed) art historians. The artist's own intentions, feelings and attitudes are not merely translated into paint.

The 'message' does not lie transparently or opaquely somewhere behind the medium; rather it is embodied within that semantically and syntactically charged, and (in the best art) *deviant* surface which we call this particular painting, *and* in its relation to other paintings. By inscribing his or her feelings and attitudes within a publicly legible medium, those private feelings, etc, are transformed. The artist, as it were, meets him or herself *and* the viewer, halfway. He or she offers *a possibility of viewing the world. Delacroix the person* may have been reactionary, elitist, a dreamer, even a vicarious sado-masochist of sorts; but because in *Sardanapolus* – the painting – his private sense of violence is inscribed in, and modified by the publicly accessible medium, the image is thereby detached from the matrix of personal obsessions in which it finds its causal origins. The style of engaging with and understanding the world which the painting offers is an individual one, but because our reading of it is not constrained by necessary reference to the actual presence of the artist himself, we are able to identify with it without the psychological pressures I have described.

Now it might be wondered why, in an essay on violence and painting, I have addressed so much attention to the question of aesthetic empathy. It is, after all, only one of a variety of responses. In this respect, it should first be noted that there is certainly no *intrinsic* connection between violence in art and the experience of aesthetic empathy. Whether we empathise with a violent work or not will be a function of the relation between the originality of its style and our own individual set of values. Indeed, many – perhaps most – of the works we identify with will have no dimension of violence at all. However, this being said, it is clear that violence does have an important contingent role in relation to aesthetic empathy. For the paintings which stake most claim to such a response are surely those in which problems and crises fundamental to our status as rational but sensuous and finite beings are wrestled with and clarified. The nature and function of violence in human life is, of course, one of the most fundamental of such problems.

The second reason why I have devoted so much attention to aesthetic empathy is to balance out the sexocentric approach. Sexocentrism tends to reduce the problem of violence in painting to the crudest moral simplicities – if the work is violent (and especially if it involves violence towards women) then to enjoy the work, is to enjoy it on the oppressive basis of sexuality in a patriarchal society. To suppose that this is a sufficient explanation of the enjoyment of violent painting is, however, not only an insult to the intelligence of many male and female viewers, *it is to degrade painting* itself. For it is only the *mediocre* work which orientates itself exclusively to the setting forth of violence. In the best creations, violence is re-presented; that is to say we do not enjoy the violence as such, but rather the way an individual fellow-being has here coped with it and shown it for what it is. To empathise with such a vision is, in effect, to acknowledge that we need not be passive in the face of violence. Indeed, it is to *know* that some other human being has shown how a stand might be taken, and that we can stand with them.

I shall conclude this study with an explanation of two omissions. First, in emphasising aesthetic empathy as a response to violence, I have concentrated on what I take to be the most important variety of distinctively aesthetic responses. My discussion, therefore, does not pretend to be exhaustive. In particular, I have not addressed the question of the sublime. The reason for this is that sublimity's special province of application is in relation to our aesthetic appreciation of great magnitudes of vastness or power, or the evocation of them through art.[1] The sublime, in other words, is applicable for the most part only to a very few violent paintings – namely those dealing with catastrophe and its aftermath. I shall address this question at length elsewhere.

The second and more important omission is that which is implied by my concentrating on the relation between violence and painting alone, rather than on the relation between violence and other modes of visual representation such as photography and film. The reason for this omission is that these latter modes of representation will require a substantially different analysis from the one appropriate to painting. This is because painting and photography (and the arts derived from the latter) have a fundamentally different ontological structure, which will, in consequence, tend to produce different cognitive readings and psychological effects. In the case of painting, for example, it is rare that we respond to it just in terms of its violence of content or treatment. We know that paintings are not simply mechanical reproductions of reality. They are images which interpret the world. Hence we are predisposed to regard them as complexes of narrative, expressive and aesthetic signification, which set forth a particular style of viewing the world. The photographic arts are, in contrast, fundamentally mechanical reproductions of various aspects of visual reality. In recent years, of course, a great deal of work has been done to show that the camera is not an innocent eye. Its images can be staged, manipulated and even, to some degree, fabricated. But the fact that so much theoretical work has been required in order to clarify this fact is itself of great significance. It show that we are strongly re-inclined to read photographs at the level of their basic code alone, ie as mechanical copies of the visual. This in turn means that we tend not to look for any broader and more complex levels of signification. Hence, if we encounter a photograph of some violent scene, we will tend to respond to the violence as such. This at least is the present state of our culture's literacy in relation to the reading of photographs. But, of course, this may change . . .

Notes

1 See, for example, chapters 6 and 7 of my *The Kantian Sublime – From   Morality to Art*, Oxford University Press, Oxford, 1989.

J P COCKBURN, *VIEW TAKEN IN THE VALLEY OF THE GRANDE CHARTREUSE*, FROM *VIEWS TO ILLUSTRATE THE ROUTE OF MONT CENIS*, 1822

CHLÖE CHARD
Rising and Sinking on the Alps And Mount Etna
The Topography of the Sublime in Eighteenth-Century England

Sublimity and the foreign: pleasure and guilt

The moments of reflection ... on the uneasy hours of this beloved parent, were the only moments that passed without pleasure, amounting sometimes to rapture, when, as they approached the Alps, the most sublime and magnificent views of nature were opened to her astonished view.

Accustomed of late to the flat, monotonous, and uninteresting views round London, she had frequently sighed for the more animating landscapes of her native country, and had no ideas of beauty superior to that which is formed by those green and undulating hills, in some places fringed half-way up by beech woods, in others rearing their tufty mounds, covered with sheep on one side above the once impenetrable forests of the weald, on the other gradually declining towards the apparently boundless ocean that forms the English channel.

But when she saw the rich and luxurious country, which nature, 'with all her great works about her,' spreads before the astonished traveller, between Lyons and Civita Vechia, the port from whence Montalbert determined to embark for Sicily, in order to avoid both Rome and Naples, her mind was exalted by scenes so much superior to any she had ever formed an idea of either from the efforts of the pen or the pencil, she seemed transported to a world of higher rank in the universe than that she had inhabited while she was in England; and she was of an age and disposition to forget, or at least be indifferent to those circumstances which can hardly fail to remind English travellers, that, though other countries may have more bold and attractive scenery, their own is that where life is enjoyed with the greatest comfort.[1]

Nature never designed Man to be a grov'ling and ungenerous animal, but brought him into Life, and placed him in the World, as in a crouded Theatre, not to be an idle Spectator, but spurr'd on by an eager Thirst of excelling ardently to contend in the Pursuit of Glory. For this purpose she implanted in his Soul an invincible Love of Grandeur, and a constant emulation of whatever seems to approach nearer to Divinity than himself. Hence it is, that the whole Universe is not sufficient for the extensive Reach and piercing Speculation of the human Understanding. It passes the bounds of the material World, and launches forth at pleasure into endless Space. Let any one take an exact Survey of a Life, which in its every Scene is conspicuous on account of Excellence, Grandeur and Beauty, and he will soon discern for what noble Ends we were born. Thus the Impulse of Nature inclines us to admire, not a little clear transparent Rivulet that ministers to our Necessities, but the *Nile*, the *Ister*, the *Rhine*, or still much more, the Ocean. We are never surprised at the sight of a small Fire that burns clear, and blazes out on our own private Hearth, but view with Amaze the celestial Fires, tho' they are often obscured by Vapours and Eclipses. Nor do we reckon any thing in nature more wonderful than the boiling Furnaces of Etna, which cast up Stones and sometimes whole Rocks from their labouring Abyss, and pour out whole Rivers of liquid and unmingled Flame. And from hence we may infer, that whatever is useful and necessary to Man lies level to his Abilities, and is easily acquired; but whatever exceeds the common size is always great, and always amazing.[2]

The first of these two passages – an extract from the Gothic novel, *Montalbert*, by Charlotte Smith, published in 1795 – offers an account of the journey from England to Italy undertaken by the heroine, Rosalie, with her half-Italian husband. The initial sentence of this passage begins by noting the ties of filial affection which bind Rosalie to England, and the worry and unhappiness produced by these ties. Very swiftly, however, it becomes clear that the distresses of the family and the familiar have been introduced only to be displaced by the pleasures of the foreign. While the heroine, we are told, still has 'moments' when she remains preoccupied with the familiar, the subject who utters the description and narrative entirely abandons these 'moments' as a topic of discussion, and embarks on a hyperbolic account of the aesthetic delight experienced by Rosalie as she crosses the Alps. This delight is overtly linked to the heroine's abandonment of the familiar for the foreign: 'she seemed transported', we are told, 'to a world of higher rank in the universe than that she had inhabited while she was in England'.

By the adoption of this rhetoric of hyperbole, the subject of the description – who is defined as female by identification with the female author named on the title page of the novel – establishes a claim to have travelled across the Alps herself, and experienced similar aesthetic pleasure. In declaring this similarity of response, she provides an unequivocal endorsement of Rosalie's response of rapture.

This response is also, at the same time, accorded a second form of endorsement: it is defined as a reaction shared not only by the traveller who tells the story of the heroine's journey but also by any traveller of taste and discernment. This additional endorsement is produced by fusing the pleasures of travel with the pleasures of the sublime – a fusion which allows the description to invoke the authority of contemporary aesthetic theory, and, beyond this body of theory, the authority of Longinus, the ancient theorist of the sublime. The account of Rosalie's experience of sublime exaltation incorporates extensive echoes of the section of Chapter 35 of Longinus' *Peri Hypsous*, which is quoted above – in William Smith's translation, *Dionysius Longinus on the Sublime* (1793) – just after the passage from *Montalbert*. Rosalie displays not only the same 'Love of Grandeur' as Longinus' protagonist, 'Man', but also the same proclivity for self-elevation (an elevation 'to a world of higher rank in the universe') which drives Longinus' 'human Understanding' beyond 'the bounds of the material world'. It is suggested, in addition, that she experiences a pleasure in the 'ocean' – one of the features cited in *Peri Hypsous* as an object of human admiration – and that, in doing so, she displays the same impatience of 'bounds' which is emphasised in the passage quoted above (and which she also exhibits in her eagerness to move outside the boundaries of London, and her delight in moving across the geographical boundaries of the Alps).

The account of the journey through the Alps, however, follows a plot which entails a dramatic reversal: the traveller uttering the description suddenly detaches herself from the heroine's responses very sharply indeed, arguing that Rosalie's pleasure in Alpine scenery is at least partly dependent on a forgetfulness of the fact that England, whatever its aesthetic disadvantages, is nevertheless the country 'where life is enjoyed with the greatest comfort'.

This reversal to imprint on the description of foreign sublimity the traces of guilt: the pleasure in which the speaking subject shares is defined as a pleasure which requires a hurried gesture of disownment. The form assumed by this gesture of disownment invites the reader to interpret the gesture as one prompted, specifically, by a guilt which attaches itself to the pleasures of travel: the heroine's rapturous enjoyment of the foreign, it is suggested, has entailed a culpable neglect of the merits of the familiar. Since the pleasures of the sublime are fused with the pleasures of the foreign, the guilt which attaches itself to these latter pleasures also attaches itself to the former. In denying that she is as unequivocally enraptured by foreign sublimity as the heroine, the speaking subject also denies that she is in the grip of a guilt-laden desire to escape the familiar.

Yet further encouragement to read this denial as the effect of guilt is supplied by the position of this passage within a moralising narrative of travel: the account of Rosalie's forgetfulness serves as a prolepsis of the sufferings which she has to endure very soon after her journey across the Alps, as a result of her marriage to a semi-foreigner, and her decision to abandon the familiar for the foreign.[3]

'Comfort' and usefulness: bathos, irony, and the dismissal of the sublime

In issuing her reminder of the advantages of the familiar, the traveller locates these advantages within the ability of England to provide 'comfort'. The selection of this quality at such a juncture is disconcerting, since it at once places the advantages of England in question: in 18th-century travel writing – a genre to which the Gothic novel constantly appeals, as a source of authority on foreign places and how best to deal with them – comfort is regularly presented as a quality to which only the undiscerning will attach any great importance.[4] While travel writings often include complaints about foreign discomforts, they never define the comforts of England as the primary merit of that country: praise of England usually claims to be motivated by some more elevated human emotion, such as the love of liberty.[5] The passage's previous invocation of Longinus, moreover, classifying Rosalie's experience of sublimity as an instance of the 'invincible Love of Grandeur' implanted in the human soul, allows 'comfort', the quality set in opposition to enjoyment of the Alpine sublime, to be placed within the category of the 'useful and necessary' – and therefore, more damningly, within the category of that which is 'easily acquired'.

The term *comfort*, then, at the very end of this final half-sentence, produces a strong effect of bathos: the reader's expectations that England might be accorded some more remarkable or admirable quality are suddenly disappointed. This effect of bathos, however, while it weakens the insistence on the merits of England, nonetheless provides an extremely powerful means of dismissing the sublime – and, with it, the pleasures of the foreign: the anticlimactic mention of mere comfort proclaims unequivocally the collapse of the rhetoric of hyperbole through which the traveller has endorsed Rosalie's enjoyment of the foreign sublime. The dismissal of sublimity is all the more uncompromising for its employment of the very rhetorical device which, since Pope's *Peri Bathous: or, Of the Art of Sinking in Poetry* (1727), had been defined by its relation of opposition to the sublime.[6]

The banishment of hyperbole, through this effect of bathos, is accompanied by a more widely diffused effect of irony: once the term *comfort* had been uttered, it becomes possible to read the final half-

sentence, retrospectively, not only as a guilty denial of pleasure, but also as a passage in which the subject who utters the description recognises, ironically, her own limitations: in detaching herself from the heroine's enjoyment of elevated pleasures, she defines herself as a more imperfect traveller, incapable of sustaining such elevation amidst the ominously unspecified 'circumstances' of Italian discomfort. (This half-sentence can, in addition, be read as one which invites an equally ironic recognition of the artificiality of the generic conventions which require that Rosalie should be 'indifferent' to comfort: Gothic heroines invariably display a truly heroic power to assume the role of perfect travellers, and succeed in extracting pleasure from the foreign landscape amidst sufferings and horrors far greater than any which Rosalie has so far endured.)[7]

This ironic recognition of limitations, of course, emphasises yet more strongly the abandonment of the sublime: as already noted, the passage, through its reference to Longinus, clearly defines the experience of sublimity as one which entails an overwhelming desire to move beyond 'bounds' and constraints.

A further effect of the introduction of irony into this passage is to invest the category of the 'useful' with a value and attraction of its own, supplying the place of the more elevated virtues which have been denied it: the 'useful' quality of comfort is defined as one which must be valued wherever human beings are prepared to display the endearing quality of modesty, and recognise the difficulties of sustained aspiration.

An analogous revaluation of the useful through an ironic recognition of human imperfection is found in a late 18th-century travel book, Patrick Brydone's *Tour through Sicily and Malta* (1773). A large section of this travel book is devoted to Mount Etna – one of the sites selected by Longinus as an instance of grandeur and vastness. Brydone emphasises the sublimity of the view from this mountain, and of the 'tremendous gulph' within the mountain itself – 'the vast cells and caverns when so many lavas have issued'. After recounting the story of Empedocles throwing himself into this 'gulph' – and hoping, in his vanity, that the world will believe that he has been 'taken up to heaven' as a god – the traveller muses further on the sublime character of the spot from which he beholds these 'vast cells and caverns':

> However, if there is such a thing as philosophy on earth, surely this ought to be the seat of it . . . The meditations are ever elevated in proportion to the grandeur and sublimity of the objects that surround us; and here, where you have all Nature to arouse your admiration, what mind can remain inactive?
>
> . . . It would appear, that in proportion as we are raised above the habitations of men, all low and vulgar sentiments are left behind; and that the soul, in approaching the aethereal regions, shakes off its earthly affections, and already contracts something of their invariable purity. – Here, where you stand under a serene sky, and behold, with equal serenity, the tempest and storm forming below your feet: The lightning, darting from cloud to cloud, and the thunder rolling round the mountain, and threatening with destruction the poor wretches below; the mind considers the little storms and thunder of the human passions as equally below her notice. – Surely the situation alone, is enough to inspire philosophy, and Empedocles had good reason for chusing it.[8]

At this point, however, there is an ironic – and bathetic – reversal, in which the traveller modestly acknowledges his own human limitations, and his need for the useful comforts of the 'humble habitations' which lie below him. His 'elevated' response to sublimity is now invested, retrospectively, with an element of the vanity displayed by Empedocles on the same spot:

> But, alas! how vain are all our reasonings! In the midst of these meditations, my philosophy was at once overset, and in a moment I found myself relapsed into a poor miserable mortal; was obliged to own, that pain was the greatest of all evils; and would have given the world to have been once more arrived at

these humble habitations, which but this moment I looked down upon with such contempt. – In running over the ice, my leg folded under me, and I received so violent a sprain, that in a few minutes it swelled to a great degree, and I found myself totally incapable of putting my foot to the ground.[9]

Travel writing: the dissipation of guilt

The ironic dismissal of sublimity in Brydone's account of Mount Etna displays, however, one very important point of divergence from the dismissal of sublimity in Montalbert: while the experience of the sublime is defined as an experience which may incorporate an element of vanity, it is not presented as one tainted by the guilt of rejecting the familiar. The traveller who ironically describes his moment of literal and figurative 'sinking' does not, like the traveller who describes Rosalie's experience of sublimity, issue a guilty denial of his previous pleasure in the landscape. He does not even express any strong reservation about this pleasure itself. He merely proclaims, modestly, than he is subject to human limitations, and cannot, therefore, rise uninterruptedly to the elevated realms of sublimity.

18th-century travel writings, in fact, more frequently employ a strategy of revaluation of the useful and familiar which does not entail any dismissal of sublimity, and which therefore renders the absence of guilt yet more conspicuous than in Brydone's description of his fall.

The travel writings which display the greatest preoccupation with the sublime, in the 18th century, are those concerned with the topography of the Grand Tour – in particular with Italy, the country which is assigned a central place within this topography. In narratives of travel through Italy, the traveller constantly demands striking and dramatic objects of observation, and defines the quality of drama and excitement as part of the entertainment which the foreign is expected to provide. Very often in descriptions of the landscape this demand for drama assumes the form of a demand for sublimity, grandeur and vastness, qualities which – apart from the relatively few instances where they are located in works of architecture – are invariably situated within wild, 'savage', barren and mountainous regions. Where the landscape is defined as one which is 'beautiful', 'elegant', cultivated and useful to humankind, rather than sublime, vast, wild and devoid of practical usefulness, the traveller complains that it fails to provide a sufficient degree of dramatic foreignness, and displays, instead, the 'tameness' or 'insipidity' which in travel writing are regularly associated with the familiar rather than the foreign. Henry Swinburne's *Travels in the Two Sicilies*, for example, comments on the natural scenery around Taranto: 'the banks that inclose the bay are so gently sloped off as to create no very striking effect; there is a tameness in the prospect not unlike the insipidity of the artificial lakes and elegant swells in our fashionable gardens in England, totally different from the bold beauties of Italian landscape.'[10]

Expressions of pleasure in sublimity, therefore, proclaim an abandonment of the familiar for the superior excitement of the foreign. These expressions of pleasure, however, also serve to deprive the foreign of an alternative source of pleasure, which is emphasised very strongly indeed in earlier accounts of Italy: the 'useful' pleasure of untrammelled natural fertility. By the ruse of constantly praising the Italian landscape for its sublimity, 18th-century travel writing ensures that the 17th-century classification of Italy as a predominantly fertile and cultivated country is replaced by a classification in which wildness and barrenness assume a major role. The traveller's pleasure in the sublime is therefore freed from the guilt that is attached to the enjoyment of most other aspects of the foreign in literature of the Grand Tour: it is this very pleasure in foreign sublimity which allows the pleasures of fertility and cultivation to be transferred from the foreign to the familiar.

The removal of guilt however requires that the pleasure which is subtracted from the foreign – the pleasure of fertility – should be accorded the same intensity as the additional pleasure which the foreign acquires – the pleasure of the sublime. 18th-century travel writings do in fact continue to invest the landscape of fertility and usefulness with pleasure, by allowing the demand for drama to assume a second, rather different, form, in which the traveller actually proclaims the virtues of the beautiful, fertile, cultivated and useful landscape. These writings define the drama of the foreign as a quality located not only in the effect of unmixed sublimity but also in the effect of contrast. Travellers constantly express pleasure in contrasts between savage and barren natural scenery, on the one hand, and gentle, fertile, and cultivated countryside, on the other. In order to construct the greatest possible opposition between the two forms of landscape, both wildness and fertility are presented as qualities which are present in extreme forms, and which provoke extreme – and sharply contrasting – emotional responses. The response which is employed to affirm the extremity of fertility, beauty and usefulness is invariably one of intense pleasure; any suggestion of 'tameness', within this context, removes much of the desired element of drama from the contrast. The landscape of sublimity and wildness, on the other hand, is regularly presented as a source of horror and terror – responses which, in descriptions praising unmixed sublimity, are defined as paradoxically pleasurable, but, in passages of contrast, are more closely related to fear than to delight. Brydone's account of Mount Etna, for example, includes the comment:

> It is indeed a curious consideration, that this mountain should reunite every beauty and every horrour; and, in short, all the most opposite and dissimilar objects in nature. Here you observe a gulph, that formerly threw out torrents of fire, now covered with the most luxuriant vegetation; and from an object of terrour, become one of delight.[11]

The same alternation between a demand for sublimity – depriving the foreign of the pleasures of fertility – and a demand for contrast – emphasising the attractions of these latter pleasures – is also found in the Gothic novel. Within the Gothic genre, however, the guilt of enjoying the foreign is considerably more difficult to dissipate than in travel writing. The heroine's pleasure in the foreign landscape is regularly defined as one which the traveller describing this pleasure can only endorse because of the specific circumstances in which the landscape is enjoyed: where Gothic heroines leave their own native regions, it is usually emphasised that their encounter with foreign sublimity is not a voluntary one. The journeys of Gothic heroines through sublime and mountainous countryside are almost invariably forced upon them by feudal oppressors, who threaten them with rape and murder; in the face of these threats, the heroine usually turns to the landscape as a source of distraction and emotional relief.[12]

In *Montalbert*, however, the heroine is an Englishwoman who voluntarily undertakes a journey to Italy. The usual device by which the Gothic novel dissipates its supplementary burden of guilt is absent, and the culpability which both travel writings and Gothic novels usually manage to keep at bay, within descriptions of the landscape, is therefore imprinted very strongly indeed on the account of Rosalie's intense pleasure in the sublimity of the Alps.

The exemplification of sublimity

Both travel writings and Gothic novels, then, in 18th-century England, cite a multiplicity of specific examples of sublimity: the traveller eagerly seeks out points on the topography of the Grand Tour which offer either sublimity on its own or a dramatic contrast between sublimity and beauty. Travel books not only distribute examples of sublimity throughout the topography of the Grand Tour, but also map out a series of individual locations which constitute established starting-points for debate about the sublime – a series beginning with the Alps and progressing through the Appenines, the cascade at Terni, St Peter's in Rome, and Vesuvius, to culminate in Mount Etna.[13]

In describing these instances of the sublime, travel literature necessarily establishes a reference to aesthetic theory, by invoking definitions and principles which have been formulated within the genre of the aesthetic treatise. An ability to refer to aesthetic theory, in order to identify instances of sublimity, and thereby succeed in deriving a pleasurable drama from the foreign, is defined as an essential qualification for the traveller who is to participate fully in the practice of travel on the Grand Tour.

It might therefore be expected that English 18th century aesthetic treatises would display a symmetry with travel writing, and would define the ability to refer to the foreign and extract instances of sublimity from it, as an essential qualification for the theorist who concerns himself with the sublime. The reader of an essay on the sublime might expect to find, within the discussion of general principles, frequent references to the points on the topography of the Grand Tour which are cited as established starting-points for the discussion of sublimity in travel books. These expectations are further encouraged, moreover, by the fact that 18th-century essays on the sublime invariably situate themselves – either by direct or indirect references to *Peri Hypsous* – within the same tradition of Longinus. The account of the human love of grandeur in natural objects, in Chapter 35 of Longinus' treatise, itself names four geographically specific examples of sublimity – the Nile, the Ister (or Danube), the Rhine and Mount Etna. All four of these could, during the 18th century, have been included in an extended version of the Grand Tour, and one of them, Etna, was often included in the more limited, conventional Grand Tour. As a result, they can quite readily be defined as objects of the specific varieties of pleasure – including the pleasure of escape from the familiar – associated with foreign travel.

Smith's edition of *Peri Hypsous* – one of the standard 18th-century editions of Longinus' treatise – brings the 'Love of Grandeur' into a particularly close conjunction with the pleasure of encountering the foreign by its repeated introduction of the theme of travel. The prefatory 'Account of the Life, Writings and Character of Longinus' declares that 'searching for the particular Passages and Incidents of the Life of *Longinus*, is like travelling nowadays thro' those Countries in which it was spent', and embarks on a long account of the 'continual Scenes of Devastation and Ruin' which these countries present to the traveller. The translator then observes that Longinus himself spent his youth travelling and that later in his life he was employed by 'Zenobia, Queen of the East'. In addition, the notes to Chapter 35 – following the notes to Zachary Pearce's parallel Greek and Latin texts of the treatise, published some years earlier – append to Longinus' description of Mount Etna the description of this volcano in Book III of the *Aeneid* – the work of literature which more than almost any other serves as a metonym for travel.[14]

English aesthetic treatises, however, diverge very sharply both from travel writings and from Smith's *Dionysius Longinus on the Sublime*, in their reluctance to name particular points on the topography of the foreign as examples of sublimity. Since most of these aesthetic treatises define a certain degree of unfamiliarity as essential to the sublime, they do in fact suggest that the foreign is more likely to supply instances of sublimity than the familiar.[15] However, essays on aesthetic questions name so few specific geographical or architectural features in the course of their discussion of general principles, that they never allow the pleasure of the sublime to be fused with the pleasures of foreign travel as consistently and unreservedly as in works of travel writing. Wherever such a fusion does take place, it is accompanied by a gesture of concealment: examples of foreign sublimity are only cited in commentaries in which it is possible to disguise the mapping-out of the topography of the sublime as a topography of foreign travel.[16]

One such gesture of concealment consists of the adoption of a general category of objects as an example, defining these objects in such a way as to make it clear that they must be located within the foreign rather than the familiar, but refraining from any specific naming of foreign places. Burke's *Philosophical Enquiry into the Origin of our Ideas of the Sublime and Beautiful*, for example, cites 'the grand appearance of the ancient heathen temples' as an instance of 'the artificial infinite' produced by 'succession and uniformity of parts'.[16]

A second commonly-adopted gesture of concealment – which is employed in the passage just quoted, alongside the refusal to specify – is the reference to the ancient world, which uses a reference to distance in time as a means of masking the allusion to distance in space. On the one hand, of course, an emphasis on historical distance actually reinforces the element of alluring exoticism introduced by the discussion of a foreign location. On the other hand, however, this element of exoticism is masked by the appeal to a field of knowledge rendered familiar by Classical education. The strategic usefulness of any allusion to objects associated with the ancient world, in investing the foreign with a familiarity of this kind, is indirectly recognised in Hazlitt's essay 'Byron and Wordsworth'; Hazlitt criticises Byron for describing a domain of the foreign which, since it is littered with remnants of the Classical past, is too easily accessible to too general and undiscriminating an audience: 'The author of the Lyrical Ballads describes the lichen on the rock, the withered fern, with some peculiar feeling that he has about them: the author of Childe Harold describes the stately cypress, or the fallen column, with the feeling that every schoolboy has about them. The world is a grown school-boy, and relishes the latter most.'[17]

The reference to the ancient world also masks the allusion to travel by positioning the subject who utters the commentary as a scholarly compiler and annotator, proceeding primarily through the consultation of textual sources and deriving his authority from expertise in the interpretation and strategic deployment of these sources. Since the consultation of texts is assumed to be a largely sedentary activity, an invocation of the authority of the scholar readily masks any rival invocation of the authority of the traveller, describing objects of eye-witness observation – and masks, too, any suggestion that such eye-witness observation – entailing as it would a journey from the familiar into the foreign – might provide an appropriate or desirable means of assessing these objects and commenting on them.[18]

In aesthetic treatises, the device of reference to the ancient world allows the inclusion of highly specific exemplifications of the sublime in ancient architecture. Despite the fact that many essays on the sublime, by reference to Longinus, invest the works of nature with a much greater potential for sublimity than the products of human architectural endeavour, several of these same essays name precise examples of the sublime in ancient edifices, and exemplify the natural sublime only by reference to general categories of objects, such as mountains, vast plains and expanses of water.[19] Addison's writings on 'The Pleasure of the Imagination', for example, name no geographically specific example of 'greatness' in nature, but cite at least seven instances of this quality in ancient architecture and sculpture, arguing that, in the achievement of greatness, 'we find the Antients, especially among the Eastern Nations of the World, infinitely superior to the Moderns'. At one point in this argument, the theorist, while maintaining a stance of scholarly speculation, directly defines the ancient monuments of Egypt as objects to be encountered through travel: 'In Egypt *we still see* their Pyramids, which answer to the Descriptions that have been made of them; and I question not but *a Traveller* might find out some Remains of the Labyrinth that covered a whole Province, and had a hundred Temples disposed among its several Quarters and Divisions' (italics added).[20]

Displays of Classical scholarship, masking the reference to travel, are also introduced through appeals to the power of association: Archibald Alison's *Essays on the Nature and Principle of Taste*, for example, argues that 'the majesty of the Alps themselves is increased by the remembrance of Hannibal's march over them'.[21]

A further form of reference to the ancient world which serves to disguise the fusion of the sublime and the foreign is, paradoxically enough, the appeal to Chapter 35 of Longinus' *On the Sublime*. The topography of the sublime which Longinus maps out in this chapter is, indeed, as already argued, clearly defined in the standard 18th-century translation of Longinus as a topography of foreign travel. Nevertheless, by citing examples of sublimity which have already been named by Longinus, an aesthetic treatise classifies the sublime as an object of speculation which specifically requires expertise, as opposed to the on-the-spot experience of particular buildings and geographical features which is conferred by foreign travel.

Most aesthetic treatises do not, however, simply reproduce Longinus' list of examples: once the reference to the ancient text has been established, by naming one or more of these examples, other instances of sublimity, taken from the domain of the foreign, can be smuggled in alongside them. The subject who provides such lists of examples still adopts the position of a scholarly commentator, revising and annotating an established topography of the sublime. At the same time, however, he also establishes a discreet claim to experience of travel, or, at least, to a fascination with the unfamiliar.

A number of treatises, for example, add to Longinus' list of examples the very mountains which, since they provide a point of entry to Italy, ineluctably classify the sublime as a pleasure which forms part of the experience of travel on the Grand Tour.[22] Baillie's *Essay on the Sublime* delicately emphasises the need to add instances of mountains to the Longinian topography by a paraphrase of Longinus which includes a particular concentration of references to 'elevation'. Having noted the 'elevated Pleasure' occasioned by the Nile, Danube and Ocean, the *Essay* swiftly appends the Alps and Pyrenees to these Longinian examples: 'A flowery *Vale*, or the Verdure of a *Hill*, may charm; but to fill the Soul, and raise it to the *Sublime* Sensations, the earth must rise into an *Alp*, or *Pyrrhenean*, and *Mountains*, reach to the very *Heavens*.'[23] Gerard's *Essay on Taste* also adds the Alps to a slightly pared-down version of the Longinian topography: pointing out our relative indifference not only to 'a small rivulet' but also to 'a narrow valley', the treatise continues: 'it is not on a little hill, though cloathed with the most delightful verdure, that we bestow the epithet *sublime*: but on the *Alps*, the *Nile*, the ocean, the wide expanse of heaven, or the immensity of space uniformly extended, without limit of termination.'[24]

Displaced exemplification: Burke
There are two 18th-century accounts of the sublime in which even the safely 'scholarly' topography of the foreign derived from Longinus appears, at first glance, to be excluded: Burke's *Philosophical Enquiry* and the sections on sublimity in Blair's *Lectures on Rhetoric and Belles Lettres*. Both these works, however, do in fact include highly displaced exemplifications of the sublime, which incorporate within them equally displaced invocations of Longinus.

Burke's *Enquiry* includes extremely few specific references to buildings and geographical features. At the very end of the treatise, several geographical references are nevertheless introduced, not into a discussion of the sublime in nature and architecture, but into an account of the nature of verbal language. A piece of description is put forward as one which has been concocted by Burke – through an apparently arbitrary selection of subject-matter – in order to illustrate the argument that words fail to present a visual image to the mind, even when they name visually apprehensible objects. This piece of description, however, just happens to offer a fairly extended account of one of the examples of sublimity cited by Longinus:

> Suppose we were to read a passage to this effect, 'The river Danube rises in a moist and mountainous soil in the heart of Germany, where winding to and fro it waters several principalities, until turning into Austria and leaving the city of Vienna it passes into Hungary; there with a vast flood augmented by the Saave and the Drave it quits Christendom, and rolling through the barbarous countries which border on Tartary, it enters by many mouths into the Black sea.' In this description many things are mentioned, as mountains, rivers, cities, the sea, &c. But let anybody examine himself, and see whether he had had impressed on his imagination any pictures of a river, mountain, watery soil, Germany, &c …[25]

Burke exemplifies the sublime, then, in this passage, through the rhetorical figure of preterition – the figure in which something is said by means of a declaration that it is not being said. The *Enquiry* denies that the description of the Danube provides any 'pictures', but nonetheless suggests some of the visual images which the reader might have formed, had such picture-formation been possible – and, by the selection of the object described, established a reference to Longinus which strongly invites the reader to endow the river with the visually apprehensible qualities of grandeur and vastness. Continued allusions to vastness confirm this reference to *Peri Hypsous*: the enormous extent of the Danube is emphasised by the lengthy enumeration of lands through which the river flows (including a casual reference to 'several principalities' which, it seems, are not worth specifying in such an extended itinerary), and by a direct allusion to the 'vast flood' which marks its course through Hungary.[26]

The account of the Danube also invokes Longinus by its suggestion of an impatience of boundaries: the river '*leaves* the walls of Vienna', and '*quits* Christendom' (italics added), on its way to a final casting-off of its own boundaries, as it flows 'by many mouths' into the Black Sea. These allusions are, in themselves, sufficient to inscribe within the description – and within the commentary which cites it – a desire for escape from geographical constraints: in other words, a desire for the pleasures of travel. Such a desire is registered yet more insistently by the specification of the impatience of boundaries as an impulse which propels the river away from the more familiar regions of the foreign, towards the exotic 'barbarous countries which border on Tartary'. The subject of commentary is positioned both as a scholarly commentator on Longinus and as a would-be traveller, investing the Danube with increased pleasure – derived both from increased vastness and from increased exoticism – as he traces its course towards remote and unfamiliar parts of the world.

A few pages later, the *Enquiry* once again emphasises the pleasures of travel, by quoting another formula of words which, it claims, fails to excite visual images in the mind. In this case, there is no immediate echo in Longinus, and no immediate reference to the sublime; the exposition of the pictures which we fail to visualise concerns itself initially with the practice of travel to Italy and then with Italy itself, and with summer. By a metonymic elision between the two words which refer to these last unpictured pictures – one naming a warmer country, and the other naming the warmest season of the year – a desire for the pleasures of travel is registered very strongly indeed:

> If I say, 'I shall go to Italy next summer,' I am well understood. Yet I believe no body has by this painted in his imagination the exact figure of the speaker passing by land or by water, or both; sometimes on horseback, sometimes in a carriage; with all the particulars of the journey, Still less has he any idea of Italy, the country to which I proposed to go; or of the greenness of the fields, the ripening of the fruits, and the warmth of the air, with the change to this from a different season, which are the ideas for which the word *summer* is substituted …[27]

Having introduced the theme of travel, Burke then sustains it, and links it to Longinus and the sublime, by a quotation from the *Aeneid* which he puts forward just as the discussion of Italy and summer comes to an end. The *Enquiry* now suggests that the failure of words to excite visual images actually endows verbal language with a particular potential for sublimity. To illustrate this point, Burke quotes Virgil's 'admirably sublime' account of 'Vulcan's cavern in Etna, and the works that are there carried on', in Book VIII of the *Aeneid*, and denies that any picture other than a 'wild and absurd' one is being formed within this passage. Through this extended denial, he nevertheless introduces into the *Enquiry* the very geographical feature which provides a point of conjunction between Longinus' range of examples and the country which Burke has just presented as one which excites a desire for foreign travel – and which, indeed, is more unmistakeably linked to travel than any other, since it occupies a central place in the topography of travel mapped out by the traditional version of the Grand Tour.

Displaced exemplification: Blair

Blair, in *Lectures on Rhetoric and Belles Lettres*, follows a strategy similar to that adopted in Burke's *Enquiry*: he offers no geographically specific examples when addressing himself directly to the question of 'sublimity in objects', but soon introduces one of Longinus' instances of grandeur once he embarks on a discussion of 'the sublime in writing'. A large portion of the lecture concerned with this latter topic is devoted to emphasising the precariousness of the sublime as a literary effect, and the constant danger of lapsing into bathos – or 'the Frigid' – which accompanies any attempt to achieve sublimity.[28] 'When a writer is aiming at the beautiful only,' Blair maintains, 'his descriptions may have improprieties in them, and yet be beautiful still … But the case is quite different with the Sublime':

> There, one trifling circumstance, one mean idea, is sufficient to destroy the whole charm. This is owing to the nature of the emotion aimed at by Sublime description, which admits of no mediocrity, and cannot subsist in a middle state; but might either highly transport us, or, if unsuccessful in the execution, leave us greatly disgusted, and displeased. We attempt to rise along with the writer; the imagination is awakened, and put upon the stretch; but it requires to be supported; and if, in the midst of its effort, you desert it unexpectedly, down it comes with a painful shock.[29]

After a brief initial example, the lecture cites a description from Virgil which 'is censurable … in this respect': the description of Mount Etna in Book III of the *Aeneid*. The reference to *Peri Hypsous* which is established simply by the object described is reinforced by the fact that the passage quoted is precisely the same as that which both Pearce's Greek and Latin edition and Smith's English edition of this work append to its description of this mountain. 'Here', Blair comments, 'after several magnificent images, the Poet concludes with personifying the mountain under this figure, "eructans viscera cum gemitu", belching up its bowels with a groan; which, by likening the mountain to a sick, or drunk person, degrades the majesty of the description.[30]

Commenting further on these lines from Virgil, Blair cites another passage which demonstrates yet more clearly the danger that Mount Etna will become the site of bathos rather than sublimity:

> The debasing effort of the idea which is here presented, will appear in a stronger light, by seeing what figure it makes in a poem of Sir Richard Blackmore's, who, through a monstrous perversity of taste, had chosen this for the capital circumstance in his description, and thereby (as Dr Arbuthnot humorously observes, in his Treatise on the Art of Sinking) had represented the mountain as in a fit of the cholic.
>
> > Ætna, and all the burning mutinous find
> > Their kindled stores with inbred storms of wind
> > Blown up to rage, and roaring out complain,
> > As torn with inward gripes and torturing pain;
> > Labouring, they cast their dreadful vomit round,
> > And with their melted bowels spread the ground.[31]

In referring to *Peri Bathous: or, Of the Art of Sinking in Poetry* (a treatise which is almost invariably ascribed to Pope rather than to Arbuthnot), Blair allows Longinus's classification of Etna as an instance of grandeur to be further destabilised. *Peri Bathous* is composed of a multiplicity of ironic reversals of *Peri Hypsous*. One of these reversals is incorporated in the comment on Blackmore's description of Etna – that is, in the section of the treatise invoked by Blair. Etna, it is revealed, has, notwithstanding the claims of Longinus, already been claimed for bathos: Horace, in search of the sublime, struck his Head against the Stars; but Empedocles, to fathom the profound, threw himself into Ætna. And who but would imagine our excellent Modern had also been there, from this description?'[32]

While indirectly invoking this reclassification of Etna, however, and emphasising the ever-present danger of bathos, Blair nonetheless insists on the sublimity of the mountain itself, allowing the pleasure of this sublimity to resurge several times amidst the general despondency of the commentary. The first resurgence of pleasure occurs when the

theorist is introducing the lines from the *Aeneid*: the description in question, he informs the reader, 'is that of the burning mountain Ætna; *a subject certainly very proper to be worked up by a poet into a sublime description*' (italics added). After quoting this description, Blair again allows bathos in writing to be displayed by sublimity in the natural object:

> It is to no purpose to tell us, that the Poet here alludes to the fable of the giant Enceladus lying under mount Ætna; and that he supposes his motions and tossings to have occasioned the fiery eruptions. He intended the description of a Sublime object; and the natural ideas, raised by a burning mountain, are infinitely more lofty, than the belchings of any giant, how huge soever.[33]

A page later, after the quotation from Blackmore, the pleasurable sublimity of Etna is again allowed to imprint on the commentary, this time through the more oblique strategy of employing metaphors of warmth and refulgence which echo the previous references, in Blair's commentary, to the interior fires which invest Etna with such drama: 'Whenever a great and awful object is presented in nature …; thence, if you can catch the impression strongly, *and exhibit it warm and glowing*, you may draw the Sublime' (italics added).[34]

This account of the need to 'catch the impression strongly' itself forms part of an argument which, after all Blair's warnings about the propensity of the sublime to collapse into bathos, defiantly affirms the power of sublimity to triumph over the bathetic. The sublime in nature is classified by Blair as the only proper source of the sublime in language. The task of the writer, in striving for the sublime, is, the lecture suggests, to preserve a continuity between nature and language which allows the sublimity of the former to imprint itself on the latter. In order to fulfil this task, the writer has to reject one of the sources of sublimity listed by Longinus – the 'Application of Figures' – and turn instead to the 'Boldness and Grandeur in the Thoughts' which is noted in *Peri Hypsous* as the 'most excellent' source of the sublime:

> If it shall now be enquired, What are the proper sources of the Sublime? My answer is, That they are to be looked for every where in nature. It is not by hunting after tropes, and figures, and rhetorical assistances, that we can expect to produce it. No: it stands clear, for the most part, of these laboured refinements of art. It must come unsought, if it comes at all; and be the natural offspring of a strong imagination.
>
> Est Deus in nobis; agitante calescimus illo.[35]

By turning to the power to 'catch the impression' of sublimity which 'a strong imagination' can supply, Blair therefore reverses the plot of sublimity destroyed by bathos which the lectures has so far been charting – and which is adopted in the passages from *Montalbert* and Brydone's *Tour through Sicily and Malta* quoted above: the brisk dismissal of the tropes and figures which destroy sublimity encourages the hope that these agents of bathos will readily be vanquished by those writers possessed of the requisite imaginative abilities.

In stating that the proper sources of the sublime are to be found in nature, and emphasising the need to exhibit the writer's impression of natural objects 'warm and glowing', Blair, in addition, strongly emphasises the value of immediacy of response. This immediacy is placed in direct opposition to the mediatory strategy of 'hunting after tropes, and figures, and rhetorical assistances'. By constructing an opposition of this kind, between reprehensibly mediated and commendably unmediated transcriptions of nature, Blair ineluctably defines the sublime in nature as something which the poet can only hope to describe in an adequate manner if he enjoys the opportunities for on-the-spot observation and immediate response which form part of the privileged experience of the traveller. The imaginative experience of the sublime in nature is, through this discussion of the sublime in writing, fused very uncompromisingly indeed with the experience of foreign travel.

The fusion between sublimity and travel is one which is also achieved much more indirectly through the reference to *Peri Bathous*. In the comment on Blackmore's description of Mount Etna which is quoted above, the satirist asks ironically, after mentioning Empedocles' plunge into Etna, 'And who but would imagine our excellent Modern had also been there, from this description?' On the one hand, the suggestion that Blackmore might be imagined to have followed Empedocles into Etna simply emphasises that his verses on the mountain have indeed 'sunk' to the 'depths' of poetical impropriety. On the other hand, the question acquires its irony from an awareness of the utter impossibility of viewing these verses as the result of an immediate, eye-witness experience of the geographical feature which they describe. A poet who entangles himself in such ludicrous rhetorical complexities, it is suggested, cannot possibly have 'been there', and viewed the eruptions of Etna in person. Since Blackmore's description is rejected absolutely, the commentary, in noting the absence of any inscription of personal experience within this description, cannot help but suggest that the verses in question might have been rather less disastrous if Brydone had, in fact, enjoyed the benefits of first-hand observation conferred by travel on the Grand Tour.

Guilt in the aesthetic treatise

On the one hand, therefore, discussions of aesthetic theory in 18th-century England register a strong desire to exemplify the sublime by reference to foreign and exotic locations; in one of the very few cases where an English example of sublimity is cited, a contemporary review of the treatise in question silently substitutes a more exotic landmark: Burke's chapter on 'difficulty', which uses Stonehenge to illustrate the principle that 'when any work seems to have required immense force and labour to effect it, the idea is grand', is summarised by the *Critical Review* as follows: 'When any work seems to have required immense force or labour to effect it, such as the pyramids of Ægypt, – the imagination immediately recurs to the greatness and power of the builder.'[36] On the other hand, this desire to fuse the sublime with the foreign is subjected to severe constraints: the precise exemplification through which such a fusion is accomplished is invariably masked or displaced. What is it, then, in the rhetorical structure of the aesthetic treatise, which precipitates the introduction of strategies of concealment and displacement which are absent from travel writings of the same period? One difference between the two genres which might provide a means of interpreting these strategies is the absence, in the aesthetic treatise, of the endorsement of beauty and usefulness which, in travel writings, serves to dissipate guilt. Both Pearce and Smith, in their commentaries on *Peri Hypsous*, register grave unease with the rejection of the useful in chapter 35, as a quality incompatible with sublimity.[37] Nonetheless, 18th-century essays on the sublime invariably maintain Longinus' opposition between vast, sublime objects and small, useful objects, and invariably present the former as the source of a more powerful and ennobling response.[38] At the same time, these essays incorporate the assumption that mere 'beauty' and usefulness are more likely to be found in the familiar landscape of England than in the dramatic, 'striking' landscape of the foreign – the same assumption which is embodied in travel writings alongside a more enthusiastic acclamation of beauty.[39]

It is possible, therefore, to read the constraints placed on the exemplification of the sublime metaleptically, as effects which point back to a specific cause: the guilt of abandoning the familiar which attaches itself to the theorist's desire to invest the sublime with the joys of foreign travel, and which the aesthetic treatise fails to dissipate by any revaluation of familiar usefulness.

This reading follows, in its general outline and a few of its details, a model of interpretation formulated by Freud, in response to his own thoughts on the foreign, in the essay 'A Disturbance of Memory on the Acropolis' (1936). In the course of his analysis of the eponymous 'disturbance of memory', Freud identifies the desire to travel with a desire to escape the familiar and the family, and fuses both desires with a feeling of 'greatness'. The description of this feeling echoes very strongly Longinus' accounts of sublime elevation – even mentioning

the 'ocean' as one of the objects which prompts such a response. After noting 'the limitations and poverty of our conditions of life in my youth', Freud comments:

> My longing to travel was no doubt also the expression of a wish to escape from that pressure, like the force which drives so many adolescent children to run away from home. I had long seen clearly that a great part of the pleasure of travel lies in the fulfilment of these early wishes – that it is rooted, that is, in dissatisfaction with home and family. When first one catches sight of the sea, crosses the ocean and experiences as realities cities and lands which for so long had been distant, unattainable things of desire – one feels oneself like a hero who has performed deeds of improbable greatness.[40]

At the same time, however, Freud identifies in part of his response to the foreign a disturbance of pleasure which he interprets as the product of guilt: while still at Trieste, considering a suggestion that they should travel on to Athens, he and his brother have experienced a gloomy – and unfounded – conviction that this extension of their journey will prove impossible:

> But here we come upon the solution of the little problem of why it was that already at Trieste we interfered with our enjoyment of the voyage to Athens. It must be that a sense of guilt was attached to the satisfaction in having gone such a long way: there was something about it that was wrong, that from earliest times had been forbidden. It was something to do with a child's criticism of his father, with the undervaluation which took the place of the overvaluation of earlier childhood.[41]

The 18th-century and Romantic sublime has often been linked in various ways to the narrative structure of the Oedipus complex, as mapped out by Freud.[42] 'A Disturbance of Memory' is quoted here, however, not in order to introduce this narrative structure into the discussion of exemplifications of sublimity, but, rather, in order to raise the possibility of reading 18th-century aesthetic treatises as works which covertly embody the same structure of guilt and pleasure – a guilt and pleasure attached to the escape from the familiar – which Freud's essay, written during a decade in which the pleasures of travel were proclaimed with particular emphasis, is able to acknowledge openly.[43]

Aesthetic treatises, then, vaunt as hyperbolically as possible the pleasures of an experience of sublimity which necessarily entails an impatience of boundaries, yet, when they extend this impatience to the disregard of geographical boundaries, register a constraint and disruption of pleasure that can be read as a metalepsis for guilt.

Whenever the desire to exemplify the sublime is registered, however, this desire can also be seen as bearing the imprint of a further guilt, attached to a further disregard of boundaries: the disregard of the boundaries of genre. In exemplifying the sublime, and excluding the familiar as a source of examples, aesthetic treatises begin to convert themselves into works of travel writing. By placing constraints on this impulse towards self-transmutation, they proclaim the need for a strict observance of generic limits, paying deference to the 'law of "do" or "do not" which, as everyone knows, occupies the concept or constitutes the value of *genre*'.[44] As a result of this deference, the disregard of these generic limits is defined as dangerously and culpably transgressive.

Freud's open declaration of a pleasure in travel which merges with the pleasure of a Longinian 'greatness' can be seen, therefore, as one which is only made possible by the essay's ingenious blurring of its own generic self-definition. 'A Disturbance of Memory' is described in the sub-title as 'an open letter', and employs the flexibility of the letter form to assume, both sequentially and simultaneously, the attributes of a psychoanalytic treatise, a fragment of autobiography, a piece of speculation in the tradition of Longinus and – above all else – a work of travel literature.[45]

The author would like to thank Simon Pembroke for his generous help with the problems which she encountered in referring to ancient literature; Dr Pembroke is not, of course, responsible for any remaining inaccuracies in her allusions to ancient texts. She would also like to thank Todd Longstaffe-Gowan for discussing with her some of the arguments put forward in this article.

1   Charlotte Smith, *Montalbert*: A Novel, 3 vols, London, 1795, II, pp 143-4.

2   *Dionysius Longinus on the Sublime: Translated from the Greek, with Notes and Observations, and Some Account of the Life, Writings and Character of the Author*, edited and translated by William Smith, London, 1739, pp84-6.

3   After the birth of a child, Rosalie finds herself in the midst of an earthquake in Sicily. Her husband, meanwhile, is away in Naples, attempting to placate his proud and vindictive mother, the Signora Belcastro, who remains unreconciled to his marriage. The heroine is then herself removed to Naples, while unconscious, by the libidinous Count Alozzi; to escape his attentions, she writes to the Signora Belcastro. Soon after, she is mysteriously imprisoned and taken to a remote castle.

4   John Moore, *A View of Society and Manners in Italy*, second edition, 2 vols, London, 1781, first published in 1781, II, pp97-99, for example, criticises those travellers 'whose senses are far more powerful than their fancy', and who when making the journey from Rome to Naples spend their time 'fretting at Italian beds, fuming against Italian cooks, and execrating every poor little Italian flea that they meet with on the road.'

5   *ibid*, II, pp 501-2, see, for example, the traveller's approbatory account of 'those just and equitable laws which secure property, that mild free government which abhors tyranny', in 'the boisterous island of Great Britain'.

6   See, for example, Chapter II of this treatise, in *The Works of Alexander Pope, Esq*, 4 vols, Edinburgh, 1764, III, pp63-112; p65: 'The taste of the bathos is implanted by nature itself in the soul of man; till, perverted by custom or example, he is taught, or rather compelled, to relish the sublime.'

7   In Ann Radcliffe's novel *The Romance of the Forest* (1791), for example, the heroine, Adeline, while travelling through Savoy, is highly conscious of 'the forlornness of her circumstances' (She is described at this point in her adventures as 'an orphan, desolate, helpless, and flying from persecution and her country'), but nonetheless finds herself 'lost in admiration of the astonishing and tremendous scenery around her' (edited by Chloe Chard, Oxford, 1986, p236, p235, p240).

8   First edition, 2 vols, London, 1773, I, pp187-96, 196-7, 199-200, 200-202.

9   1, 202.

10 Second edition, 2 vols, London, 1790 (first published 1783-5, II, pp45-6.

11 *ibid*, I, p173. The passage continues: 'Here you gather the most delicious fruit, rising from what was but lately a black and barren rock. Here the ground is covered with every flower; and we wander over these beauties, and contemplate this wilderness of sweets, without considering that hell, with all its terrours, is immediately under our feet; and that but a few yards separate us from lakes of liquid fire and brimstone.'

12 In Ann Radcliffe's novel *The Mysteries of Udolpho* (1794), for example, the heroine's journey over the Alps, as well as a later journey over the Appenines, are imposed on her by the villainous Montoni (edited by Bonamy Dobrée (Oxford, 1980), p160-70 and 222-27. Where the heroine is not actually travelling as a prisoner of the oppressor, she is often fleeing from him – in which case her travels are, of course, equally involuntary. See, for example, *The Mysteries of Udolpho*, pp449-462.

13 The relative degrees of grandeur exhibited by the Alps and the Appenines are discussed in Hester Lynch Piozzi, *Observations and Reflections Made in the Course of a Journey through France, Italy, and Germany*, 2 vols, London, 1789, II, 154-5. An analysis of the sublimity of the cascade at Terni is included in the same travel book, II, pp154. Moore, I, pp401-3, argues that the sublimity of St Peter's is diminished by the fineness of its proportions. For an account of the sublimity of Vesuvius, see Martin Sherlock, *Lettres d'un voyageur anglois* (London[Geneva?], 1779), pp72-3. The contrasting sublimity and beauty of Etna are described in Thomas Watkins, *Travels through Switzerland, Italy, Sicily, the Greek Islands to Constantinople*, second edition, 2 vols, London, 1794; first published in 1792; see also Brydone, I, pp187-96, 196-7 and 173 (*op cit*).

14 William Smith, iii-iv, v, ix; Pearce, *Dionysii Longini De Sublimitate Commentarious*, London, 1724, pp118-19. Not all editions of the treatise, of course, directly invest these four objects with an evident foreignness. The identity of Longinus has actually been too vaguely defined for the readers to be strongly encouraged to construct an authorial voice which surveys the five natural features from the standpoint of a distinct geographical affiliation – although Smith's suggestions, in his introduction to the treatise, that Longinus was born either in Syria or Athens, and was definitely a Greek, confer a certain exotic distance on all the four named features (See iv-v).

15 See [John] Baillie, *An Essay on the Sublime*, London, 1747, p8: 'Yet notwithstanding we have demonstrated that the *Vastness* of the Object constitutes the *Sublime*, to render the Sublime perfect, two Things are requisite; a certain degree of *Uniformity*, and that by long Custom the Objects do not become familiar to the Imagination' See also pages 11-12 of this same treatise, Edmund Burke, *A Philosophical Enquiry into the Origin of our Ideas of the Sublime and Beautiful*, edited by James T Boulton, Oxford, 1987; first published in 1757, p31, Alexander Gerard, *An Essay on Taste*, 1759, London, 1971; first published in 1759, p81, and [Henry Home,]

Lord Kames, *Elements of Criticism*, first edition, 3 vols, London, 1762, I, pp144, 215-6.

16 p74, p75.

17 William Hazlitt, in *Romantic Critical Essays*, ed by David Bromwich, Cambridge, 1987, pp120-122; p121.

18 Eye-witness observation is accorded particular importance in late 18th-century definitions of travel: travel writings of this period are particularly anxious to emphasise that the traveller has observed the objects of commentary in person. Even historical narratives are often incorporated in accounts of visual scrutiny: see, for example, Piozzi, I, 381 '*I have examined the place* where Sylla massacred 8000 fellow-citizens at once ' (italics added).

19 Chapter 36 of William Smith's *Dionysius Longinus on the Sublime* contains the remark: 'In the Works of Art we have regard to exact Proportion; in those of Nature, to Grandeur and Magnificence' (p87). A version of this argument is included in Joseph Addison, 'The Pleasures of the Imagination', in Richard Steele and Joseph Addison, *Selections from the Tatler and the Spectator*, ed by Angus Ross, London, 1988, pp364-406; p378 'There is something more bold and masterly in the rough careless Strokes of Nature, than in the nice Touches and Embellishments of Art.' See also James Beattie, 'Illustrations of Sublimity', in *Dissertations Moral and Critical*, London, 1783, pp605-655; p617: 'The most perfect models of sublimity are seen in the works of nature.'

20 p381, p381, p382.

21 Edinburgh, 1790, 17-18; the passage continues 'and who is there, that could stand on the banks of the Rubicon, without feeling his imagination kindle, and his heart beat high'. As this example demonstrates, the argument that the sublimity of objects may be enhanced by their historical associations allows an aesthetic treatise to name as examples of the sublime not only works on architecture but also natural features of the foreign terrain.

22 A reference to the Grand Tour is, of course, clearly established by the account of the journey through the Alps in *Montalbert*. The description of this journey specifically notes the way in which Rosalie and her husband will depart from the usual itinerary of travellers on the Grand Tour, by avoiding Rome and Naples – thereby establishing that itinerary as one in relation to which their travels must necessarily be defined.

23 p5.

24 pp13-14. In Lord Kames's *Elements of Criticism*, the Alps are not directly incorporated in a paraphrase of Longinus, but are introduced into the discussion of the sublime with sufficient promptness, after a footnote providing such a paraphrase, to define them as candidates for inclusion within an augmented version of it; on the page following the passage to which this footnote refers, Kames declares: 'In some objects, greatness and elevation concur to make a complicated impression. The Alps and the pike of Tenerif are proper examples'. (I,264,265) Beattie's 'Illustrations of Sublimity', incorporating a reference to *Peri Hypsous* within the argument that 'that which is great is not always good', forms, add two new examples which both ostensibly reinforce the reference to the ancient world: 'Troy in flames, Palmyra in ruins, the ocean in a storm, and Etna in thunder and conflagration, are magnificent appearances, but do not immediately impress our minds with the idea of good.' While Troy is removed from the topography of contemporary by the reference to the 'flames' which mark a particular point in its history, however, Palmyra is described precisely as the contemporary, ruined city visited by travellers on extended versions of the Grand Tour (pp605-655; p613).

25 p167.

26 The description of vastness is, of course, rendered particularly hyperbolic by the plot which the passage follows: it begins with the river as a mere rivulet – the feature which Longinus places in direct opposition to the 'great, and ... amazing', and traces a progressive increase in size which, by the time it has reached Hungary, had accomplished its transformation into an instance of greatness.

27 p170.

28 In the course of his discussion of this danger, Blair uses the term 'the Frigid' (Hugh Blair, *Lectures on Rhetoric and Belles Lettres*, first edition, 2 vols, London, 1783,1,78), with direct reference to Longinus (see William Smith, p8 and 9-12), but, at the same time, indirectly invokes Pope's concept of bathos, by an allusion to *Peri Bathos*. (This allusion is discussed below. In *Peri Hypsous*, the quality denoted by the term *bathos* is equated with hypsos, or the sublime, rather than placed in opposition to it.)

29 I, p73.

30 I, pp73-4. The full quotation is as follows:
———Horrificis juxta tonat Ætna ruinis.
Interdumque atram prorumpit ad æthera nubem,
Turbine famantem piceo, et candente favilla;
Attollitque globos fammarum, et sidera lambit.
Interdum scopulos avulsaque viscera montis
Erigit eructans, liquefactaque saxa sub auras
Cum gemitu glomerat, fundoque exæstuat imo
Aeneid, III. 571
Blair appends to this quotation the following footnote:
The port capacious, and secure from wind,
Is to the foot of thundering Ætna joined,
By turns a pitchy cloud she rolls on high,

By turns hot embers from her entrails fly,
And flakes of mounting flames that lick the sky.
Oft from her bowels massy rocks are thrown,
And shivered by the force, come piece-meal down.
oft liquid lakes of burning sulphur flow,
Fed from the fiery springs that boil below. DRYDEN
In this translation of Dryden's, the debasing circumstances to which I object in the original is, with propriety, omitted.

31 I, p74.
32 *The Works of Alexander Pope*, III, p83.
33 I, p73; I, p74.
34 I, p75.
35 William Smith, p16; Blair, I, 75. Jean-François Lyotard, 'The Sublime and the Avant-Garde', in *Art Forum*, April 1984, pp36-43, p38, notes the 'unsureness' with which Longinus' treatise hovers between very different accounts of sublimity: 'The author was a rhetorician. Basically, he taught those oratorical devices with which a speaker, of whatever style, can persuade or move an audience … However, when it comes to the sublime, major obstacles get in the way of rhetorical and poetic regulations …'.
36 In the *Critical Review, or, Annals of Literature*, 70 vols, London, 1756-90, III, 1757, pp361-374; p366.
37 Pearce expresses this unease in a note to Chapter 36 (p119), which Smith translates into English in his commentary on the same chapter (p177): '*Longinus* in the preceding section has said, that Men view with amaze the celestial Fires (such as the Sun and Moon) tho' they are frequently obscured; the case is the same with the burning Mountain Ætna, tho' it casts up pernicious Fire from its Abyss; but here, when he returns to the sublime Authors, he intimates, that the Sublime is the more to be admired, because far from being useless or amusing, it is of great service to its Authors as well as to the Public. Dr. *Pearce*.'
38 See, for example, Blair, *op cit*, I, pp61-2: 'What are the scenes of nature that elevate the mind in the highest degree, and produce the sublime sensation? Not the gay landscape, the flowery field, or the flourishing city; but the hoary mountain, and the solitary lake; the aged forest, and the torrent falling over the rock.' See also Beattie, *op cit*, p613: 'a clear fountain is not a grand object, though in many parts of the world it would be valued above all treasures'.
39 As noted above, the argument that familiarity threatens to destroy the sublime is one which strongly suggests that it is in the topography of the foreign, rather than that of the familiar, that instances of sublimity will be found. Alison, pp326-8, notes more directly 'the difference or inferiority of the scenery of our own country, to that which we were accustomed peculiarly to admire'.
40 In *The Standard Edition of the Complete Psychological Works of Sigmund Freud*, gen ed James Strachey, 24 vols, London, 1955-74, XXII, 1964, pp237-248; 246-247, 247.
41 p247.
42 See, for example, Thomas Weiskel, *The Romantic Sublime: Studies in the Structure and Psychology of Transcendence*, Baltimore and London, 1976, *passim* (especially pp10-11,91-4,100,103,105,203).
43 Paul Fussell, in *Abroad: British Literary Traveling between the Wars*, New York and Oxford, 1980, 15-23, emphasises very strongly the desire to escape which is expressed in English writings of both the 1920s and 30s; the delights of the foreign are described with unreserved enthusiasm not only in the travel literature of these two decades, but in a variety of other genres as well. Fussell's analysis could convincingly be extended beyond the limits of works written in English, or by native inhabitants of England.
44 Jacques Derrida, 'La loi du genre/The Law of Genre', in *Glyph* 7, 1980, 176-232; p203. The account of this 'law of "do" or "do not" ' continues: 'As soon as the word "genre" is sounded, as soon as it is heard, as soon as one attempts to conceive it, a limit is drawn. And when a limit is established, norms and interdictions are not far behind: "Do not" says "genre," the word "genre," the figure, the voice, or the law of genre.'
45 p239.

ABOVE: THE SPHINX AND PYRAMIDS OF GIZA, FROM F L NORDEN'S *TRAVELS IN EGYPT AND NUBIA*, 1757; *BELOW:* THE GIZA PYRAMIDS AND THE SPHINX, FROM PART IV OF JOHANN BERNARD FISCHER VON ERLACH'S *ENTWURFF EINER HISTORISCHEN ARCHITEKTUR*, 1721

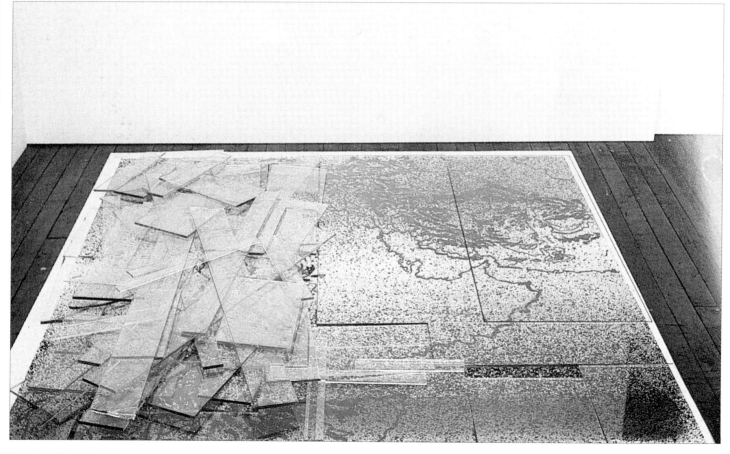

ABOVE: ANA MANDIETA, *UNTITLED (TREE OF LIFE SERIES)*, 1977, EARTH-BODY WORK WITH CLOTH, OAXACA, MEXICO; *BELOW*: JOSHUA NEUSTEIN, *MAP UNDER GLASS*, 1987

IRIT ROGOFF
The Discourse of Exile
Geographies and Representations of Identity

Any critical examination of the relation between geographical materialities and the representations of coherent identities reveals that these do not complement or construct one another in a direct or causal manner. The mere appearance of flags or of recognised national entities within identifiable boundary lines, of landscapes which invoke the attributes of national, regional or continental characteristics or the representation of specific linguistic practices does not necessarily signify a set of shared homogeneous values operating from within one shared collective identity.

While critical discourses have dealt with such inconsistencies at great length, the world of visual representations has continued to mask the possibilities for difference which exist within the locus of geographical signification. Even within such work as the series of gigantic black and white flag paintings executed by the Dutch artist Armando during the early 1980s, with all their irony and play on absence of colour as signification and on aspects of ceremony and bombast which make up the rituals of collective identities, the discourse remains one which is locked into an assumed and automatic relationship between such signs and named identities.[1]

Contrary to readings which conflate geographies and identities and link both to a historical determination of the homogeneous, collective and shared nature of cultural enterprise, the following discussion posits the strategic function of cultural displacement and dislocation and the ways in which these are pictorially constructed and signified. Focusing on the work of Ana Mendieta (Cuban/American) and Joshua Neustein (German/American) an attempt is made to look at issues of perspective (Neustein) and iconography (Mendieta), with their critical view of the positivistic logic of the sign and the temporality of sequentiality, as the main platforms on which pictorial cultural coherence has been founded. Furthermore it is argued that the disruption of such traditions through geographical and cultural exile and dislocation has opened up possibilities for the incorporation of alternatives and plural perspectival vantage points and pictorial references which forge new cultural conjunctions that are constructed out of difference and disjuncture rather than similarity and continuity.

Within the realm of visual representation the issue of materiality; of alternative modes of visually codifying specific, located and named entities is central. The vantage points from which these are established and depicted are equally central, for as Edward Said has characterised his own experience: 'My background is a series of displacements and expatriations which cannot ever be recuperated . . . the fact that I am always in and out of things, and never really of anything for very long'.[2] It is thus not only the signs and symbols of specific realms of belonging which are significant to their ability to signify but the vantage point from which they are viewed and described. Above all else, the issue these visual discourses of place and identity point to is that of positionality, the newly arrived at, oblique and circuitous ways in which the self is positioned in relation to the great traditions, be these epistemic structures, the signification of specific location and its national/cultural identification or gendered narratives and histories. I am fully aware of the radical differences between the artists I am discussing; Neustein is a first-world man and Mendieta is a third-world woman. Neustein makes art objects within the artistic paradigm of Modernism and Mendieta made ephemeral and transient works in nature out of humble materials while attempting to shift the artistic paradigm she worked in. Above all else Neustein is alive and well and working in New York, his work having opportunities to change direction and alter form, while Mendieta is dead and the production part of her artistic practice has come to a tragic and premature end. These differences however are important for the problematisation of the degrees of pluralities which exist within the visual discourse of exile and the varied forms it assumes. Hopefully the contextualisation of the discussion in the work of two such different artists will help to thematise the margins as somewhat more complex than 'other' to the centre.

It is precisely because this effort cannot be contained within conventional systems of sign interpretation that it opens up possibilities of the representation of displaced identities. If the representations of geographies as in Neustein's map-making of the world and in Mendieta's reconstruction of acculturated earth-plots do not work toward the signification of traditionally identified affiliations and locations, perhaps their resistance works towards a revised understanding of identity. The fact that these can be further differentiated by gender-related issues and practices opens up possibilities for visual discourses of gender and culture which work across one another. Traditionally, coherent cultural identity has been seen as transcending such aspects of difference as gender or language, whilst anchored in a shared participation in an overall historical narrative. Introducing these as further degrees of inherent difference with clear cultural manifestations may help to redefine positionality away from the traditional concept of rootedness within one specific and coherent given culture. How to make visible the invisible fragmentation of the subject which works against traditions of cultural coherency is the question being asked by many contemporary artists and how to do so within the inherited language of signification and therefore disrupt its supposedly simple legibility is equally the subject of much contemporary critical discussion. In a recent piece in which he attempts to frame some of the issues related to the interrogation of identities between Post-Modern and post-colonial culture, Homi Bhaba speculates that:

> It is this familiar, Post-Modernist space of the Other (in the process of identification) that develops a graphic historical and cultural specificity in the splitting of the post-colonial or migrant subject. In place of the 'I' institutionalised in the visionary, authorial ideologies of Eng Lit or the notion of 'experience' in the empiricist accounts of slave history – there emerges the challenge to see what is invisible; the look which cannot 'see me', a certain problem of the object of the gaze which constitutes a problematic 'referent' for the language of the self . . . What is transformed in the Post-Modern perspective is not simply the 'image' of the person, but an interrogation of the discursive and disciplinary place from which questions of identity are strategically and institutionally posed.[3]

Ana Mendieta – landscape as the geography of the body

I have been carrying on a dialogue between the landscape and the female body (based on my own silhouette). I believe this has been a direct result of my having been torn from my homeland (Cuba) during my adolescence . . . I am overwhelmed by the feeling of having been cast from the womb (nature). My art is the way I re-establish the bonds that tie to the universe.[4]

In a letter written in the early 1980s Ana Mendieta tells of an 'African custom which I think . . . is analogous of my work . . . The Men from the Kimberly go outside their village to seek their brides. When a man brings his new wife home, the woman brings with her a sack of earth from her homeland and every night she eats a little bit of that earth. The earth will help her make the transition between her homeland and her new home'.[5] Mendieta and her sack of earth had gone through a process of 'deterritorialisation'. Caren Kaplan describes this as 'A term for the displacement of identities, persons and meanings that is endemic to the Post-Modern world system'.[6] This is founded on Deleuze and Guattari's use of the term deterritorialisation to locate the moment of alienation and exile in language and literature. Kaplan suggests that deterritorialisation describes the effects of a radical distanciation between signifier and signified in which meanings and utterances become estranged. This defamiliarisation enables imagination, even as it produces alienation, in Deleuze and Guattari's words 'to express another potential community, to force the means for another consciousness and another sensibility'.[7]

Mendieta's actual displacements were numerous and repeated, from Cuba and her family at the age of 13 she moved to the United States, then to study at Iowa University, to life in New York City's Soho, to work in Mexico and Cuba and finally to work in a studio in Rome. These were accompanied by a series of artistic moves from a Minimal mode to an increasingly Conceptual art involving actions, objects and documentation. The changes taking place within here artistic practice were thrown into sharp relief by her increasing awareness and incorporation of the emergent discourses of cultural criticism involving gender, race and the cultural signification of certain sign-systems into her overall understanding of her art.

There is little nostalgia or illusion about the recuperation of previous cultural coherencies in any aspect of Mendieta's work. Her actual return to Cuba as an adult on working visits she had prepared for through works in the Cuban section of Miami where she made a figure-like form out of the hair of Cuban exiles in Miami collected from local hairdressing salons. This figure she attached to a local tree much used in ceremonial rituals by the immigrant population of the city. Every aspect of this complex project is inscribed with an understanding of loss, transition and emergent immigrant realities which build on but do not emulate or continue the original practices. Within this artistic project in Miami we can observe no nostalgic hankering after some semblance of either the 'real' or 'original' culture, but rather a recognition of its supposedly secondary level of existence as a displaced immigrant community to be a potent cultural reality. Of her actual return she wrote: 'I was afraid before I went there because I've been living with this obsessive thing in my mind – what if I found out it has nothing to do with me?'[8] Between these lines we can read the presence of conflicting cultural traditions and of the artist's own location of herself within entirely opposite and conflicting political and ideological systems of state Communism and Capitalist democracy. The interludes in Mexico and Rome thus assume a form of cultural mediation; Mexico being a host to many exiled Latin Americans who can relocate their preoccupation within a Spanish culture which has sustained itself continuously and has an acute and fully articulated awareness of its own heritage. Rome on the other hand is the source of the other culture which made up Ana Mendieta's world of reference, the Western tradition founded in Classical Antiquity and Roman civic practice. All of these journeys do not speak only of disruption but also of the collecting of tools, images and references which would help the work transcend the boundaries the artist wished

to dissolve. These include the various definitions of the type of work which qualifies for the category of 'art', the sites and locations which are considered credible for its display as art objects and, above all, the conventional linear histories into which this artistic practice could be slotted.

Mendieta's process of deterritorialisation has been effected through a framework of feminism, third-world cultural politics and first-world avant-garde art practices of the late 1970s and 1980s. The relation of these elements to the great traditions has gone through a series of sharp dislocations which were brought to an abrupt halt with her violent death in 1985 at the age of 36.[9] The scope of the project she had begun was enormous and can be seen as only partially completed, but transience and discontinuity are inscribed in every aspect of this project and its untimely ending does not in any way diminish or qualify its significance. Both her premature death and her declared state of exile can, in hindsight, work in a derogatory way to sentimentalise readings of her work, rather than towards a recognition of the critiques of concepts of time and space as traditional cultural values that she was working to deconstruct. Mendieta's work of the last decade of her life has been closely bound to the earth. She worked through tracing the silhouette of her body on earth, sand, tree trunks and fields in the environs of Iowa City where she had done her studies and in the Oaxaca region of Mexico and the hills near the city of Havanna, Cuba. The works themselves use a rich variety of materials including gunpowder, fire, wood, paint mixed with blood, cloth and many others. Some of these have been eased into situ with a great delicacy that works to echo the existent lines of rock or earth formations while others have been etched through blasting or set up by fire with the intention of imposing their form on the landscape through extreme contrast. Free-standing silhouettes raised high on to the skyline and set alight like the military banners of ancient armies on the march, served to light, illuminate and transform the horizon for a series of eerie moments and then collapse into small piles of ashes and charred fragments. The transient status of the works, sites abandoned to either destruction or to change according to climactic and other conditions, echoes other states of transience all linked to an earth which defines everything but cannot be adhered to in any way. They function like a contemporary production of site-specific archaeology which proceeds to play havoc with conventional notions of cultural time, of past and present and yet, in defying cultural time as a progressive sequence, they do not attempt to impose some other non-specific notion of timelessness.

The project which Mendieta embarked on could best be described through Deleuze and Guattari's parallel concept of 'reterritorialisation'. As Caren Kaplan understands this concept, its value:

> lies in the paradoxical movement between minor and major – a refusal to admit either position as final or static. The issue is positionality. In modern autobiographical discourses, for example, the self that is constructed is often construed to be evolving in a linear fashion from a stable place of origin towards a substantial present. In Post-Modern autobiographical writing such a singular linear construction of the self is often untenable or, at the very least, in tension with competing issues . . . Much of contemporary feminist theory proposes a strategy of reading and an analysis of positionality similar to Deleuze and Guattari's concept of 'becoming minor'. In working with issues of race, class and sexualities, as well as gender, feminist discourses have come to stress difference and oscillation of margin and centre in the construction of personal and political identities.[10]

Mendieta's process of reterritorialisation then is the construction of a collective history based on gender as well as on race and on cultural specificity. The artistic materials and tools that she employs in this project are: matter versus contour as the essence of a personalised geography, and place or 'site' (ie, determined by choice rather than fate) as opposed to location. In these she is working against the grain of dominant artistic traditions in her total abnegation of all forms of boundaries. To begin with the works are made predominantly out of doors and remain there except for their photographic representation thus negating the cultural boundaries in which works of art are produced and displayed – studios, galleries, museums. Generically too these works defy definition and containment within a given style or mode, since they differ from both earthworks and from pure body-art by combining the two and by playing on the tension between a performance art and a continuous slow deterioration of the pieces in nature. The works themselves are also without boundaries since there is no exact place within their sites where they either begin or end. Thus they cannot be framed or bound within conventional artistic or geographical territorialities. Their extreme materiality, sensuous, brutal, culturally and physically suggestive, plays the role of foregrounding quality, texture and substance as opposed to definition.

Lest all of this sound like an attempt at an archetypal 'feminine' artistic practice, I hasten to say that Mendieta's work cannot be summed up as a representation of the dreaded biologically essentialist 'feminine'. This is due primarily to her ability to find a balance between universality and specificity. She carved, sculpted, dug, blasted, fired and painted figures inspired by the mythological metaphors of the Great Mothers, Gaea, Hades, Mother Earth, etc in and on the many sites worked through, but their universality is purely a function of their reception by European Western traditions. For Mendieta, a rigorous student of the religions and rituals of the Spanish and Latin American cultures, predominantly the Santeria in Cuba in the Middle Ages, these have a concrete historical specificity.[11] Such a cultural and historical concreteness is in turn echoed in the ways that her work repeatedly negotiates a set of images and a set of materials with different sites. Her own vigilant insistence on concretising the experience and its representation points to the fact that our responses to specificity requires that it be within an acculturated hand's reach; a historical tradition in which we ourselves are positioned, a museum or an accessible or recognisable location. The fact that these works take place in an unknown hill in Mexico or Cuba does not make their location any less specific. Nor does their historical moment take the form of a nostalgic hankering for the primeval, the ahistorical and the timeless. The predominance of female figures in the iconography is not to do with an attempt to repopulate the world with a universal female form on which every mythical narrative and allegory can be hung, but rather that of giving concrete visual forms to lost narratives by 'siting' them. This lost, timeless quality has been projected on them by a Western historical narrative that constructs and determines place and designates time and excludes other narratives that cannot be located parallel to itself. I find Mendieta's restless travels, her constant search for sites, her insistence on named geographical locations for her works to be the most telling part of her historical reterritorialisation. Her very playfulness with regard to the transposition of culture in time and place leads to a new understanding of the strategic sense of knowledge and its deployment. Her invocation of myths, religions, symbols and materials seems to me, for all their transience and ephemerality, to stress the strategic and geographical as opposed to the temporal dimensions of human historical narratives. Geographies and their signification thus emerge not as the sites of secure and coherent identities but rather as those of disruptive interventions in the historical narratives of culture.

Mendieta's process of reterritorialisation, of constructing what Said characterises as 'a new world to rule', of making a collective gendered history rooted in a particular Latin American tradition and then consciously displaced again and again is attractive precisely because it points to future possibilities rather than to closure. In 'becoming minor', in exploring that revolutionary potential that the recognition of difference and the negation of boundaries liberates at the heart of the great traditions, Ana Mendieta confers a rich potential reworking on the condition of exile.

Joshua Neustein – mapping out strategies of dislocation
Geography (is) the eye and the light of history . . . maps enable us to contemplate at home and right before our eyes things that are furtherest away.

Johan Blaue, *Le Grande Atlas*, Amsterdam 1663[12]
Map-making as a form of decorative art belongs to the informal, pre-scientific phase of cartography. When cartographers had neither the geographical knowledge nor the cartographical skill to make accurate maps, fancy and artistry had free rein.

J Wreford Watson, 1972[13]
Joshua Neustein's recent paintings of maps plunge us directly into the midst of a major contemporary debate concerning the relation between object and subject in image-making and their foundations in epistemic structures. These paintings of maps, which abdicate neither their right to the status of art nor to their obvious association with cartography, serve as a visual discourse on a major post-structuralist polemic, namely the location of theories of cognition within the framework of ideological positions. In their very insistence on their right to live out such a duality and in their formal properties which combine a scale alien to map-making with an austerity alien to picture-making, Neustein's maps continually demand a confrontation between the conventions of both traditions and most importantly between their implications as modes of perceiving the world.

The two modes which are here juxtaposed are the tradition of scientific linear perspective and that of mapping as an artistic form. Linear perspective as thematised by Alberti was not just the process of binding the picture to vision and visual perception but also the definition of what he chose to term a picture; it was not just a surface but a plane serving as a window that assumed a human observer whose eye level and distance from that plane were the essential factor in determining its rendition. The making of the picture was therefore defined by the positioned viewer, the frame and the definition of the picture as a window through which an external viewer looks. The emergent humanist approach of the Italian Renaissance, an approach which increasingly foregrounded the new role of the spectator in relation to the picture, was carried into the pictorial world itself when Alberti insisted that all appearances of things are purely relative. Furthermore it is the human figure alone which is capable of providing the measure of whatever else the artist cares to represent.[14] The consequences of affording man (the positioned viewer) the central determining role were, to begin with, as Erwin Panofsky noted, the dissolution of any pictorial equality and the establishment of a qualitative process in which each planar direction and each object were measured in terms of their own intrinsic worth.[15] This process however had far greater implications than the provision of a fully articulated technique for the organisation of pictorial space. As Panofsky saw, the history of so-called 'scientific' linear perspective could equally be seen as the triumph of a sense of reality which is founded on a notion of objectivity and on the creation of a distance between subject and object. Similarly it could be described as a triumph of overcoming the irrational will which denies the distance between subject and object. Most importantly however the increasing refinement of linear perspective allowed for a fixing and a systematisation of external reality and for a furthering of the individual ego which controlled this process.[16] The legacy therefore is the construction of a world view which is founded in notions of objectivity and rationality and the recognition of a central beholder who possesses these qualities and reconstructs the world according to their rationale. Within such a reconstruction there is little room for a plurality of narratives or view points or the recognition of realities constructed through the binary opposition of difference, being enacted out. Furthermore the logocentric reconstruction of space cannot be played out without the colonisation and appropriation of that space and its insistent anchoring to the beholder.

The mapped view on the other hand suggests an encompassing of the world, without, however, asserting the order based on human measure that is offered by perspective pictures.[17] At its centre we find the astonishing concept of the unpositioned viewer and its essence insists on the plausibility of the view from nowhere. This dispensing with the positioned viewer who upholds an entire logocentric construct therefore allows for a pluralism which transforms the mapped view into a variety of modes such as collective, national or individual narratives. For all of its expression through easily recognised conventions of knowledge the mapped view in picture-making nevertheless recognises that 'the geography of the land is, in the last resort, the geography of the mind'.[18] Joshua Neustein's maps can therefore be located within a new discursive space which is formed out of the tensions between these two positions. They encompass within themselves an entire range of contemporary dialectical tensions and binary opposites which form a challenge to the traditional concepts of epistemology. To my mind these maps can be read as the formulation of a theory of cognition which is in itself imbued with doubt concerning both the empirical basis and the spirit of logical positivism on which any theory of cognition must be founded. Instead we find presences, easily read cartographic texts, which in their very corporeality signal fundamental absences and challenge the conventions of the systematised relations between perception, verification and representation. Thus for all of their cartographic detail these maps set up a strategic resistance to being read empirically and challenge language as a way of understanding texts. Within their space the domination of a fixed position is abdicated while, simultaneously, normative codes of empirical verification are constantly spun around in an interior debate on the nature and validity of representation.

If these images are not maps according to the traditional European conventions of cartography as picture-making, what are they? Increasingly they strike me as being meditations on issues of boundaries and definitions and the interactions between the two. These have their genesis in the mid-1970s in a series of works done in Israel such as *Territorial Imperative* and *Sculpture for a Moving Border* which form a speculative visual discourse on the illusory nature of the stability of borders. In the first instance these works have to be viewed as site specific as they provide a reflection on a particular socio-political situation in which borders serve a supreme function. The geographically limited state of Israel encompasses within its recent history a wide range of shifting borders: ones designated by international mandates and others resulting from armed combats, green lines which signal memories and intentions and heavily fortified ones which protect all the previously specified borders contained within them. Historically too, the narrow strip of land which is modern Israel is traversed with the ancient borders of numerous conquests and settlements, each of which defined its achievements by establishing its boundaries. Within the perpetually volatile political situation and amidst the considerable internal debates on the validity of what is being defined by the different sets of boundary lines which signify the different sets of political and ideological beliefs, clearly distinguishable borders have become a parallel to the achievement of coherent identities. The proximity between how boundaries both determine and undo identity have been described by Edward Said:

> Just beyond the perimeter of what nationalism constructs as the nation, at the frontier separating 'us' from what is alien, is the perilous territory of not-belonging. This is where in primitive times people were banished and in the modern era, immense aggregates of humanity loiter as refugees and displaced persons.[19]

While not wanting to privilege biography as an analytical tool, one must nevertheless recognise the degree that correlations between moving borders and shifting identities, play a consistently central role in Neustein's work. The maps, he says, 'began in 1980 with the intention of mapping out the whole world as a form of 21st-century landscape.'[20] To begin with they seemed to be charting out a geography of the heart, since many of them had at their centre the city of Danzig, Neustein's birthplace and the point from which he set out to, what he calls, 'refugee' throughout the world. This city of Danzig which he set up as a kind of medieval *coeur du mond* is placed within vast expanses of unspecified and undifferentiated European and Asian terrain. This process of non-empirical location is further complicated when we begin to ask which Danzig is being referred to? Free city of the German Reich between 1872 and 1918, free international city of the Weimar Republic populated by Germans but located in Poland, or is it Gdansk, birthplace of the Polish Solidarity movement of the 1980s? What emerges then are parallels between moving borders and shifting identities which cannot be tied down to national or cultural entities and cannot be signified by conventions of cartography. Instead declarations of subjectivity replace pretences of objectivity within these maps, defying the traditional view of cartography as the manifestation of increasing human control over the world through knowledge, skill and articulation. These grand schemes are supplanted with narratives of memory, of dislocation and incoherence in which the small recognised spot which is Danzig is set bobbing about in the vast dark expanses of its continent, its geographical location affording it neither continuity nor coherent identity. So much for the positioned viewer and for the vast bodies of rational knowledge at his disposal to construct and chart coherent narratives of development and continuity.

In the later maps of the past two or three years the continents have been separated into clearly defined autonomous entities. Their interiors, however, are unmarked and unspecified by the signification conventions of other epistemic structures such as national entities or geographic terrains. Executed in steel-grey tones with severe black outlines and occasionally enlivened by metallic hues and pearlised surfaces, these works invoke a playful legitimation and attestation to their seriousness of purpose through their austere monochromatism. Equally their surfaces are marked by a seemingly detailed concern with topography and terrain which are indicated by formations of fine black powder to denote mountains, rivers, etc. It is only after considerable scrutiny that the viewer realises that these details do not in fact indicate any reflected realities of the supposedly mapped surface. Instead they formulate an illusionary visual language of cartographic credibility and proceed to deploy it for purposes of critical obfuscation rather than enlightened clarification. In the first instance it is the fact that these images do not agree to function in the way in which we expect them to function that alerts us to their real discourse, a discourse which stand in for bodies of knowledge and which perpetuate assumptions about verifiable realities.

If these textural and tonal suggestions with which Neustein covers his maps are not in fact the significations of geographical realities, what are they instead? Perhaps they refer to atmospheric qualities, contributing a dimension of individuation to these continents whose interiors are so undefined. It is these endless playful dualities constantly enacted out on the surface of the work, which make their close observation so rewarding; the interiors are fluid, open to limitless redefinition, suspending all the rules and conventions of transmitting knowledge visually, while substituting some nebulous notion of atmosphere for all the unnamed entities which we always knew to fill those boundaries. But what kind of atmosphere is this? Is it the banality of continental stereotypes or is it the signification of genuine stratospheric hazes and cloud membranes which serve to further obscure that which we are so hard at work trying to decypher? Neustein himself says of maps that 'they have elusive defining properties and a certain virtue of indiscernibility', alerting us, the viewers, that strategic plays with the very concept of decoding are being set up before us.[21] Instead we are presented with large-scale outlines of continents, executed with painterly bravura and whose very corporeality emphasises all that is absent – the impossibility of rendering that which constructs them from the inside in the form of myriad coexisting pluralities. Like Michel Foucault in 'This is Not a Pipe', Neustein too makes claims that visual language is discourse, not reality and that the way in which one alludes to the other within late-Modernism has to be carefully rethought, particularly when it is harnessed to images which are supposedly self-evident conveyors of objective information.

Of late, Neustein's maps have acquired a further layer of objects, most of them *objet trouvées* which are superimposed over the painted surfaces of the maps. The nature of the objects themselves seem extremely humble to begin with – metal cones, sticks and grids, geometric shards of glass, etc. Their juxtaposition with the maps engages however two very different levels of language, neither of which is usually subject to any form of critical interrogation. Does *Grid over Europe*, 1987, allude to some aspect of the continent's present state or is it another atmospheric component that combines with the lines and textures to enhance the work's realism and corporeality? Rather than these they seem to be the signification of another discourse, one that is parallel to the usage of cartographic images as purveyors of absolute knowledge and in which these maps-cum-art-objects are in turn viewed as commodities. The artist himself says of them that, 'The platforms, objects of industry, that are superimposed over the maps are not so much planar dimensional extensions of the map matrix as they are scrutinies, discrete annunciations of commodified products.'

In other discourses, such as those of mass-media advertising, the combination of maps and markers of industrial production have undergone an almost complete process of commodity fetishisation and have become the signification of distances traversed by modern means of transportation or of markets conquered and goods distributed over vast global expanses. For Neustein however, they serve to enhance the liberating potential of the mapped view which does not serve specific and easily identified vested interests. If anything it is the cones, grids, geometric poles and cut glass that locate the work increasingly in the sphere of art, since they also carry an entire range of meanings related to avant-garde art's break towards simplified form and abstraction as well as its use of industrial and media found objects. The hallmarks of the early, so-called 'heroic' years of Modernism and the hallmarks of epistemic structures of knowledge here combine forces to call attention to their status as language, as form of utterance behind which stand vast areas of meaning. Futhermore they help engage another dimension, that of time, into the work's sphere since these are significations of both certain, unspecified continuity, of histories and legends, languages, and images which together make up the global culture. Superimposed on these are the archaeological artifacts of industry and the fallen debris of space satellites. The very impossibility of their coexistence within separate time frames, maps them as eternal and unchanged except by the occasional disaster of nature or conquest by man while industrial objects reflecting only the 'present' of their production, is strongly protested in these works. The very counter-epistemic nature of Neustein's maps, the unspecified interiors of the outlined continents, provide conceptual refutation of such convenient assumptions. Similarly the industrial debris is mobilised to denote the limitation of the visual base of cognition as in *Map Under Glass*, 1987, in which the numerous shards of transparent glass piled over half of the map serve as the very opposite of the glassed surface of a framed work which protects it and facilitates its viewing. At the same time as it obfuscates the image, the glass surface, surmounted on a set of legs and assuming the form of a low table, introduces a whole range of puns concerning 'coffee-table art' and other ways in which real presences have been packaged as decorative commodities. The transformation of the maps and industrial debris from easily decoded conventions to strategic interrogations of the way in which processes are inevitably imbued with meaning and loaded with ideological positions have here been achieved by their reformulation as art. Not however in the classic sense of early Modernism which serves to undermine the holy status of art but by engaging in the contemporary issues of the discourse on representation and the validity and legitimacy of images as conveyors of meanings. The strategies of dislodging and dislocating which Joshua Neustein embarks on in these works are not determined by biographical narratives, although they are surely informed by them, but by a Modernist concept of engaged art which is invisibly linked with other concurrent discourses being debated within the public sphere. Their very ambition in combining several modes of signification within a discussion of the validity of representation and the codification of the epistemic foundations of knowledge lends them an aura of remarkable optimism. What Gramsci had termed 'the pessimism of the intellect which is countered by the optimism of the will' is here played out via a highly individualised rewriting of the assumptions of both knowledge, on the one hand, and memory, on the other. The mapped view, previously the stronghold of the unpositioned viewer, is expanded to encompass limitless plurality of which difference is conceptually constituted.

Notes

Part of this text appeared in the exhibition catalogue *Joshua Neustein*, Exit Art, New York, 1987. I would like to thank Exit Art's director, Jeannette Ingberman, for inviting me to contribute the text and for making great editorial efforts on its behalf.

1 Armando's flags are reproduced in the catalogues for *Documenta VII*, Kassel, 1983, Vol I, p 48.
2 Edward Said in an interview with Imre Salusinsky (ed) *Criticism in Society*, pp 122-148.
3 Homi K Bhaba, 'Interrogating Identity' in *Identity – The Real Me*, ICA Documents 6, London, 1987, p 5.
4 Ana Mendieta, unpublished statement quoted in *Ana Mendieta – A Retrospective* (Exhibition Catalogue), New Museum of Contemporary Art, New York, 1987, p 10.
5 *ibid*, p 31.
6 Caren Kaplan, 'Deterritorialization – The Rewriting of Home and Exile in Western Feminist Discourse' in *Cultural Critique* Vol II, 1985, pp 187-198.
7 Gilles Deleuze and Felix Guattari, 'What is a Minor Literature' in *Kafka – Towards a Minor Literature*, trans Dana Polan, Minnesota, 1986, p 17. Quoted by Kaplan, *op cit*, p 188.
8 Ana Mendieta, *op cit*, p 33.
9 Mendieta died in circumstances which have not been clearly determined, her husband the artist Carl Andre was acquitted of the accusation of causing her death.
10 Kaplan, *op cit*, p 189.
11 *Ana Mendieta*, *op cit*, p 28.
12 Quoted by Svetlana Alpers, *The Art of Describing*, Chicago, 1983, p 159.
13 From an unpublished lecture entitled 'Mental Distance in Geography: Its Identification and Representation' given at the 22nd International Geographical Congress in Montreal 1972 and quoted by Alpers, *op cit*, p 126.
14 John White, *The Birth and Rebirth of Pictorial Space*, London, 2nd ed 1967, p 122.
15 Erwin Panofsky, 'Pespective as Symbolic Form' in *Aufsatze zu Grundfragen der Kunstwissenschaft*, Berlin, 1964, p 101.
16 *ibid*, p 123.
17 This argument is taken from Svetlana Alpers extensive discussion of 17th-century Dutch painting, 'The Mapping Impulse in Dutch Painting' in Alpers, *op cit*, pp 72-119.
18 J Wreford Watson, *op cit*, Alpers, p 125.
19 Edward Said, 'The Mind of Winter – Reflections on Life in Exile' in *Harpers* Vol 269, No 1612 SE 1984, p 51.
20 The artist's diary, August 26 1987.
21 *ibid*, September 3 1987.

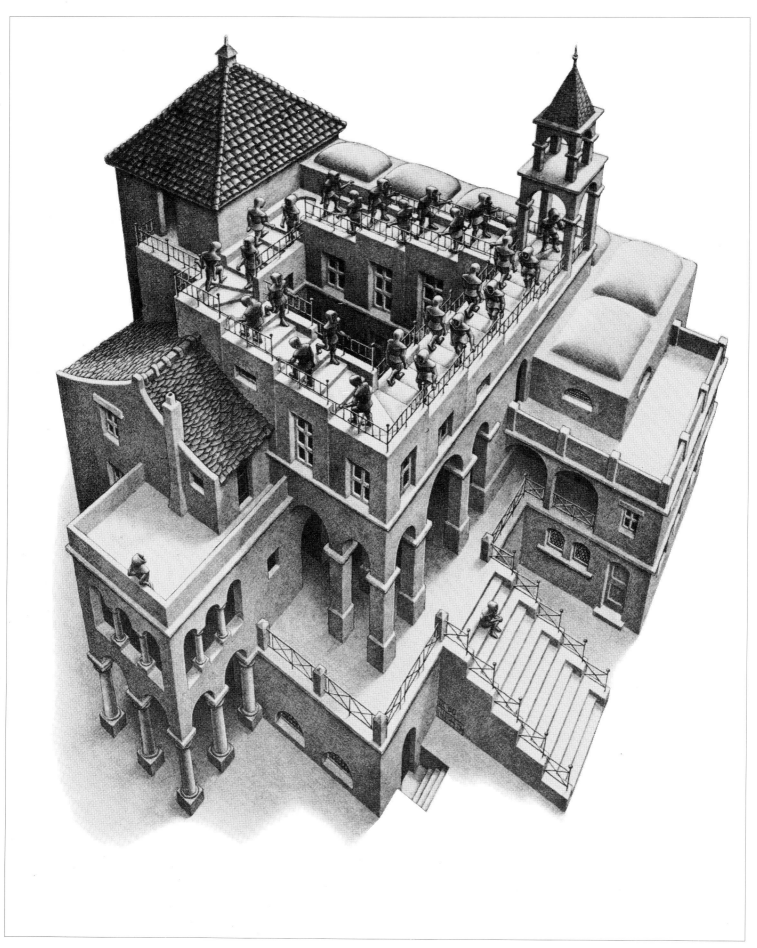

M C ESCHER, *ASCENDING AND DESCENDING*, 1960, LITHOGRAPH

DAVID WOOD
Escher and Calvino: Thinking Eccentrically about Time

Thinking eccentrically about time

Whether time is thought of as objective ('out there') or subjective ('in us'), the commonest form of naivety is to suppose that its structures are exhausted by simple, serial succession. No one with a memory, or a capacity for planning ahead could ever be content with that. And no musicians deploying complex patterns of rhythmic and melodic repetition could begin to find it satisfying. Far more rewarding is the exploration of time as complexly structured or constituted, a project which can cut across questions of subjectivity or objectivity.

All art, whether kinetic in its performance (music, drama, opera) or requiring temporal synthesis in our experience of it (painting, literature, sculpture, architecture) is essentially bound with questions of temporal articulation. Philosophers, for whom time has been one of the deepest mysteries, have on the whole been strangely unadventurous in their thinking on these matters. There are exceptions, however, and Nietzsche, Husserl and Heidegger are some of the obvious names to mention.

Committed as philosophy has been to legislating for the production and reproduction of identity, and to theories of representation and signification that serve these functions, time has usually been seen either as a dutiful servant underpinning identity through repetitive succession, or as the bringer of death, destruction or dispersion. In attempting to bring out the creative and productive role of time, philosophy is pushed to its limits, and can best venture further on the rafts of art and literature.[1]

Moving outwards from philosophy it is possible to distinguish five different levels of the productive constitution of time:[2]

1. as taking place in some sort of purified experience. Here we would situate a phenomenological account of time such as is provided by Husserl's theory of inner-time consciousness.
2. as constituted in or through human existence. Heidegger's account of our being-in-the-world – a central dimension to which is the importance of human finitude – (being-towards-death and the structure of resoluteness) provides the obvious model.
3. as constituted in and through historically specific human practices. We could think here of the highly structured time (at every level from the day to the year) of the farmer (agricultural time), or of the institutional time described by Foucault (disciplinary time) – the time of the time-table.
4. as constituted via the bound signification of narrative.
5. as constituted via processes of unbound signification.

As suggested above, it is in art and literature that the most fertile examples of the more complex structures are found, and this will be illustrated through some of the graphic work of Escher and some of the writing of Calvino. The focus will be on the implications of the last two of the above levels, but first a word about the others.

These levels each pick out distinguishable shapes of a gradually more complex inter-twining of language and time. This interweaving is not however something that befalls an otherwise clear distinction between signification and the temporal. (The power of Derrida's *différance*[3] rests on their fusion at the most fundamental level.) And it can be argued that neither time-consciousness nor the temporality of human existence are entirely pre-linguistic, but would contain the seeds and sproutings respectively of linguistic signification.[4]

Foucault's discussion of institutional time is of a time that subjects bodies to routines of daily life via grids and time-tables. Time is complexly constituted as a set of successive meanings by the imposition of a spatialising grid. By 'spatialising' I mean that the order of the day is best understood as following out the consequences of a written timetable in which the future is predicated on the past, in which the structure of the evening is to be found at the bottom of the time-sheet.

Signs here are in operation, but in the most rigidly controlled way, ordered according to numerical succession and to conventions of grid representation. An infinite complexity (of division and sub-division) is possible, and daily, weekly, monthly, yearly cycles introduce a nestedness of succession not found in simple serial time. But the role of signification is (in principle) strictly limited.

In *narrative*, matters are different. They are also essentially problematic, because quite what counts as a narrative is itself a theoretical issue. Here narrative is to be construed, minimally, as committed to a representation of a productive continuity of action in time. This is not meant to be infinitely elastic. Nor is it meant to resolve the questions that these terms – representation, productive, continuity, action and time – each pose. Together they spell out what I mean by the 'bound' signification of narrative. *Bound signification* involves an articulation of signs bound to an ulterior organising pattern of representation. The most obvious example of that would be a plot. Now it may be that many, or most, or all emplotments are themselves vehicles for the enactment of deeper structures. The structural analysis of narrative found in Lévi-Strauss' account of myth, or Barthes' essay of that name,[5] finds, in effect, the working out of logical formulae, and values like productivity (comes to something, says something) and continuity, arguably involve some primitive commitment to the preservation and/or restitution of identity. And it might perhaps be useful to so characterise the basic commitment of the idea of productivity in our general characterisation.

The inter-twining of the structure of time with that of narrative is both rich and subtle. For Ricoeur, the two are in the end difficult to separate, and in this respect, Ricoeur[6] is endorsing the original suggestion that there may be an intimate connection between time and signification. We are now in a position – with the help of Escher and Calvino – to pose a question which can perhaps be posed more easily than answered. It is this: Is there not in what has been said so far, a tacit limitation to the processes of signification that are allowed to structure time? For all the ways in which narrative gives depth and intelligibility to our understanding of time, is it not still restricted to understanding signification in an essentially representational way? And what alternative possibilities for thinking eccentrically about time might there be? With this question we arrive at our final category: time as constituted via processes of unbound signification.

Before reading Escher and Calvino this category might be thought to be guarded by a question mark. Now, I think, an exclamation mark must be added.

Escher: time and representation

Describing his development as an artist, Escher confesses his early obsession with the perfection of his graphic techniques. This involves control over one's tools, 'above all', he declares, 'one's own two hands.' He later describes this as 'a state of self-delusion', shattered by 'a moment when it seemed as though scales fell from my eyes.' The movement is not merely from hands to eyes, but from scaled to unscaled eyes. Escher reworks the visual equivalent of Nietzsche's 'ears behind ears'. 'Ideas,' as he put it, 'came into my mind, quite unrelated to graphic art'. And yet the accompanying:

> desire . . . to communicate [these ideas] to other people . . . could not be achieved through words, for these thoughts were not literary ones but mental images of a kind that can only be made comprehensible to others by presenting them as visual images.

This is surely unpromising. As we approach Escher, he seems to be walking past us rather than towards us. We have suggested possibilities of signification beyond representation, pointing perhaps to a 'poetics of time', and yet Escher goes out of his way to say how words cannot capture his deepest insights.

Indeed this inadequacy of language renders precarious the very 'introduction' in which these words appear.[7] Most curiously, given that their success in aiding our understanding his images would constitute a paradox of self-reference not entirely alien to the structure of some of his graphic pieces, we might come to doubt at a deeper level whether words were so poor.

Perhaps predictably, Escher notices this end and, in this very same introduction, confesses:

> reading over [my remarks] about the particular representational quality of my prints, I feel it may be rather illogical to devote so many words to it . . . however . . . most people find it easier to arrive at any understanding of an image by the roundabout method of letter symbols than by the direct route.

Linguistic mediation, he is claiming, is merely a pedagogical necessity. What about visual images? Are they any different? Escher says he is trying to communicate what he revealingly calls 'a specific *line* of thought'. He writes:

> The ideas basic to [these reproductions] bear witness to my amazement and wonder at the laws of nature [*elsewhere*: 'the enigmas that surround us'] which operate in the world around us.
> He who wonders discovers that this is itself a wonder.

But if language is inadequate, why does he think visual representation can capture these 'ideas'? Again, he confesses that strictly, they cannot.

> A mental image is something completely different from a visual image and however much one exerts oneself, one can never manage to capture the fullness of that perfection which hovers in the mind, and which one thinks of, quite falsely, as something that is 'seen'.

Eventually he says:

> I manage to cast my lovely dream in the defective visual mould of a detailed conceptual sketch.

Escher's difficulty is not new. Philosophers have usually expressed the problem the other way round. Confronted with how we can have an idea of a triangle, which was not itself isosceles, or right-angled or scalene . . ., Kant invented the idea of a transcendental *scheme*, which would mediate between sensory specificity and the idea. Escher is, as it were, describing his grasp of a schema, and his puzzlement over how to represent it. Kant explains this by saying that such schemata *exist only in thought*.

Time forces a certain foreshortening of the argument, but there is something of an analogy between the *ideas* that Escher is talking about, and what, after Kant, could be called transcendental schemata.

Kant, let us recall, distinguishes between the schema of *a sensible* concept (dog, triangle), by which concepts are connected to images, and the schema of a pure concept of understanding, ie, the categories (of substance, cause, possibility, modality etc). These schemata Kant calls '*a priori* determinations of time in accordance with rules'.[8] Now Kant admits that '[the application of] . . . this schematism of our

understanding . . . is an art concealed in the depths of the human soul, whose real modes of activity nature is hardly likely ever to allow us to discover, and to have open to our gaze.' We may wonder whether this opening to the gaze is not what Escher is describing when, he says, the scales fell from his eyes, or whether Kant's remarks are not a salutary warning against trying to *use* the idea of a schema to illuminate anything.

There is the further difficulty that Kant's account would seem to take us back to the first pre-linguistic level of the constitution of time associated with Husserl and phenomenology.

Is Escher not a false trail?

Consider the series of Escher's lithographs that includes *Waterfall, Ascending and Descending, Three Spheres, House of Stairs,* and perhaps *Belvedere*. Each has to be understood both in relation to time, and as interfering in productive ways with the rules of representation. And it is helpful rather than an artificial introduction to think of our interpretation of complex wholes as a *synthesis*. In the case of these drawings, in which we are presented with lines, steps, routes for the eye to follow, such synthesis not only *takes* time, but involves an imaginative traversal of a path. It involves a synthesis close to that suggested in a narrative. We imagine the prisoner carrying on walking up and up and up, and yet going round and round, *not* getting any higher. Our experience will not gel. There is a break between local success (taking each step) and global failure. It doesn't add up. It is as if we are supplying an *a priori* rule of synthesis and finding it unravelling behind us.

If we recall Escher's remarks about visual images being inadequate to his ideas, it seems perhaps that it is not for the obvious Kantian reasons that his ideas are too pure for any particular image to capture, but that they are not ideas such as could provide a rule for a representation, or even a properly ordered unfolding of a representation. Here representation functions curiously as a way of showing something about the relation between representation and what transcends it. Escher is using representation to point beyond itself. In this is prefigured not just the wider possibilities of the language that he claimed inadequate, but a mode of signification not immediately attached to the real, not reducible to representation. Escher does for drawing what Calvino does for language.

This claim about Escher can perhaps be further clarified. What is the relation between one step and the next in *Ascending and Descending*? It is surely not one of mere proximity, but of signification. The surrounding lines mean 'this step is going up'. And the succession of steps mean 'these steps are going up'. And yet reflection soon tells us, these steps *cannot* be going up. A formal principle intervenes: we cannot keep going up and returning to the very same place. Our belief in simple succession is shattered. It is not merely (which we know) that a series of steps can constitute an entirely different level of Being from that of its elements – compare a tune to a note. But what is generated (in this case) is a whole (a circle) which belies the very principle (going up) being used to generate the series.

If we were to extract a principle from this, it would be that local temporal intelligibility, together with intelligible transitions between one such locus and the next, may not add up to an intelligible whole, even if it is possible to produce an intelligible representation of that whole. It is perhaps a sign of the relative neutrality of art in this respect, and the continued need for philosophy that it itself does not judge the status of such representations. On the traditional view, we would be warned against the dangers of representation, which can make seem plausible what is not. Rational assessment tells us that things cannot be the way they seem. But suppose the *real* were not itself entirely free from representation? If one took the horizontal structure of human action (including goals, conditions of action, networks of possibility) always to supply a representational dimension to every action, then a sequence of such actions could be envisaged in which the intelligibility of the whole rested on the finite horizons of each step. A pessimist might suppose, for example, that the historical pursuit of truth, freedom or happiness had just that structure, that the enthusiastic perpetuation of the series rests on amnesia about the past. If Escher were thought to have supplied a model for that, we would no longer be talking about the gap between representation and reality, but the non-linear structure of 'real' time. The gap between part and whole also needs further development. Whether one thinks in terms of horizons, or local rationalities, what is being proposed takes a different shape looked at from the other end. For if there is some sort of rule governing the whole series (eg 'walking/flowing up but not getting any higher') this rule would not be embodied in the *elements* of the series. In other words, and to generalise, the intelligibility of temporal sequences does not require that the same structures be repeated at different levels, and indeed may require the opposite.

The direct implication of this is to counsel against the misguided attempts to subject the temporal organisation of human behaviour to a single principle (such as goal-directedness). It may even be more efficient to allow the temporally linked units of such behaviour to retain a rule-governed opacity.

If a first reflection on the set of Escher's lithographs selected here suggests the dangerous power of representation to suggest forms of coherence that could not be realised, subsequent thoughts suggest that when we are dealing with the real as temporally constituted, the very distinction between representation and reality may be the proper subject of our doubts. This is not to invite fuzzy talk, but to suggest the organised interarticulation of representation and reality.

Calvino: the time of desire

We have used Escher very selectively as a springboard for reflection. While there is no question of trying to make generalisations about art (or anything else) from such a small base, more light might be cast on this dim but fertile area by explaining another example from a quite different genre: Italo Calvino's *If on a Winter's Night a Traveller*, a book which I must admit I have not even finished. I have read it three times from cover to cover, I have read the blurb on the back, but I am not done with it. This interim report might perhaps begin with an observation from the book's cover, that 'in its course a whole shelf of novels are begun and – for reasons at the time entirely reasonable – never finished.' For here we have the inkling of a connection with Escher, all of whose connections are, at the time, *reasonable*, but ...

The aim of this analysis will be to draw out the implications of the basic moves by which the book is constructed for thinking eccentrically about time. It will be argued that it is Calvino's relatively unbound use of signification that plays the major role. It will be further claimed that these moves have implications beyond the book.

It will have escaped no-one, however, that Calvino is not content to organise the book in an odd way, from which we can construct certain possibilities of thinking about time. There are also numerous theoretical claims about time scattered throughout the book. We have not long started the book when we read that:

> Long novels written today are perhaps a contradiction: the dimension of time has been shattered, we cannot love or think except in fragments of time each of which goes off along its own trajectory and immediately disappears. We can rediscover the continuity of time only in the novels of that period when time no longer seemed stopped and did not yet seem to have exploded, a period that lasted no more than a hundred years.

And yet even in this remark we meet the difficulty that will confront every attempt to distill a thesis about time from the utterances made within the book – there is no privileged voice to rely on. And even if there were, these remarks, as so many, cannot be unambiguously attributed to the author, as they are bound up with the author's reporting of the thoughts of his reader. And perhaps the necessary confusion of voices is one of the themes of the book.

There are however ways in which it makes sense to attribute positions to Calvino, namely by interpreting the way he organises the remarks his characters make. And it is in this way that a discussion of the themes of the book as well as of its organisational structure can be developed. For it is in both respects that it opens up a signifying time. The impact of the book may result from the paralleling of these two.

At the thematic level the most persistent and general theme is desire, we might almost call it metaphysical desire. One can find in Lacan a thesis about the relation between language (the symbolic) and desire, which argues that language constitutes a radical *break* with a pre-symbolic relation to the world. And through all its capacities for references, for description, language cannot restore that original unbroken relation. We can give the name 'desire' to that impossible quest to re-establish, through language, a pre-linguistic unity with the world. A satisfactory story (a pleasing narrative) would be one which produced and sustained the illusion that, at the level of the meaningful organisation of time, the word and the world were one. Calvino makes thematic the desire that underlies this into a theme and ruthlessly exposes it in a number of ways. That such desire is constitutive of reading is made abundantly clear by the long contradictory series of ideal books described by Ludmilla:

> I prefer novels that bring me immediately into a world where everything is precise, concrete, specific ...
>
> The book I would like to read now is a novel that gives the sense of living through an upheaval that still has no name ...
>
> The novel I would most like to read at this moment should have as its driving force only the desire to narrate, to pile stories upon stories without trying to impose a philosophy of life on you, simply allowing you to observe its own growth ... Each novel, each desire, offers another version of some re-established contact with the world, a contact that would dispense with signs. The first is precise, concrete, specific; the second, a living through; the third; a natural narrative development.

And yet this book is not only made of unfinished books, but makes incompleteness thematic. In the diary of Silas Flannery, we read:

> On the wall facing my desk hangs a poster someone gave me. The dog Snoopy is sitting on a typewriter, and in the cartoon, you read the sentence, 'It was a dark and stormy night ...' and the impersonality of that *incipit* seems to open the passage from one world to the other, from the time and space of here and now to the time and space of the written word; I feel the thrill of a beginning that can be followed by multiple developments, inexhaustibly ...

But the spell is always broken . . .

> The facility of the entrance into another world is an illusion: you start writing in a rush, anticipating the happiness of a future reading, and the void yawns on the white page.

And if this is the writer's experience, it only mirrors the experience of the reader, who either finds unprinted blank pages signalling a discontinuity in the story he's reading, or is interrupted in his reading early on etc.

> The Reader is beset by mysterious coincidences. He told me that for some time, and for the most disparate reasons, he has had to interrupt his reading of novels after a few pages.

Is he bored? No.

> I am forced to stop reading just when they become most gripping [... and] when I think I am reopening the book I began, I find a completely different book before me.

We are being offered a symmetrical necessity of incompleteness, on the part of reader and writer.

Language makes promises, opens up desires which it cannot fulfil. To begin reading or writing another book is for hope, or desire, to spring eternal. If this is right, then the status of cimmerian books is unclear. Professor Uzzi-Tuzzi explains[9] that 'Cimmerian books are all unfinished because they continue beyond – in the other language, in the silent language to which all the words we believe we read refer.'

There are at least three different forms by which Desire determines our reading (or writing). We aim for completeness (and books respond by breaking off), we want coherence (but are met by fragmentation), we want reliable beginnings (and yet the first page already refers to a pre-existing world.

If we could generate a *thesis* from this, it would be that desire structures time through language in the form of unending and unavoidable repetitions of impossible projects, or projects possible only by the silencing of doubts about the aesthetic illusion, doubts which we are now too knowing to be able to silence.

This suggests apropos of Kant's account of the *a priori* rules of temporalisation, that these rules are not neutral with regard to the constitution of the real, but insofar as they embody such ideals as unity, identity, permanence, etc, they reflect the equally necessary workings of desire.

If we have been ruthlessly reductive about the thematic content of the book, we must be equally bold in considering the lessons its structure teaches us about the possibilities of time. I will not dwell on the multiplicity of levels, and the reflexive references between them, from author to reader, from reader 1 to reader 2, from author n to character, etc. Nor shall I comment on the structural organisation of a sequence of secondary stories around a base story. I want simply to pick out the most important and obvious device being exploited and comment on its implications for the structuring of time.

Novels can be inserted into other novels by the strategem proposed by Marana to the Sultan, 'the rudimentary expedient of . . . a character in the first novel opens a book and starts reading'. This of course is the iterative mechanism underlying the whole book. How should we describe what occurs here? From one moment to the next we can be moved, perfectly reasonably out of one story into another. The 'coherence' of this book is the most powerful testimony to the power of such a device to generate a kind of continuity out of a radical discontinuity. Through language we seem to be able to transcend any important connection between meaningful continuity and natural causality. Or rather, the causal links are reduced to an absolute minimum. The relative autonomy of signs from any natural reference allows there to be signs of signs, and hence stories about stories, and it is this that generates unbound signification. No more is the sequence tied to some underlying order or grid. The openings provided by language to different orders or levels of language, bestows on these simple linguistic devices the power to determine what does and does not count as 'continuity'. Setting can be radically shifted, characters entirely changed, 'worlds' annihilated and created. Still, the book continues.

After reading Calvino, the question one can no longer ask, and yet can hardly avoid asking – is whether what we learn applies only to the extremes of Post-Modern novels, or whether it has a wider significance. We claim that Calvino has shown us – writ large – the extraordinary scope that the self-referential powers of language give to our everyday construction of significant continuity in time. When I first read the remark of the seventh reader (near the end of the book)

that 'the ultimate meaning to which all stories refer has two faces: the continuity of life, the inevitability of death', I took it to be just another comforting reduction. But is it not precisely, if surprisingly, the continuity of life that gets reaffirmed here?

> the man with the suitcase, lost on the railway system, is the man with a past he imagines he can break free from. He can make these radical breaks but it doesn't work:
>
> > All I did was to accumulate past after past behind me, multiplying the pasts.

Or again:

> The past is like a tapeworm, constantly growing, which I carry curled up inside me.

Here the continuity supplied by the structure of nested quotation appears as a *necessity* rather than a possibility of freedom. To make a break with one's past is to become the person who has, as it were, put that past in brackets. Every discontinuity can be recuperated. But what if the continuity that we call the self were to rest on nothing more than the mechanisms of quotation that sustain this book?

Heidegger talks of a work of art as opening a world. This book too can be treated as opening a world – not just a literary one, but one in which language and existence are inter-twined. Our author of course is preparing us all the way through for just such a parallel. And in comparing reading to making love he seems to confirm Heideggerean usage: 'within both [reading and love-making] times and spaces open, different from measurable time and space.'

What is this openness? It is the effect of allowing unbound signification to contribute to the intelligibility of our lives. If this interestingly names at least something of the structuring of the text, how does it relate to the theme of Desire?

Desire has as its proper object what could be called the transcendental signified – that which is 'beyond language'. For the referential and descriptive functions of language suggest a possibility – of direct contact with the real – that language can never achieve, and that every more subtle or persistent use of language necessarily frustrates. What philosophers have thought of as identity through time was described by Nietzsche as a grammatical fiction. At one level Calvino seems to be confirming this, but it is not just the word 'I' that does the work, but the capacity of such linguistic operations as quotation, self-reference, story embeddings, to forge unbound continuities.

It might be thought that art works best when it conceals its artifice, and that conventions that drew attention to themselves would cease to function, would self-destruct. Both Escher and Calvino risked marginality by dramatically putting the conventions into play, rather than just using them. This much is received wisdom. What has been suggested here however is that this very displacement of convention releases us into whole new ways of thinking about time, in which representations of a sequence are folded back to constitute the sequence itself: thinking eccentrically.

Notes

1 I do not here specifically discuss music, despite its obvious relevance. And in some ways the challenges to traditional harmonic structures in 20th-century music far more explicitly illustrate the complexity of temporal patterning, than, say the work of Escher or Calvino. But is there not a crucial difference between musical and other 'signs'? Musical notes tend towards a kind of signifying purity or one-dimensionality, whereas the representational and/or symbolic dimensions of visual and literary signs set up a whole array of harmonic resonances that always multiply and complicate the chains of signification.

2 See part 4 of my *The Deconstruction of Time*, Humanities Press, Atlantic Highlands, 1988.

3 Wood and Bernasconi (eds), *Derrida and Differance*, Northwestern, Chicago, 1988, focuses on this 'concept'.

4 See the lengthy discussion of Husserl and Heidegger in parts 2 and 3 of *The Deconstruction of Time*, *op cit*.

5 Roland Barthes, 'Introduction to The Structural Analysis of Narrative' in *Communication* 8, 1966.

6 Ricoeur, *Time and Narrative*, trans McLaughlin and Pellauer, University of Chicago, Chicago, 1984.

7 See the 'Introduction' to Escher's graphic work, in Dutch, 1960.

8 *Critique of Pure Reason*, A145. Kant summarises these rules as relating ' ... 1 to the time-series, the time-content, the time-order, and lastly to the scope of time in respect of all possible objects.'

9 p 60.

10 See Heidegger's *Origin of the Work of Art*.